AWAKENING

THROUGH

A COURSE IN MIRACLES

DAVID HOFFMEISTER

4443 Station Avenue
Cincinnati, OH 45232, USA
+1 513-898-1364
www.awakening-mind.org

Foundation for the Awakening Mind

Second Printed Edition 2009
Awakening Through A Course In Miracles
By David Hoffmeister
ISBN 978-0-578-00818-9

This book, like every aspect of the non-profit Foundation for the
Awakening Mind, is the fruit of a collaborative effort of willing
and inspired volunteers. Thanks to all of you for your passion
in making this material available in book form so that many can
benefit from the sharing of this Inner Wisdom.

I offer my love and appreciation to the Holy Spirit and to
everyone who asked such sincere questions and shared their
intimate thoughts and feelings with great trust and deep passion.
I am forever grateful.

Love & Blessings,
David

Table of Contents

Advanced Teachings

Resources

Introduction

All through his early life David Hoffmeister was known for questioning beliefs rather than accepting conventional answers. He was inspired to seek spiritual enlightenment and in 1986 he encountered *A Course in Miracles*. He recognized the Course as the tool he sought to help him transform his mind. As he read it, David found that the Voice of Jesus in the Course supported him in his deep examination of concepts and assumptions. Jesus became David's internal teacher, answering his every question, and guiding him in the day-to-day management of his life and relationships.

David studied the Course with passionate intensity for several years and attended many Course study groups. The Voice of Jesus provided David with discernment about writings and teachings. Then the Voice of Jesus began to speak through David with authority. People began to refer their spiritual questions to him. David had several retreat experiences during which he was able to free his mind from ego chatter and enter into deep silence. It was in this manner that he ultimately experienced Enlightenment.

In 1991 David was guided to travel around the United States and Canada to share his understanding of *A Course in Miracles*. He followed Jesus' instructions to "become as a child," depending completely on the Holy Spirit for transportation, money, shelter, food and the words he spoke. David conveys a deep sense of peace, love and joy to people in Course gatherings, churches, spiritual groups and holy encounters. The Voice of Jesus told David, "Freely you have received; freely give." Thus, David has never charged for his time or his teaching. He gives his teaching materials away and is supported only by love offerings.

David has become a living demonstration of the principles of *A Course in Miracles*:

> God's will for me is perfect happiness.
> I am sustained by the Love of God.

I will step back and let Him lead the way.
I am the light of the world.

In 1996 David was guided to establish the Peace House in Cincinnati, Ohio. It became a place of meditation and a place where he could welcome those desiring to go deeply within the mind to discover the Christ.

Holy Spirit guided David to acquire computers and learn Internet technology. The result was the creation of the website, www. awakening-mind.org, which offers many resources related to *A Course in Miracles* and the metaphysics of Christ. Always a lover of music and seeing that it was another path to God, David set up a number of Music Pavilions on his website highlighting artists who share spiritual ideas through music. Also available on the site are video clips of his interviews, audio recordings of gatherings and teaching sessions, searchable archives, and writings.

David opens his mind to Holy Spirit and responds to questions on www.groups.yahoo.com/group/AwakeningInChrist.

The Foundation for the Awakening Mind is a non-profit organization that coordinates the ministry and handles donations.

In 2002, David again began to travel, this time with the help of the "Messengers of Peace." The Messengers of Peace are joined with David in sharing the Purpose of Awakening. You can learn about the current Messengers of Peace on the Awakening Mind website at www.awakening-mind.net/messengers.html

For the most advanced study and application of David's teachings on *A Course in Miracles*, visit the Teacher of Teachers website: www. miracleshome.org. It contains written materials and audio sessions of David working with students, all for free download.

The material in this book has been collected from David's e-mail messages, website postings and transcripts of his gatherings and workshops. It offers a roadmap inward to Heaven through forgiveness, as taught in *A Course in Miracles*. The Kingdom of Heaven is within. Blessed are the pure in heart, for they will see God. Ask and it will be given to you; seek and you will find; knock and the door will be opened to you.

The Goal of
A Course in Miracles

The Course* often speaks about its aim; not seeking for the light, God, or Truth, but for true forgiveness, the undoing of the ego and its thought system. Its primary focus is the Atonement, which is complete forgiveness, rather than God. God is. But the blocks to Love's awareness seem to obscure that Reality.

The theology is presented to the learner in order to help the learner to distinguish between illusions and truth so that the blocks to Love's awareness can be removed. It is not the purpose of the Course to make any words special, religious or sacred. Its only purpose is to give the split mind the tools to choose the Holy Spirit by seeing what is false, therefore healing the split.

The perceiver learned the perceptual realm of time and space, and now time and space will be used to unlearn. True religion is found not in the word, or a sacred text; it is found in the undoing of the belief that sacredness is found in form.

Quotations from *A Course in Miracles*, second edition, Foundation for Inner Peace, Mill Valley, CA 1996, are referenced by the following system.

T: Text
W: Workbook for Students
M: Manual for Teachers
C: Clarification of Terms
P: Psychotherapy: Purpose, Process and Practice

A Course In Miracles is abbreviated as "the Course" throughout this book.

S: The Song of Prayer
In: Introduction

Example:
   "All real pleasure comes from doing God's Will."
   T-1.VII.1.4
   Text, Chapter 1, Section VII, paragraph 1, sentence 4.

Come and See

Beloved One,

There is nothing left to seek for in this world when it can be exchanged for another one. No thought of gain or loss, winning or losing, success or failure ever had any meaning. Fantasy is not real and dreaming is not Being One. You are ready to awaken to Oneness. And as you awaken the whole world awakens as well. For the world was never more than a misperception. As perception becomes whole, the single mind sees only wholeness. At last you are ready to see with Inner Vision, and you realize that physical sight was nothing but the illusion of being in the dark. The Light has come and it is time to rejoice! It is time!

Teaching and learning true forgiveness is being aware that one is never upset by anything but erroneous thoughts, and that those erroneous thoughts can be released. True forgiveness is the release of all hurts, grievances and grudges that block the awareness of the Divine Love that is God-given and exists in everyone and everything. True forgiveness is releasing all anger, hatred, guilt and fear by seeing that they came from an error, a mistaken belief, in forgetting the Love of God. Living and extending inner peace is the natural result of true forgiveness, for when error has been laid aside and a healing Correction accepted in its place, peace prevails. To extend peace, one must be peaceful. To teach peace, one must learn it for oneself. No one can offer a gift they do not already possess. Likewise, peace of mind cannot be found outside one's own mind, for it depends not on the world. Peace comes from God and is a natural extension of God. Therefore prayer and meditation are advocated as means to inner peace and harmony. Religion is the experience of inner peace. Education, which is the unlearning of falsity, is but a means of coming to the experience of inner peace.

We were brought together by God to serve the plan of awakening, to treat each other with dignity, respect, kindness, and holiness, and to awaken to our Divine Love. We approach our Purpose for coming together with great reverence and devotion. It is the core of our Life in God. Our relationship is our Relationship with everything and everyone, for we live and love as God lives and loves, unconditionally, all-inclusively, and free of specialness. There is no jealousy or exclusion in Love. We join with all in experiencing the all-inclusiveness of the family of God, where no brother or sister is seen as separate or apart from the Whole of God. Our hearts are filled with Love and gratitude for our Relationship in God. We are glad that this joy is not dependent on where bodies seem to be or whether or not they seem to be together. We are created by a Pure Idea, and we are like our Source. We are Spirit as God is Spirit, and we are overflowing with thankfulness that this truth is dawning as the Mind we share. Our walk together is for the Purpose of accepting our Divine Source and laying aside all thought of the world as the source of anything.

Thank you for your devotion to Awakening!
David

A Prayer for our Joining

Beloved Child of God,

In God's Peace there is no affiliation with anything: no affiliation with any person, place, book, country, doctrine, dogma, ritual, concept, organization, or establishment. We are joined in Purpose or Content, and "joining in form" is a meaningless concept. There is no "social vision" in True Vision, for the Vision of Christ remains the only meaningful goal. In Truth we remain steadfast in our devotion to Inner Peace, Freedom, and the Love of God. Complete forgiveness is Salvation or Enlightenment (freedom from illusions), and thus transcends the "error" of believing it is possible to separate from the Love of God, from eternal Oneness. The Atonement is the realization that the separation never happened. Peace is natural. Let us not ask questions of the impossible. Let us accept and rejoice in our Oneness. Amen.

God Bless You Beloved One,
David

Uncovering the Present Moment
The Kingdom is At Hand

Beloved One,

Truth is within the mind. Yet there is a belief system that produces deception, a state of unawareness, which obscures the awareness of truth. We have an opportunity, in a deeply meaningful way, to come together and look calmly at the obstacles to Love and ask the Spirit to bring illumination. The mind which perceives itself as existing within a world of duality always operates from a dualistic belief system. Continually questioning this dualistic belief system may be perceived as unsettling and overwhelming; yet this questioning is necessary if one is to attain a constant state of peace.

There is just one Spirit, but there appear to be many thoughts, emotions, and perceptions that conceal awareness of Spirit. These are all temptations to forget Self and God. If faith is given to these illusions, there is not willingness to question the underlying false belief at the root of all misperception. It is very important for us to be open-minded and willing to let the Spirit help us unveil this false belief.

The message I am sharing is that truth is within you and that consistent peace of mind is a goal that you can and inevitably must attain, because it is the only Reality. It's a peace that comes into awareness from being tuned in to that small, still Voice within, and letting go of another voice in the deceived mind, the ego, which is the voice of conflict, fear, and death. In that sense our topic can be described like this: there are two voices in the deceived mind, and this discussion is a means to help each of us learn to listen only to the Voice for God, and thus bring an end to self deception.

This Voice for God or peace could be called one's intuition or inner guide. You may think of this Voice as an Inner Knowing, or Higher Power. What we want to do is to get beyond the words, which are forms, and go deeper. We want to join in an intention to experience clarity of mind and peace of mind. We want to come to the present moment, to the realization that right now, this very instant, one is perfect. It's not a matter of trying to build up and improve one's self.

No matter how improved or inflated the limited self seems to be, it will never be the changeless, eternal Self that God created. One must be aware of the trap of thinking that one's happiness, peace of mind, and salvation are somewhere off in the future. The linear, past-future, concept of time is part of the dualistic belief system that must be questioned. There is great joy and contentment in the experience of Now. God isn't holding out on us or dangling a carrot of eternal peace before us, saying, "Here's Enlightenment, keep reaching... oops, you missed again!" Enlightenment is right here, right now, for the mind that is ready, open, and willing to recognize it.

"The Kingdom of Heaven is at hand" means it is Now. Now is the gateway to the eternal. For time and eternity cannot both exist. All is One with God, and I am grateful for the beloved eternity which is real and true. Now is the time of Salvation!

Love,
David

Love

There is an experience that brings an end to all uncertainty and an end to all questions. The experience of Love is Divinely Inspired and changelessly eternal. Love does not come and go or rise and set like the sun, nor does it shine brightly only to fade and disappear for a time. Love is not personal or specific. It is impossible to Love something specific, for Love is Whole and knows no parts. Love is without an opposite, being Everything God creates forever. Divine Mind is God, is Love, is You, is All.

You can never leave behind or be separate from Love. Illusions will inevitably fall away, but Love remains eternal and extends on and on forever. Love is all-encompassing and cannot be limited. Love can seem to be temporarily forgotten or covered over in awareness by the belief in linear time, yet the Holy Instant of Love is always now and is ever present.

God is Love. God, being Love, is One and abstract. God, being Love, does not take different forms or come in gradations. In this world there appear to be many thoughts, emotions, and perceptions that conceal awareness of Love. Yet they are merely temptations to forget that Love is All there Is. Whenever the temptation to deny Love arises, remind yourself that You are Love and God is Love and nothing can separate the Oneness of God's Love.

God, being Love, has no opposite. God is all-knowing, all-powerful, and All-Loving. Illusions brought to Love must disappear, as darkness vanishes in the presence of Light. Love is All since God is All. God, being Love, has nothing to do with disease, depression, pain, sadness or any of the forms that fear seems to take. Illusions of time may seem to veil the Face of Love, but Love remains untouched. Love can be but Itself and knows only Itself. Love and fear, God and the world, have no meeting point. The awareness of One implies the nonexistence of the other. The five senses of the body seem to deceive for a time, but Love is revealed as One through Inner Vision the world knows not. Pray sincerely and let your prayer be a unified desire for Love, for God. Inner Vision will lead to the remembrance of the Love that You Are and God Is, a Love without opposite.

Ego is make-believe. Can make-believe be real if only Love is real? Ego is opinion. Can eternal, unconditional Love know of opinion? Ego is falsehood. Can Love, being true, have awareness of falsehood? Love is true and real and only Love is true and real. Love is One and is therefore beyond the possibility of comparison or compromise. What can the belief in duality, in past and future, have to do with eternal Love? And what could break apart Love, which is forever One?

Love extends Itself, Being What It Is. In extending, Love remains loving, for Love remains Itself. There is no loss or gain in Love, for Love is completely without lack or limits. To know Love is to know completion and fulfillment. How could Wholeness ever understand anything but Itself? And what could Love need, already Being Everything forever?

Accept now the eternal Love of God. What else could be more worthy of your acceptance? There is nothing to seek and nothing to find, only Everything to accept right now. *I* am Love. Such is the Truth. Thank You God for the simplicity of Oneness! Thank You God for Being Love and extending Love forever!

Introduction to the Metaphysics of the Separation

In the traditional story, God said to Adam and Eve, "Don't eat from the tree of the knowledge of good and evil." But the serpent lured Eve into taking an apple and she gave one to Adam. Then, according to biblical myth, they were kicked out of the Garden of Eden and that was the separation or the "fall."

The Course presents a different story. God didn't kick anyone out. Rather, the fall of man is a perceptual distortion, a vast illusion, in which the mind believed that it pulled off something that is impossible: separation from your Creator.

> Into eternity, where all is one, there crept a tiny, mad idea, [separation from God] at which the Son of God remembered not to laugh. In his forgetting did the thought become a serious idea, and possible of both accomplishment and real effects. Together, we can laugh them both away, and understand that time cannot intrude upon eternity. It is a joke to think that time can come to circumvent eternity, which *means* there is no time. T-27. VIII.6

Imagine this very powerful mind that was created in the image of the Father, turning his head and asking, "Could there be anything more than Heaven, more than Everything?" This idea is a little puff of madness. It was a totally ludicrous idea, but, instead of laughing at it, the Son of God took it seriously and then fell asleep. The Course says that giving such a powerful mind to such a totally laughable, ridiculous idea is how this world seemed to come about. The world we seem to live in is part of that sleep, that dream. The Course also says God gave an immediate answer, the Holy Spirit, which may be referred to as the still, small voice or the intuition.

Once the mind believed in the separation, it was terrified of the light because the little puff told the mind, "Now you've really done it! You've broken away from Heaven and turned away from your Creator." So the puff said, "Quick! We'll run and hide. We'll make up a world of form and since God is Spirit, He can't come after us there; we'll be safe."

In other words, this world was a projection from this tiny puff of an idea of separation. It was made as a hiding place so God couldn't enter. God is infinite and abstract. Heaven is changeless and eternal. But this world is finite and fragmented. Everything in this cosmos is always in flux; even the stars are going to burn out. It has a beginning and seems to be moving towards an end.

Once the mind fell asleep in the so-called fall, there were two thought systems: one was the fear-based thought system of the ego, the "puff," and one was the Thought from God's loving answer, the Holy Spirit. The ego's thought system, based on the premise that the impossible has happened and that fear is real, says, "If you ever go back into your mind, into that white light, and back to God, God will get you and destroy you!" And the loving answer just keeps reminding the mind, "You could never do such a thing, God is not angry at you, your Father loves you, your Father will always love you."

Imagine for a second a mind that is used to wholeness and congruency in Heaven suddenly having two irreconcilable thought systems in it. The Course says that the tension from trying to hold this split together was intolerable. The ego said, "I know how you can alleviate this terrible tension: get rid of your feelings of pain and guilt by projecting the split out onto the world." Thus we have a world of duality: up and down, male and female, good and bad, right and wrong; That is the trick of this world. Whenever we judge, whenever we condemn, the mind is projecting, saying, "That person out there is at fault."

Another word for projection is blame. You can blame your boss, blame the government, blame yourself, blame your past, or blame the dog. This is a world in which blame seems to be everywhere. The Course is saying the world was made up so the mind could blame everything out on the screen of the world, without taking responsibility for the split and without accepting the Holy Spirit's healing of the split.

These basic metaphysics give us a perspective on what the Course is talking about. Then it comes down to, "How can I apply this in my daily life?" And if you're going through a particular issue with a person, through a financial problem, or through depression, we try to be practical by talking together about what seems to be the problem; then we can trace it back in our mind to the separation.

How Did the Separation Occur?

Dear Beloved One,

Any question that the ego ever asked is only a metaphor for the one doubt that lasted but an instant: could one have a separate existence apart from one's Creator? This doubt thought seemed to cause the One Mind to separate into multitudes of parts, and this we speak of as the original error, the separation, the dream of sin that never was. There is no reason that can ever be given for something that is unreal. As there is no source for error, it can only be seen for what it is, and that is the end of all questions.

What seemed to occur in the one unholy instant was simultaneously corrected. If this were not so, the separation would have a reality of its own and the power of God would indeed be limited. What seemed to be the unholy instant never was at all. What now seems to be linear time is but a moment's madness being replayed again and again in the mind of the sleeping Son of God. Recognition of what is unreal brings an end to the concept of linear time and to all illusions and returns the Mind to the original state of the Holy Instant.

A sense of separation from God is the only lack that really needs to be corrected. This sense of separation comes only from a distorted perception of Reality, from which you then perceive yourself as lacking, and from which all seeming needs arise. One's responsibility now is to relinquish all needs but the singular need for God. There was no perceptual universe that existed before the thought of separation, nor does it actually exist now. One must see that what seems to be a multitude of images is just one error.

There seems to be a gap between you and your brother; the body's eyes report differences, and you believe them. You must seek within you and allow the Holy Spirit to correct this mad idea. Everything God created is like Him as One. Only Love can create Love, and what is temporal is not Love. Extension is of God, and this inner radiance that the children of the Father inherit from Him is eternal. Life in a body is temporary and not of God. Life is not of the body, but of the mind. To realize this is to realize Salvation. You are so worthy of God's Love and you are entitled to the perfect comfort that comes from perfect trust.

Do not waste your time on useless attempts to make yourself more comfortable within the illusions by rearranging them to suit your seeming needs and wants. The miracle is the means for you. It prepares your mind for God. The miracle prepares the mind for the acceptance of the Atonement, where God's creations are completely dependent on Each Other. He depends on you because He created you perfect. You must learn to look upon the world as a means of healing the seeming separation. The Atonement is the guarantee that you will ultimately succeed. And remember to apply this one idea, "Seek ye first the Kingdom of God and all things will be added unto you." Matthew 6:33 All is one in Christ. I love you forever and ever.

I love you forever and ever,
David

Mysticism

Simply do this: Be still, and lay aside all thoughts of what you are and what God is; all concepts you have learned about the world; all images you hold about yourself. Empty your mind of everything it thinks is either true or false, or good or bad, of every thought it judges worthy, and all the ideas of which it is ashamed. Hold onto nothing. Do not bring with you one thought the past has taught, nor one belief you ever learned before from anything. Forget this world, forget this course, and come with wholly empty hands unto your God. W-189.7.

The ultimate teaching is that one must empty the mind of the contents of consciousness. Every scrap of fear and every thought of time-space, including the thoughts about the book *A Course in Miracles*, are included in the final release. This ultimate letting go of the thoughts of the world is what I refer to as Mysticism; for the surrender of the past leads to the experience of the eternal Present. You need not concern yourself with this step at this point. It is most helpful to continue your work with the Course in earnest. The rest will surely follow. I am joined with you in the Purpose of learning complete forgiveness. And God's Plan cannot fail.

How Did the Impossible Happen?

Bill Thetford and Helen Schucman, early on while they were taking down the Course, at one point asked, "How could any of this have happened? If God is perfect, and the Son is perfect, how could the separation, the impossible, happen?" And Jesus addresses it early in the text saying, You are still looking for a historical answer as if something happened in the past.

> It is reasonable to ask how the mind could ever have made the ego. In fact, it is the best question you could ask. There is, however, no point in giving an answer in terms of the past because the past does not matter, and history would not exist if the same errors were not being repeated in the present. T-4.II.1

In order to ask, "How did the impossible happen?" there has to be an assumption beneath the question. What is the assumption? That the impossible happened! You see. If Jesus answers this question, then that makes the error real. It's another delay maneuver, especially the questions, "How did the impossible happen?" and "To whom did the impossible occur?"

Jesus says that the ego is going to ask all kinds of questions like this, to which there is no answer. But there is an experience. Seek for the experience in which those questions dissolve.

> The ego will demand many answers that this course does
> not give. It does not recognize as questions the mere form
> of a question to which an answer is impossible. The ego
> may ask, "How did the impossible occur?", "To what did
> the impossible happen?", and may ask this in many forms.
> Yet there is no answer; only an experience. Seek only this,
> and do not let theology delay you. C-in. 4

That is why all that we do when we come together is question all
of our assumptions. And when you keep doing that you can't help
but come to the experience, Ahhh! I Am! Period. The questions are
dissolved. You don't need anything after that. I am as God created
me...

> This course is perfectly clear. If you do not see it clearly,
> it is because you are interpreting against it, and therefore
> do not believe it. And since belief determines perception,
> you do not perceive what it means and therefore do not
> accept it. Yet different experiences lead to different beliefs,
> and with them different perceptions. For perceptions are
> learned *with* beliefs, and experience does teach. I am leading
> you to a new kind of experience that you will become less
> and less willing to deny. Learning of Christ is easy, for to
> perceive with Him involves no strain at all. T-11.VI.3

Opening to Forgiveness

First we learn we only seemed to be upset because of harboring
erroneous attack thoughts, though in releasing them we see our
sudden happiness and laughter is a true experience of the Lightness
and Love and Laughter that is our Spirit! Laughter is the result of
unlearning the ego way of thinking and perceiving.

It is a miracle to let go of grievances by allowing memories and beliefs and judgments to surface in awareness and then letting them go. This is forgiveness – when the temptation to perceive yourself as unfairly treated arises, surrender the thought, the perspective, the desire to be "right" about the way it was "set up" or seemed to be, and let go into the miracle. As this becomes our habit, being a miracle worker is happily discovered as our function in all situations!

We are joined in the Purpose of forgiveness, and I am grateful this is so. We shall rise together and Be Free, for such is God's Plan. And God's Plan cannot fail, being the only Plan that will work. Amen.

Many Blessings,
David

Defining Ego

- A conversation with David

Friend 1: I have a problem. The Course seems to present the concept of the ego as an evil thing, as opposed to my readings in psychology, which say that you've got to have a strong ego. This creates a real conflict in my comprehension, and you sound like you're well prepared to deal with this. [Laughter]

David: Well, let's talk about the ego, unveil it. The thing about the ego is not attempting to fight it or combat it because it loves a fight. The Course is saying just look at it. The only reason fears are maintained is because we try to look away from them.

Have you ever had a dream where you're being chased by something? You don't want to turn around and look at it. And basically Jesus is saying, "It's not fearful at all. We can look right at it, and it'll be gone like a puff of smoke."

I studied psychology and psychoanalysis. Freudian psychology described these intra-psychic forces. It basically says that, between the "id" (all these unconscious forces) and the "super ego" (the voice of morality), is the "ego." The ego acts like a mediator in that system. If it's a mediator between these two combating forces in the mind, that's where the idea of wanting to build up ego strength comes in. But all the parts – the id, the ego and the super ego – are part of what we refer to as the ego.

There is another part of the mind Freudian psychology didn't really get into, which is Spirit. When I was in psychology, I kept looking for the Spirit. I asked, "How do we integrate religion and spirituality with psychology, because they seem to be antithetical?"

Later I got into reading quantum physics. Some of the quantum physicists were talking about perception and that there's no reality in the world apart from what you think. They did double-blind experiments with particles in which they tried to take the experimenter out of the experiment, but they still found that the thoughts in the mind of the experimenter were moving the particles. They could in no way remove the mind of the experimenter from the experiment. All these things point to the idea that the world is subjective, that mind is involved in it.

I started to see that psychology wasn't really helping; it was very pessimistic. There had to be another part of the mind.

Then I started reading eastern philosophy about the Higher Self, and I had a sense that, "Yes, that resonates, there has to be a Higher Self beyond this small self."

Friend 1: I figure you've been through the Jungian approach as well. How did your approach to the ego compare with Jung's?

David: Jung took Freud's idea of the unconscious and called it "collective unconscious." He started to see that there was something, the Higher Self, beyond this unconscious. This Higher Self, Jung said, was able to communicate through dreams and through symbols with love-archetypes and so forth, and there were ways of awakening toward realization of this Higher Self.

A Course in Miracles fits well with Jungian psychology, in the sense that Jungian psychology said that there was this unconscious with all these beliefs under the surface and that you had to get in touch with the beliefs. And that's what the Course is saying. Jesus is saying that there are a lot of unconscious beliefs and until you can look at them, until you can become aware of them, then they run you. You had asked about defining the ego and there's one point at the back of the text where Jesus says that you can't have a definition for something that is nothing, which is interesting; like if I define it for you that's giving it a reality. But he says we can point to the opposite, and the ego's opposite in every single way is a miracle. Then, after he talks about the ego as the nothingness that it is, he again points to the positive, the right mind, the divinity.

Somebody asked me the other day, "So the ego has to die in the end?" And I said, "Well you can look at it that way, but you have to believe that it lived before you can believe that it can die." I've heard people that work with the Course say, "love your ego" or "hate your ego," and a lot of times when people are reading the book they will perceive that the ego is up to no good. But Jesus says you made the ego by believing in it, and you can dispel the ego by withdrawing your belief in it.

Friend 2: That's what bothers me. I feel sometimes there is so much emotion put into trying to destroy this ego, like it's replaced the devil.

David: Jesus actually says he had to do that so you wouldn't dismiss it too lightly. And that's when He introduces the idea that it's obviously just a belief. You made it by believing in it, and you can dispel it. But he says that about Satan so that it's not just brushed away, because that's part of the ego's defense mechanism, to just brush fear under, repress it or deny it, and then all of a sudden fear comes up. This is a Course in dispelling the ego, not in trying to kill it.

Friend 2: That's what bothered me, that it was a battle. I think it would be easier to just withdraw your energy from that belief system than to try to fight it.

David: In the end that's all dispelling the ego is: remembering to laugh at it. Now, when the mind is in the sleeping state, part of the mind is where the Holy Spirit lives, and the Course calls it the right mind; this is sanity. This is the connection back to Christ and the Father. And then the dark side of the mind is where the ego resides. So to say, "Love the ego," would be to say, "Love nothing." In order to truly love something, it has to exist. So the Course is definitely not saying, "Love the ego," and it's definitely not saying, "Hate the ego," because, as you were mentioning earlier, when you fight against it, it seems to just roar even more.

The ego is up to no good in the sense that the purpose of the ego is sickness, fragmentation, guilt, sin and death. And the Holy Spirit's purpose is healing and waking up. And it's important to start to tell the difference between the two, because until we can, we'll think that the ego has something to offer us. And as long as we believe it still has something to offer us, then we'll still invest in its way of thinking, and we'll still feel guilt; we'll still feel pain and separation.

Friend 3: So much of the Course talks about the ego, not because it's real but because the sleeping mind believes it's real. And to the extent that it believes in it, it has a hold. So Jesus is just saying this is how this works; this is what to look for; this is what's going on for the mind that believes in the ego. And when you can start to see what it is and recognize it for what it is, then that's the way out.

Friend 1: Yeah, but isn't ego our personality?

Friend 4: No. Your personality is your personality, isn't it?

David: All of our personalities are different. Some people seem to be aggressive and out-going, some people seem to be shy and reserved. Some people seem to be intellectuals and other people seem more feeling and sensitive. When you talk about personality there is enormous variation. Sometimes people think of them as complementary, but they may seem to conflict at times. Often between husband and wife, boyfriend and girlfriend or within a family there seem to be stark personality differences. Whenever there's conflict, it's not the Holy Spirit that's involved; there is an ego basis.

Basically the "personality self" is what the Course calls the "self-concept" with a small "s" instead of a capital "S" for Christ Self. The self-concept is part of a construction that was made when the separation seemed to happen.

The thought that you could separate from your Creator was horrifying. The separation wasn't true, but the mind believed it for an instant, the "unholy instant." The mind was so afraid it tried to run away from God into the darkness as far as it could; it started to stack up beliefs.

God placed the answer, the Holy Spirit, instantly in the mind where the problem was. But it was intolerable for the mind to hold onto both thought systems at the same time. So the mind made up the world to project on, like a movie screen. And the ego said, "Project the split out there onto the screen." Then you could forget about the split within the mind and see the duality out there on the world instead. So the sleeping mind sees a world of duality: male, female; good, bad; right, wrong; hot, cold; fast, slow...

Friend 3: Victim, victimizer.

David: Victim, victimizer. That's part of the giant optical illusion. Instead of looking in my mind and seeing I have a split in my mind that has to be healed, the trick is that the split is out there in the world. We have the good guys and the bad guys, like in the old cowboy movies. So, I split my brothers into two camps, and now I can blame and be angry at the victimizers and I can pity the victims. The Course is saying that it's a trick, it's a scam. Whenever you blame the IRS or blame your parents, your spouse, your boss or the weather, you are trying to hurl the guilt you feel, the unworthiness that you feel, away onto them. But it really doesn't solve anything; it doesn't get rid of the problem, because when you do that the mind believes that somehow your projections are going to creep back, and then it starts getting defensive. If you've ever felt angry at somebody and attacked them, you may have then feared they were going to tell your friends or whatever. As soon as the attack goes out, then it's like, "Oh, my gosh! What have I done?" Then you get defensive.

Friend 2: Is pride of the ego?

David: That's a good question, because I got messages when I was growing up to take pride in things. Is pride good or bad? Jesus talks about the ego's uses for the body, and pride is one of them. Pride is always based on form. There's a body identification: "I'm proud of my ethnic heritage. I'm proud to be an American. I'm proud of my wealth." It's all form based, world-based, because it's all externally based.

Jesus says, "Your worth is established by God. ...nothing you do or think or wish or make is necessary to establish your worth." T-4.I.7 Our Heavenly Father is the sole basis for our worth, but the ego sticks pride in there: "You can make a bigger better self." It's a trap. When you get the possessions that you thought would make you happy and the relationships that you thought would make you happy, you still feel like, "I'll be happy when..." And the ego says, "Keep playing the game. Seek but do not find. Just keep pursuing." Pride is so sneaky that you go round and round in a circle, like a cat chasing its tail.

Jesus says, "We cannot really make a definition for what the ego is, but we *can* say what it is not." C-2.4 And he goes on to describe the state of the miracle. The ego dissolves in the right mind.

Jesus also says in Lesson 223:

> I was mistaken when I thought I lived apart from God,
> a separate entity that moved in isolation, unattached, and

housed within a body. Now I know my life is God's, I have no other home, and I do not exist apart from Him. He has no Thoughts that are not part of me, and I have none but those which are of Him. W-223.1

Defining Perception

- A conversation with David

David: This is a Course in changing perception. So let's throw it out there. When you think of perception, what comes to mind?

Friend 1: In the Course it's perceived as an individual viewpoint which is coming from ego, filtered through the emotional body and generally dis-informed by the attitude body, and fairly blurry to the agenda body. [Chuckling]

David: So you're saying, *very* distorted. [Laughs] Perception involves "reading meaning into." The second lesson of the Course is, "I have given everything I see all the meaning that it has for me." And, as you were saying, it seems to be individual in the sense that two or three people can see the same accident happen and each will describe it differently.

The Course is saying that every time you're feeling upset in any way – it could be fear, anger, depression, boredom or whatever – you're making a decision in the moment, and you're choosing that emotion based on your interpretation, or your perception, of what's happening. It makes perfect sense that people could have different reactions, because each has a different filter or personal perspective. Perception is definitely a decision. When you start to apply this in your life, whether to your frustration at work, to your in-law's or to floods, you can see how backward your perception is. We don't see anything the way it truly is.

Friend 2: So I don't react to the fact of it, but to my interpretation of it.

Friend 1: Another reason why it doesn't matter.

David: [Laughs] That could be the group motto. I can see people saying, "Well, wait a minute, things *do* matter." But it doesn't matter, really, because it is based on guilt. For example, you could go down to an inner city and feel guilty about the homelessness you're seeing and think, "These people are so much worse off than I am. I feel so bad that I'm going to give them all the cash I've got in my pockets (to help me feel better.)" And the Course is saying that the act of giving money won't relieve you of your guilt; only getting clear in your perception will make you free of guilt.

And when your perception is healed, when you're in your right-mind so to speak, whatever your action, say giving a helping hand, it's done with purity because you are aware of your real intention.

So where does perception come from? Thought! Lesson 5 teaches us: "I am never upset for the reason I think." It's such a good lesson because a lot of the time our first reaction when things happen is, "I know why I'm upset. I'm upset because..."

Friend 2: The same reason anybody would be upset.

David: Yeah, "Because they did *this* to me. Wouldn't you act that way too if somebody did this to you?" And Lesson 6 states: "I am upset because I see something that is not there." It's like seeing a mirage. You're hot and thirsty on the desert and see an oasis in the distance. But when you get there, it's not there.

And Lesson 7 says: "I see only the past." I'm constantly watching the past and getting all upset because the past is where the guilt seems to occur. The past is the ego's domain and the present is where the Holy Spirit lives. The mind just wants to keep calling on the past and believing in its reality.

Friend 2: Rehashing it.

David: Yes, or in relationships; I've talked to addiction counselors who see patterns emerge in their clients. One client will say, "I married five times and the same thing keeps happening over and over. I try to marry somebody else, but the same things happen. I married five alcoholics." Or with jobs; you get a job and think, "I hate this job; I'm going to get out of this job!" And at the next job, "I hate this job!" The past just keeps repeating itself.

What the Course says is that, whenever you're thinking about the past or the future, your mind is blank, because it is stuck in past thoughts and projecting them out. That's what the world is; the world is literally the past thoughts in our minds that are projected out into the world of form. And so it's no wonder we get upset with what we're seeing with our eyes, because we're viewing a screen which is just the past, our grievances taking form. We have angry thoughts in the mind and they're in the picture show.

There are just two thought systems; there is the fear-based ego thought system and there is the Holy Spirit's thought. And so it comes down to discernment between the two. I need to be able to tell the difference between the two.

Then I need to start to withdraw my investment in ego thought. If I think the ego's offering something to me that's good, useful, or helpful, I'm going to want it to stay around; I'm going to hang onto it. The Course is getting you to ask, "How am I tapped into this thing, Jesus, and how am I invested in it, but don't know it?"

Friend 2: Like, "What's valuable to me?" I'm not going to let go of something I feel is worthwhile and gives me something. But, as I question and really change my mind, then I'm going to see proof for the new thought system out on the screen. Then I'll have experiences that witness to that new way of thinking.

David: So the question is, "What do I want?" It comes down to, "What do I really want?" And at the beginning, when you first start working with this stuff, it's like, "Yuck! I must really want guilt and fear because I seem to still be perceiving events that seem to witness to that." And the Course is saying that you really need to keep asking that question, going deeper.

When I was growing up, before the Course, the two things I wanted in life were freedom and intimacy. I thought, "Oohh, that feeling of connectedness and intimacy, I want that, I just want that so much!" And freedom, "I like to soar! I like to feel like there is nothing hanging over me." It wasn't that my goals were wrong. In the Course freedom and intimacy are nice goals, but *where* I was seeking for them was all wrong.

Friend 1: Didn't you think that those two in particular, freedom and intimacy, are juxtaposed?

David: The way I perceived it was this: when I would try to go for the intimacy, my freedom seemed to be limited. Intimacy seemed like a ball and chain.

Friend 1: Mutually exclusive goals.

David: I'm discovering through the Course that they aren't mutually exclusive. In fact, they're found in the same place; they're identical. My definition of freedom was, "I want to be able to go where I want to go, do what I want to do, do it how I want to do it, and do it when I want to do it." A real sense of no limitations.

Friend 2: Now does that mean that you wanted to find somebody who would want to do exactly what you wanted to do when you wanted to do it? [Laughter] That sounds like a fantasy!

David: The intimacy part of it was saying, "I want that feeling of connectedness. I want the feeling of being so close to someone that it's like we know each other's thoughts. I want that kind of closeness where there is no sense of separation." And my intimacy ideas had a lot of romantic ideas tied in there, too. I wanted companionship, having somebody there with me. "It's not so easy," I would say, "to be intimate if she's living in California and I'm living in New York." My idea of intimacy was that bodies must be together, preferably under the same roof, as close as possible for as long as possible.

That was my definition of intimacy.

Now, the deeper I've gone into this, gone through relationships, worked with the Course and had transformations, I've found that both of my definitions were heavily related to the body. In my definition of freedom, when I said go anywhere, do anything, it was about mobility of the body. It wasn't so much freedom of the mind. And intimacy was in terms of "get the bodies together and you're lucky if you can agree on certain things."

What I found is that relationship and true intimacy come from following the Holy Spirit, and that's also what true freedom is. That went against what I thought. I had hoped to become a fulfilled person through pursuit of those body-centered goals, but I found I really had to question them.

Now, being used by the Holy Spirit as I travel around the country and go into things with people, I feel a real sense of intimacy with people, a real connectedness, what I was always searching for. But it's certainly not in the form I had envisioned.

Coming to True Perception

Dear David,

In my job it falls to me to enforce minor laws and morals. Yet it seems *A Course in Miracles* says that anything that is not eternal is simply not real. Part of a miracle is overlooking all perceived errors and allowing the Holy Spirit to fill your mind with true perception. The Course says you give to yourself whatever you think of another person. What is the correct way to perceive?

Beloved One,

Thanks for writing. Forgiveness is always a gift to our Self because it releases the make-believe self/world/cosmos of the ego and opens the way to remembrance of Self and God. As a brother or sister is recognized beyond the body, their Innocence as a Divine creation is recognized. You have written that the "miracle is overlooking all errors..." and this is so. With the help of the Holy Spirit it is possible to look beyond error to the Light of the Atonement, Which is forever Innocent and Sinless. Pardon is always justified because the misperceptions of the ego are not real. The Golden Rule asks you to do unto others as you would have others do unto you.

See no body as guilty and you see no body to blame. The Innocence of the Spirit is apparent when one realizes that attack is impossible. A unified mind cannot attack or be attacked. And without the belief in attack, guilt has no basis. The Holy Spirit gently leads to a unified mind and a unified perception that is the forgiven world. When forgiveness has been accepted, the illusion of guilt has vanished from awareness. It is possible to perceive any seeming situation as extending Love or calling for Love. Let the Holy Spirit show you by aligning your mind with this Guidance. Healing is unlearning the ego and thus releasing every scrap of ego belief, thought, emotion, and perception.

If you are willing the way will open, for nothing can obscure the Innocence the Holy Spirit would have you behold. Blessings to miracle workers everywhere! All Glory to God!

Love always,
David

Seeing Beyond Some Common Ego Defenses

The ego cannot separate What God created as One. No thought of disharmony can withstand the Light of Truth. All things work together for good, because there is a common perspective which sees all things and happenings as illusory. In quietness are all concerns already answered and is every seeming problem already resolved.

There is nothing to fear in honest inquiry. You must stop running, avoiding, projecting, justifying and rationalizing what you think you know to be the case. Then admit that you have been deceived and be open to question all that you think you know. How else can you allow a complete change of mind about yourself, and accept your Reality as the Self God created? Stop pretending that you are an autonomous, independent person who knows something of Divine Mind. The Mind and body have no meeting point, no point of reconciliation. You are not a person with a mind. You are wholly, purely, completely Mind. True independence is not the independence of autonomy but of complete dependence on God. Surrender all ideas of what you think you are to the Holy Spirit, and allow Him to teach you to forgive and thus remember Divine Mind.

The ego states emphatically, "I no longer need a teacher!" A healed mind has no need to make such a statement. Did Jesus ever make such a statement? As long as you believe bodies, persons, and autonomous private minds have reality, you will be attracted to or repulsed by "personal" teachers, for the ego made the world and all idols to distract you from looking within and following the Teacher Who remembers your innocence. The ego wants you to find scapegoats to bear the blame and idols to raise up and cling to, that you may retain autonomy and independence as a person with a separate will, be it leader or follower, and all under the guise of "spirituality."

Open to the Teacher within, and hear Him speak to you through a variety of symbols in which you believe. The world is nothing but a representation of private thoughts. The Holy Spirit uses what was made in hate to teach the meaning of true forgiveness. Meaning is within. Meaninglessness is outside.

The ego states, "You don't need to look at the ego, just love." Can one love a world of images, something which was made to take the place of God? The world was made by belief, not by God. Can one remember love, which has been veiled from awareness by belief, without questioning such belief? Jesus has said:

> To learn this course requires willingness to question every value that you hold. Not one can be kept hidden and obscure but it will jeopardize your learning. T-24in.2 No one can escape from illusions unless he looks at them, for not looking is the way they are protected. There is no need to shrink from illusions, for they cannot be dangerous. We are ready to look more closely at the ego's thought system because together we have the lamp that will dispel it, and since you realize you do not want it, you must be ready. T-11.V.1

Don't be fooled into thinking you can forgive a world without raising to awareness the belief system that made it. The mind cannot release what it has denied from awareness, and all ego shortcuts to love are really nothing more than delays and/or distractions.

True Silence is the state in which God is remembered. Revelation is beyond all words. This deep Silence is always available, though it is very fearful to a conflicted mind, to the ego. Mental chatter, thoughts of the past and future, are the ego's attempt to deny Silence from awareness. Words are but symbols of symbols, representations of thoughts. In the Course Jesus says:

> Is the teacher of God, then, to avoid the use of words in his teaching? No, indeed! There are many who must be reached through words, being as yet unable to hear in silence. The teacher of God must, however, learn to use words in a new way. Gradually, he learns how to let his words be chosen for him by ceasing to decide for himself what he will say. This process is merely a special case of the lesson in the workbook that says, "I will step back and let Him lead the way." The teacher of God accepts the words which are offered him, and gives as he receives. He does not control the direction of his speaking. He listens

and hears and speaks." M-21.4

Here is an example of this kind of use of words:

> The Holy Spirit speaks through me today. The Holy Spirit needs my voice today, that all the world may listen to Your Voice, and hear Your Words through me. I am resolved to let You speak through me, for I would use no words but Yours, and have no thoughts which are apart from Yours, for only Yours are true. I would be savior to the world I made. For having damned it I would set it free, that I may find escape, and hear the Word Your holy Voice will speak to me today. W-296

A mind in accord with the Holy Spirit is silent. Whether the body seems to be speaking or moving is irrelevant to such a miraculous silence. The purpose or motivation the mind chooses determines the state of mind one experiences. Silence is natural, but is obscured from awareness by the choice to align the mind with the ego. The issue is never to speak or not to speak, but instead to be clear in mind of one's purpose, for that is the decision to be made. The rest merely follows.

The ego demands its freedom: "I will not be confined by another person, institution, teacher, group or set of rules. I am a free person." The ego feels free when it's not being looked at. It does not bring to awareness the law, "Ideas leave not their source," and the realization that there is no world apart from one's mind. Persons can never be free, for the mind that believes it is a person is enslaved by deception. One cannot be mind and body, spirit and matter, eternal and temporary. The concept of person is an attempt to combine or reconcile what can never be combined or reconciled. Since there is no world apart from the mind, there are no other persons, institutions, or sets of rules outside. Images can seem to act out the belief in control, but they no more than symbolize the illusion of control, since God did not create control. Freedom from control cannot, therefore, come to a mind which believes it is a person in a world external to itself.

Freedom comes only to a mind that realizes it has dreamed the entire world and that the world is merely a world of ideas. The forgiven world is quickly forgotten and the Kingdom of Heaven, life eternal, is true freedom.

Perhaps you have avoided someone, using the justification that they were trying to control you or your spiritual journey. Perhaps you feel safer or even happier because they are away. Your mind is powerful. Powerful enough to make a world, to make up bodies and construct institutions within time and space. Only a mind that believes itself to be a body, a person, in a world of other persons and institutions, groups, external to itself, could perceive itself as capable of being controlled, institutionalized, or feel happier because a body is not around. One is responsible for choosing peace. Nothing can happen to oneself apart from what the mind desires, and if one wholly desires the peace of God and nothing else, that must be one's experience.

The ego always focuses on specifics and persons, past and future, for it has no awareness of the Holy Spirit's purpose in the present. When you notice that your mind is preoccupied with such senseless musings, choose again. The miracle will remind you that the false is false, and you will feel the ease of your position on High, above the battleground. There is no peace, no safety, and no security on the battleground of thoughts of persons and specifics. Be clear on what you really want, and you will not feel the need to pay attention to the world of images. The truth is the light within.

I Do Not Perceive
My Own Best Interests

- A conversation with David

David: The issue the deceived mind has with this Course is that the Course is saying that God is your author. God created you like Himself. He is Spirit. He created you Spirit. You are an idea in the mind of God.

How many of us go around thinking of ourselves as an idea? A person, maybe; a linear person with a past and a future, and all of the associated attributes, characteristics and traits. But just the pure idea in the image of our Father?

The Course is saying God is your Author, and you are Authored by God. The deceived mind has an issue with that. The deceived mind believes it is a body. Or, if it is more sophisticated, it believes it is *in* a body. It believes it is time-bound and form-bound.

The deceived mind attaches to form; it gets caught up in sales of houses, in families and in outcomes. It is really caught up in the script, so to speak. It has denied that it is Spirit. It is terrified of that Spirit. It is afraid to let go.

You get so used to relying on yourself, on your resume, on your past history, on the bankable skills that you need to survive. The Course turns the tables around and says, "I've got a purpose and a mission for you. You need to help wake our brothers up and you'll wake yourself up in the process." But doubt crops up, "I don't know about this." That's when you need to trust.

It is like Jesus sending the disciples out two by two and saying "Don't take an extra pair of shoes." But, you think, "This is the 20th century; it's a dog-eat-dog world!"

Friend: You'll get chewed up and spit out!

David: Not only that, people will also say, "If I quit judging like you are talking about and give it up big time, life is really going to get boring." Jesus says in the Course, "Make this year different by making it all the same." T-15.XI.10.11 People read that and say, "Blah. Yuck! Sameness! Why do I want to have everything the same?"

Let's look at the Course:

> Before you can make any sense of the exercises for today, one more thought is necessary. At the most superficial levels, you do recognize purpose. Yet purpose cannot be understood at these levels. For example, you do understand that a telephone... [A telephone starts ringing in the background and the group breaks into laughter.]...is for the purpose of talking to someone who is not physically in your immediate vicinity. What you do not understand is what you want to reach him for. It is this that makes your contact with him meaningful or not. W-25.4

That is a great thing to use as a contrast. You can agree and say, "I know what a phone is for." We've learned what objects are for. Jesus is trying to reach the mind at that level, but he also throws in, "Yet purpose cannot be understood at these levels." So there has to be a purpose that is guiding us that transcends all of this. In fact, if you pop over to lesson twenty-eight, He gives a concrete example.

> You could, in fact, gain vision from just that table, if you would withdraw all your own ideas from it, and look upon it with a completely open mind. It has something to show you; something beautiful and clean and of infinite value, full of happiness and hope. Hidden under all your ideas about it is its real purpose, the purpose it shares with all the universe. W-28.5

That's a phenomenal idea, that you could receive salvation from even a coffee table. What is a table for? A table is to put things on so bodies can sit around. It is at the level of the body. You see how it comes back to body identification?

Friend: It makes it convenient for the body.

David: There it is. It comes back to that. When you think about all these ambitions, they all trace back to the comfort of the body, the convenience of the body. It comes back to the authorship idea and the body identification idea.

Everything traces back to body identification. That is a very deep basic idea. The Course is about slowly letting go of that body identification. Jesus was always so defenseless. What would there be to defend other than the body? Yet when they arrested him, and all throughout his mission, he was defenseless. How could that be possible unless he was convinced that he wasn't that little slab of flesh?

> It is crucial to your learning to be willing to give up the goals you have established for everything. The recognition that they are meaningless, rather than "good" or "bad," is the only way to accomplish this. The idea for today is a step in this direction. W-25.5

That covers it. The ego would love to have us believe that the Holy Spirit is trying to coerce us to do something. It is only when you get to the point where you see something is not good or bad, that it is nothing, that you don't feel coerced or like it's a sacrifice to give it up.

All we have to do is withdraw the goals we have established for everything. The real meaning is right there, obscured by these other goals.

Friend: Therefore the goal for everything, I guess, is to be forgiven? How do you experience the goal of giving up all the meanings that you have attached to things?

David: You give it up through recognizing that it doesn't have any value. Sometimes the meaning of relinquishment or give up has a lot of connotations and charges. There is the belief in sacrifice there. The deceived mind believes that you have to give up something. As long as you believe that *nothing* is *something*, then it is going to seem like a sacrifice. You have to make a lot of metaphysical connections to start to see that you are giving up nothing.

I really like the part at the back of the book where it talks about relinquishment of judgment. Jesus says it is not that you shouldn't judge, it is that you can't. You are not capable. He says,

> It is necessary for the teacher of God to realize, not that he should not judge, but that he cannot. In giving up judgment, he is merely giving up what he did not have. He gives up an illusion; or better, he has an illusion of giving up. M-10.2

This world is illusion. When you reach the point of, "Ah ha! It is nothing," it is realizing that you never had to give up anything. The whole point is just the idea of holding onto an intention, trusting it and just letting it carry you. That is the only answer I could give of how you come to that.

> In no situation that arises do you realize the outcome that would make you happy. Therefore, you have no guide to appropriate action, and no way of judging the result. What you do is determined by your perception of the situation, and that perception is wrong. It is inevitable, then, that you will not serve your own best interests. Yet they are your only goal in any situation which is correctly perceived. Otherwise, you will not recognize what they are. W-24.1

Friend: So I'm trying to be detached in all different ways and turn it over to Holy Spirit?

David: Yes, we're talking about perception here. We were just talking about, "I give the meaning to everything I see." That is what perception is, the meaning I give to what I see. So it's not so much, "what am I here to *do*?" It's more like, "with which lens am I looking at all of this?"

We also hear and say, "I know I created this, and I know I would create something else if it wasn't this. But the word "create" is used very carefully in the Course. In relation to the world Jesus uses words such as "made" and "invented," as in "I have invited the world I see." Jesus always reserves the words "create" and "creation" for Heaven, pure abstract Oneness.

Friend: It is guilt-inducing even to think I created this for myself.

David: Yes. In the Course the word creation is not even used in connection with the real world because even it is made up. It is not Heaven, which is beyond the realm of perception.

Another way to think of it is in the time sense. Life seems to be linear: the past is behind me, here I am now, and I've got these things to deal with in the future. But the Course teaches that the script is written.

During that tiny instant of madness when all of the perceptions that ever could be were spun out, in the same instant the Holy Spirit made the real world, which took away all meaning of guilt, judgment and fear, and it has a fresh perception of the world. But if the real world is there, then *why* am I concerned at all with outcomes?

Jesus says that our perception is wrong. We need to keep going into "Why is my perception wrong?" Because the world spun out the way it is going to go. The script is written – over and done. So, the question now is more like, "What do I have control over?" That is another thing people have a big reaction to. They say, "I feel strapped down thinking that things have to be the way they are going to be. Is my free will being violated here?"

There is a part in the Rules for Decision section where it says that there is no way of avoiding what must happen. Clearly, if that is the case, the only choice we have is how we look upon the situation. And that means it is a perceptual problem. As we go on we are going to get some big insights into what is going on with our perception.

Friend: So you are saying the script is written, it can't be changed?

David: I don't believe in Determinism. The Course says you do have choice left, and the only choice you have is the meaning that you will give to the script playing in front of you. You are free to choose your own interpretation. Jesus says that your will does not have anything to do with this world. Your will is in Heaven. Your will is complete happiness in your Father's Will. It doesn't meaningfully translate. Your will seems to be imprisoned while you are in this world. So, there isn't any point talking about that or equating it with choice. But you *do* have a choice on how you look at the script.

You can see it differently. There is a way to look at it with the Holy Spirit, there is the miracle which results in peace, and then there is the ego lens in which case you get hopping mad or fearful or depressed in some way.

Now you need to get really clear on this choice. You need to get clear on these two lenses. Why in the world, why would anyone in their right mind look through the ego's lens? No one in their right mind looks through the ego's lens. When they are in their right mind they are looking with the Spirit: "Help me please to be clear on this insanity so that I can be sane. I want to be sane, I want to be peaceful."

> If you realized that you do not perceive your own best interests, you could be taught what they are. But in the presence of your conviction that you do know what they are, you cannot learn. The idea for today is a step toward opening your mind so that learning can begin. W-24.2

I know what I like and what I dislike. These are my favorite things and these are my least favorite things. The ego thinks it knows what it likes and what it dislikes. It also thinks it knows what is in its own best interests. Because if it knows what its likes are and what its needs are, then the mind is closed, saying "I already know, Jesus. I don't need to take your hand. I am a person, I am a body, I've got my dislikes, I've got my likes, and I deserve it." That is part of what it means to be a special person. And here we come with these lessons that say you can't even perceive your own best interests till you know what they are. So that is going to take extending our minds a bit and opening up. Even with the simple things, I don't know what is best for me.

> The practice periods should begin with repeating today's idea, followed by searching the mind, with closed eyes, for unresolved situations about which you are currently concerned. The emphasis should be on uncovering the outcome you want. You will quickly realize that you have a number of goals in mind as part of the desired outcome, and also that these goals are on different levels and often conflict. W-24.4

If you take that in and start to do the searching in your mind, you may have outcomes related to family, to relationship. You may have outcomes about career or financial outcomes. Then there may be things about wanting world peace, or saving the dolphins, or a particular personal interest. Maybe you feel strongly about political issues; there are certain outcomes tied into that.

Friend: So are outcomes expectations?

David: Yes. He is saying in that last line, "these goals are on different levels and often conflict." For instance when we were talking about when you really wanted to be home. And then going into work to do this sales job, there is something else that you want.

When the seeming fall took place, one of the earliest beliefs was the belief in levels, levels of need. You hear that you have to take care of your body, you have to take care of your spirit, you have to take care of your emotions and your mind; in spiritual terms you might hear about different levels, that you have to have them in balance. There weren't any levels before the fall. The levels actually are made up and they are part of the system.

Jesus is saying that the problem is that you have all these different outcomes and all these different goals in mind because you perceive yourself as a person on all these different levels. You are doing a juggling act. As we go on we will see that there is no way that all these problems could ever be solved on all these different levels. It is absolutely impossible to do it. It is insane and frustrating because it is impossible. Doesn't it seem that the Truth, if there is such a thing as Truth, would be simple?

As you go on with the Course you will see that there is only one problem and one solution. "Oh, this is too good to be true!"

> In applying the idea for today, name each situation that occurs to you, and then enumerate carefully as many goals as possible that you would like to be met in its resolution. The form of each application should be roughly as follows: *In the situation involving ___, I would like ___ to happen, and ___ to happen*, and so on. Try to cover as many different kinds of outcomes as may honestly occur to you, even if some of them do not appear to be directly related to the situation, or even to be inherent in it at all. W-24

David: "In the situation involving my sales, I would like...."

Friend: ...everything to turn out like I want it to!

David: If we go back to our "script is written," you can see how bizarre this is. If the script is already written and the outcome is already going to be the outcome and there is nothing in the world that can be done to alter the outcome, the only thing that the mind has to choose is the lens that it will see it through.

Friend: You are saying that there is no choice in outcomes. Doesn't that imply that the world of form is real?

David: It is not real. The only reason that it is not real is because it occurred during the unholy instant. Remember how we said that when the tiny puff of an idea was taken seriously, it all spun out, and it all occurred in the past. Jesus tells us constantly about the past in the Course. It is gone. It is gone into an ancient instant; it is over and done with.

Jesus keeps saying, "Guys, we are all in the present, it is all right here – all of it!" And literally that is the sense that there is no reality to the script.

God did not create the world, so God does not have anything to do with the perceptual world. If you take the basic idea of the Course at the beginning, "Nothing real can be threatened, nothing unreal exists," T-In., well, where does that put the world?

But we don't want to go from the top down, that only Heaven is real and all else is illusion, because what Jesus is saying is that He knows we believe in the world and so to go from the top down would be inappropriate or at the least unhelpful. We could not understand. We need to start with metaphor. The whole book was written at the ego level because Jesus starts with the premise that you believe in the world. You believe you are a person in the world. So, for your learning, we're going to have to start by taking the problems and situations that you believe you really have.

Friend: What about incarnation, though? From what I understand, the script is already written; this may be my tenth incarnation and I may have five more to go before I finally let go of everything and can forgive. Is that what you are saying? That I am dreaming this dream for the tenth time?

David: Jesus addresses reincarnation and says that if it helps strengthen your belief in the eternal then it may still be a useful belief. But it is still defined in a sense of *place*. The belief that the soul is immortal and eternal, and yet entering the finite and being contained there, must be questioned. The metaphor that I found helpful is that the mind is set back, watching things come up on the screen, as if you were sitting in a recliner flipping through the channels on the television. That's another analogy for reincarnation. More and more images keep coming onto the screen regardless of the channel. What seems to be death in this world isn't a real ending. It is like, what is next? As long as there is still guilt in the mind, as long as I still believe I can seek for idols in this world and as long as I can still find something more valuable here that is not in Heaven, I keep asking for more scripts. Okay, change the channel!

All that gives me the perspective that what Jesus is saying is real. It is like Jesus is right with me saying, "Come outside to the light."

Friend: And that can happen in an instant. But I wonder how many more incarnations? I feel conflict, it seems like you can control it, but you can't.
David: Well, the one thing you have choice on is *when*. At the very beginning of the book, at the introduction, Jesus says, "Free will does not mean that you can establish the curriculum. It means only that you can elect what you want to take at a given time." T-In.

Free will does not mean that you can establish the curriculum. It certainly seems on the surface that I am choosing to study *A Course in Miracles*, but in the ultimate sense that is not even a choice. We don't even have a choice in *how* we are going to wake up, the so called path we take.

But the *when* is our choice. There will come an instant when the mind clearly sees the faults, as Jesus did, that is the choice that is left up to the mind. That's where the will and the choice come in. Without trying to figure it out in a form sense, you can go nuts trying to analyze: is this the right book, the right person, the right relationship?

Friend: But now the question becomes, "Is it helpful?"

David: It is the second period one goes through in the Development of Trust; "...he must now decide all things on the basis of whether they increase the helpfulness." M-4.I.A.4 That implies that you can make a choice, that you can make a decision to do something in the world that will increase the helpfulness. As opposed to "the script is written" which is really a deep idea, it doesn't even enter in until pretty late in the workbook.

Once the mind can work its way down through all the false beliefs, it will come to "Ah, this is it, it is so simple." Instead of choosing between billions and billions of things in the menu of the world, it is really just a simple choice, and that is between the Holy Spirit and the ego.

> If these exercises are done properly, you will quickly recognize that you are making a large number of demands of the situation which have nothing to do with it. You will also recognize that many of your goals are contradictory, that you have no unified outcome in mind, and that you must experience disappointment in connection with some of your goals, however the situation turns out. After covering the list of as many hoped-for goals as possible, for each unresolved situation that crosses your mind, say to yourself: *I do not perceive my own best interest in this situation.* And go on to the next one. W-24.6-7

The situation is going to turn out like it is going to turn out. Situations don't turn out simultaneously two different ways. So really, what it is saying is that it's the goals in your mind that are conflicting. You have conflicting expectations in your mind. Like Saturday night when you would rather be home doing something fun, and on the other hand you thought, "I want to go in and make the sale," so you had conflicting goals. I want to do both, what am I going to do here?

This sets us up for the next lesson, because if I have conflicting goals and expectations, then I'm willing to admit that is my problem: I don't have a unified goal. I have a lot of things going on in my mind. And where did these things come from? If I could just find the source for all these thoughts that are coming up in my mind — they are all straying up from something — that would solve it.

These are humbling exercises and Lesson 25 turns it up a little bit more:

> I do not know what anything is for. Purpose is meaning. Today's idea explains why nothing you see means anything. You do not know what it is for. Therefore, it is meaningless to you. Everything is for your own best interests. That is what it is for; that is its purpose; that is what it means. It is in recognizing this that your goals become unified. It is in recognizing this that what you see is given meaning. W-25.1

That is pretty tight! Everything is for your own best interest. You can see why this gets back to "the script is written" in a sense. That the script is done and every single thing that happens is for my own best interest. Why don't I see it like that? There must be something going on in my mind if I could lose my peace over not making the sale or a girlfriend leaving me.

It is all in Divine Order. But as long as you perceive yourself as having different levels, conflicting levels with conflicting goals, you can't see the Divine Order. It is right under your nose. Everything is perfect; there is not a pinhead that is out of place. And we have to say, "Help me, because I am not seeing this, here. I am not experiencing that everything is for my own best interest."

Friend: That is why we set the goal for peace.

David: If you go forward with peace as the goal, Jesus says you will perceive everything as coming to meet that goal. If you go into a situation and you are so single-minded that this is the most peaceful and joyful situation that you could ever imagine, then no matter how people are reacting, you don't see the negatives, you don't see the things that would take you away from the goal because you are so focused on the goal.

Friend: Perception is projection. If it doesn't fit the goal, then it doesn't get in.

David: What is interesting about the Course is that it talks about projection and denial. The mind has lots of tricks that it uses to deny and confuse. If you really follow the thinking of the Course then you find what the defenses are being used against is the love of God.

This is interesting! That is what the defenses are defending against. They are defending against the Holy Spirit coming to the mind and saying, "You are perfect just the way you are." The deceived mind is terrified of this light. But the plus side of it is when you see that if the deceived mind uses them against the love of God or the Holy Spirit, what is it that the defenses are defending? The self-concept, a concept that has been made, a false idol that is not eternal. All of the defenses are being employed to defend this little concept, this tininess that you believe you are.

So now we will get into the core of it: all those expectations and all those goals and all those different levels.

> You perceive the world and everything in it as meaningful in terms of ego goals. These goals have nothing to do with your own best interests, because the ego is not you. This false identification makes you incapable of understanding what anything is for. As a result, you are bound to misuse it. When you believe this, you will try to withdraw the goals you have assigned to the world, instead of attempting to reinforce them. W-25.2

Your goals are about future careers, relationships and romance, maintaining this image of who you think you are. This image is splintered on many levels, so, if you look at it mindfully, you will say, "Gosh, what a mess." You will ask yourself: "What am I going to pick first?" And maybe push the change of mind into the future: "Once my finances get cleaned up, or once my daughter gets married I will have a little space here." Or try to change circumstances: "Gosh, I just wish I had some sun, it has been raining so many days here."

What the Course is saying is just take a look at all your goals to get the sense that they are all ego goals. It can be kind of overwhelming when you start to look at that.

I was watching the movie *Gandhi* and one reporter said to him, "You look like an ambitious fellow," and Gandhi responded, "I hope not." Something inside of me took a little leap. Because everything I've ever heard in my life, from every source I'd ever heard, was that ambition is the making of your self, striving to gain something.

Jesus talks about the Holy Instant, when you just totally still your mind from all the pursuits and all the projections, all the chasings and strivings and are quiet and still enough to realize, by golly, right here, right now, this instant, you are whole and complete. You are everything; and all of the pursuits and all of the chasings, comings and goings are part of the ego.

Maybe you strive and are into this ambition stuff. So, all you could do, all any of us can do is say, "Okay, I want You to help me step by step, point by point, lead me out of ambition. Lead me out of wanting things to be different than they are, out of trying to pursue and strive."

Everything that is pursued is for the self-concept: fame, pleasure, money and sexual conquests. Some people are ambitious for misery.

> Another way of describing the goals you now perceive is to say that they are all concerned with "personal" interests. Since you have no personal interests, your goals are really concerned with nothing. In cherishing them, therefore, you have no goals at all. And thus you do not know what anything is for. W-25.3

Let's just think about this. If you didn't have personal interests, how would you get into an argument? What would you argue about? When conflict comes up in families and at work, there is a conflict of interest involved. So what we have there is a bunch of self-concept illusions battling with another bunch of self-concept illusions.

Above the battleground there is peace and calm, because it is just a clash of illusions. But that is not the way it feels if I believe I am one of those self-concepts. Because then I will defend. In male and female issues, if I identify with male, I will defend men etc.

The special love relationship is saying, "I am going to find another person who will agree with me, who will share my personal interests." Finally, I think I've found that person; it seems like I've succeeded in pulling away from the abstract level of God in Heaven and found in form the thing that will finally make it work, that will get rid of these terrible feelings of worthlessness, guilt and fear.

What it actually is doing is taking on another self-concept and making it a God substitute. That is why all special relationships in this world are doomed to the hate part, "Because you let me down. I put all my emotional eggs in your basket, and you were supposed to help me get over this unworthiness and guilt I feel."

A lot of rejection goes on in significant relationships. The whole idea of the holy encounter is to say, "My ego, my personal goals, my interests are not who I really am and I need to give up who I think I am. I need to give up these personal goals."

Friend: Because that is the only way that I will ever come to the recognition of who I am, is getting the other stuff out of the way.

Releasing Common Ego Errors and Awakening

Beloved One,

To escape the ego belief system and recognize Enlightenment it is necessary to expose unconscious ego beliefs and see their nothingness. The approach to Truth involves negating everything believed to be real that obscures the awareness of Truth. Once this negation is complete, it is obvious that the Truth is true and only the Truth is true. This is Enlightenment, pure and simple. *So our shared Purpose is to expose and remove the obstacles to the awareness of Love's Presence.*

There are two main categories of ego errors:

The first is metaphysical errors, which always involve level confusion or seeing causation in form. Causation is solely of the mind. Right-mindedness sees causation where it is and welcomes the Guidance of the Holy Spirit.

The second category is transfer-of-training errors. Transfer-of-training errors always include the attempt to make exceptions to the miracle. By making no exceptions, the Atonement, or complete forgiveness, dispels the ego entirely.

The ego's complexity makes *A Course in Miracles* difficult, yet Wisdom reveals the simplicity of the Course. If you understand that the ego is death and that a synonym for the ego is reciprocity, then you will grasp that reciprocity is death. By reciprocity I mean giving in order to get something in return. True Giving, as God Gives, asks for nothing, for Wholeness has no needs or desires and therefore simply radiates and extends. Human beings cannot understand Wholeness, for the persona is the mask drawn over the Wholeness of Being. The personality self thinks it has an autonomous existence and strives to become a better self with better circumstances, not seeing the mask of the cosmos as a mask. Persons never reach Divine Silence, for the person construct can never know what it was made to hide. Silence is the natural State of Divine Mind and can only be accepted exactly as It is.

There have been many books written about *A Course in Miracles* that reflect the personal interpretations of their authors. Everything you read, hear, or watch presents an opportunity for discernment, and you will know the Holy Spirit's Peaceful Interpretation by the experience of peace. Until the peace of mind is a consistent experience, be assured that one of the two ego categories of errors mentioned above is still being valued and chosen. And this means that something of the world still holds value and attraction. *A Course in Miracles* calls this the attraction of guilt, pain, and death. No one in their right mind chooses guilt, pain, and death, for these are always wrong-minded decisions. What we shall do is expose these faulty decisions and show that they offer nothing that you want.

First, there must be a metaphysical context for what I am speaking about. Meta means beyond, and our context for understanding will always be beyond the physical. Time has no reality whatsoever, yet, before it will disappear from awareness, it must be turned around and viewed from a healed Perspective. As time is a linear construct, let me use the analogy of a line in geometry as an example. If you look at the line from anywhere *outside* the line, you see a line. Likewise, observed from the ego, time appears to be a long line stretching into billions of years.

If the line is looked at from *within* the line, however, there is no line; there is only a point. Similarly, observed from the Holy Spirit, time is only a single point. And, to the Holy Spirit, time is over. The Holy Spirit sees the entire cosmos as a singular point of terror, a tiny tick, a mad idea that was corrected immediately and therefore is gone. Present Love remains all that is real and true.

Dreaming a distorted cosmos of time and space is the definition of the belief that time is not over. This is the belief that the separation from God is current, and also in some strange way, valuable. For if the past was not valued, it would no longer be remembered and called forth in awareness. The illusion of linear time is the calling forth of an ancient instant that has no reality or existence. Another analogy that may serve as a helpful example: when you look at stars at night you are perceiving burning gases that have long since burned out but still seem to be present. The same can be said about everything specific you perceive in the cosmos.

The first fifteen Workbook lessons in the Course are an introduction to the new Perspective of time I am sharing with you now. These lessons can only have meaning if you are willing to release the ego's linear perspective of time and the things of time. In the Light of all of the above, let us review Workbook lessons 51-53, which are review lessons of the first fifteen lessons:

Nothing I see means anything. The reason this is so is that I see nothing, and nothing has no meaning. It is necessary that I recognize this, that I may learn to see. What I think I see now is taking the place of vision. I must let it go by realizing it has no meaning, so that vision may take its place. W-51.1.(1)

I have given what I see all the meaning it has for me. I have judged everything I look upon, and it is this and only this I see. This is not vision. It is merely an illusion of reality, because my judgments have been made quite apart from reality. I am willing to recognize the lack of validity in my judgments, because I want to see. My judgments have hurt me, and I do not want to see according to them. W-51.2.(2)

I do not understand anything I see. How could I understand what I see when I have judged it amiss? What I see is the projection of my own errors of thought. I do not understand what I see because it is not understandable. There is no sense in trying to understand it. But there is every reason to let it go, and make room for what can be seen and understood and loved. I can exchange what I see now for this merely by being willing to do so. Is not this a better choice than the one I made before? W-51.3. (3)

These thoughts do not mean anything. The thoughts of which I am aware do not mean anything because I am trying to think without God. What I call "my" thoughts are not my real thoughts. My real thoughts are the thoughts I think with God. I am not aware of them because I have made my thoughts to take their place. I am willing to recognize that my thoughts do not mean anything, and to let them go. I choose to have them be replaced by what they were intended to replace. My thoughts are meaningless, but all creation lies in the thoughts I think with God. W-51.4.

I am never upset for the reason I think. I am never upset for the reason I think because I am constantly trying to justify my thoughts. I am constantly trying to make them true. I make all things my enemies, so that my anger is justified and my attacks are warranted. I have not realized how much I have misused everything I see by assigning this role to it. I have done this to defend a thought system that has hurt me, and that I no longer want. I am willing to let it go. W-51.5. (5)

I am upset because I see what is not there. Reality is never frightening. It is impossible that it could upset me. Reality brings only perfect peace. When I am upset, it is always because I have replaced reality with illusions I made up. The illusions are upsetting because I have given them reality, and thus regard reality as an illusion. Nothing in God's creation is affected in any way by this confusion of mine. I am always upset by nothing. W-52.1. (6)

I see only the past. As I look about, I condemn the world I look upon. I call this seeing. I hold the past against everyone and everything, making them my enemies. When I have forgiven myself and remembered Who I am, I will bless everyone and everything I see. There will be no past, and therefore no enemies. And I will look with love on all that I failed to see before. W-52.2. (7)

My mind is preoccupied with past thoughts. I see only my own thoughts, and my mind is preoccupied with the past. What, then, can I see as it is? Let me remember that I look on the past to prevent the present from dawning on my mind. Let me understand that I am trying to use time against God. Let me learn to give the past away, realizing that in so doing I am giving up nothing. W-52.3. (8)

I see nothing as it is now. If I see nothing as it is now, it can truly be said that I see nothing. I can see only what is now. The choice is not whether to see the past or the present; the choice is merely whether to see or not. What I have chosen to see has cost me vision. Now I would choose again, that I may see. W-52.4. (9)

My thoughts do not mean anything. I have no private thoughts. Yet it is only private thoughts of which I am aware. What can these thoughts mean? They do not exist, and so they mean nothing. Yet my mind is part of creation and part of its Creator. Would I not rather join the thinking of the universe than to obscure all that is really mine with my pitiful and meaningless "private" thoughts? W-52.5. (10)

My meaningless thoughts are showing me a meaningless world. Since the thoughts of which I am aware do not mean anything, the world that pictures them can have no meaning. What is producing this world is insane, and so is what it produces. Reality is not insane, and I have real thoughts as well as insane ones. I can therefore see a real world, if I look to my real thoughts as my guide for seeing. W-53.1. (11)

I am upset because I see a meaningless world. Insane thoughts are upsetting. They produce a world in which there is no order anywhere. Only chaos rules a world that represents chaotic thinking, and chaos has no laws. I cannot live in peace in such a world. I am grateful that this world is not real, and that I need not see it at all unless I choose to value it. And I do not choose to value what is totally insane and has no meaning. W-53.2. (12)

A meaningless world engenders fear. The totally insane engenders fear because it is completely undependable, and offers no grounds for trust. Nothing in madness is dependable. It holds out no safety and no hope. But such a world is not real. I have given it the illusion of reality, and have suffered from my belief in it. Now I choose to withdraw this belief, and place my trust in reality. In choosing this, I will escape all the effects of the world of fear, because I am acknowledging that it does not exist. W-53.3. (13)

God did not create a meaningless world. How can a meaningless world exist if God did not create it? He is the Source of all meaning, and everything that is real is in His Mind. It is in my mind too, because He created it with me. Why should I continue to suffer from the effects of my own insane thoughts, when the perfection of creation is my home? Let me remember the power of my decision, and recognize where I really abide. W-53.4. (14)

My thoughts are images that I have made. Whatever I see reflects my thoughts. It is my thoughts that tell me where I am and what I am. The fact that I see a world in which there is suffering and loss and death shows me that I am seeing only the representation of my insane thoughts, and am not allowing my real thoughts to cast their beneficent light on what I see. Yet God's way is sure. The images I have made cannot prevail against Him because it is not my will that they do so. My will is His, and I will place no other gods before Him. W-53.5. (15)

What is being undone in the Great Awakening is the perception of linear time and the identification with a linear identity that is of the ego's making. Guilt, although an illusion, seems real in awareness as long as you perceive yourself as part of linear time. The Holy Spirit stirs the sleeping mind so that it may first observe the cosmos and experience identity from the perspective of Wholeness in the Present, and then gently Awaken unto eternity. A happy dream of forgiveness precedes the gentle Awakening unto Pure Oneness.

The Holy Spirit returns to awareness the power of the mind and the all-inclusiveness of the mind. The awareness of power and inclusiveness go together, since only the ego's insane attempt to judge, compare and project blocks the vastness and inclusiveness from awareness. To reject is to judge against, and this produces the optical delusion of consciousness I call distorted perception. Inclusiveness is the forgiven world, and everything of the cosmos is perceived from the Present Healed Perspective of the Holy Spirit.

Forgive the past and let it go, for it is gone. Only a Blessing remains, and the Big Picture is readily available to behold.

Blessings of Peace,
David

Answering the Call

Hi David,

I have been a very serious student of the Course for 2½ years now. I have felt called to concentrate on the Course so that I might travel and teach it. This call prompted me to search more intensely on the web for *A Course in Miracles* and I found your website a couple of weeks ago. What a marvelous website you have! It has been so helpful to me! As a Course person who has been "called" to walk the earth, I would like to know more of what your experiences were. Thank you.

Beloved One,

Thanks for sharing your heart with such openness. You are being Called, and everyone is Called. In this world, the ego's voice and goals can seem to crowd out the Holy Spirit's Voice, and though everyone is Called, few seem to listen and Answer. To Answer is simply to be happy, for God's Will is for Perfect Happiness. The time-space cosmos was made as a mechanism to avoid the Perfect Happiness of the Kingdom of Heaven. Yet in Answering the Call there can only be happiness. It is my joy to meet with you while I am in California and explore everything entailed in Answering the Call.

Trust in the Holy Spirit is the key to Awakening. To the extent you are able to trust the Holy Spirit you will increasingly be aware that you have no problems. The ego was a limit placed on communication, and as you are willing to communicate you will attract communication to you. A simple life of listening, trusting and following will transfer the lesson of forgiveness to encompass your entire perception. Healed perception is integrated perception, and in this not one person, place, or thing is held apart from the blessing the miracle brings. Trust would settle every problem now, and a simple life of trust will yield immediate results in terms of peace of mind.

Salvation is not for sale. Enlightenment is not for sale. Those who would truly Give offer freely what has been received from the Holy Spirit. Rituals fall away as the mind yields to Divine Spontaneity. The desire to "get" dissolves in True Giving. Travel can be a symbol for the willingness to share and the willingness to Flow, to accept and not expect. What shows up is perfect in that it is orchestrated and provided by One Who Knows your best interests in every seeming situation. Everything is for one's best interests in healed perception. To surrender is to yield the personal perspective in favor of the Flow.

If you would trust, do not attempt to activate the past, organize the present, or plan the future. If there are plans to be made, you will be told of them by your Inner Wisdom and they will be for the benefit of everyone. The miracle meets every perceived need in one gentle perspective, and leaves a blessing for all.

I am with you all the way, and we cannot fail in a Plan destined to Awaken all in Oneness and Love. Take my hand and we shall skip along singing and rejoicing as we go. For we but seem to travel in happy dreams of forgiveness, all the while safe at Home in God.

Leave the structure of the ego's world with Me and enter into another world of happy, peaceful perception. There is no loss in this exchange, for dreams of pain are over now. Leave the world of giving to get, of paying to partake, of repeating past mistakes.

Come join me in the real world, a world inspired by joy that knows not of a fear of consequences. You have a Great Gift to share, for you are Divine Love Itself. Nothing can hold you back from your appointed function, for God goes with Us All Now. One moment of Trust can change the entire outlook. Come and See.

Blessings of Love Forever and Ever,
David

Ideas Leave Not Their Source

Dear David,

In the Workbook, Lesson 167, it states, "Ideas leave not their source." I have heard you and other students of the Course quote this short sentence, but I do not understand the meaning of this statement, and I respectfully request your clarification. In kindness and love.

Beloved One,

Thanks for writing. In Heaven this idea means Christ remains in the Mind of God and can never really "leave." With regard to this world, the idea means that there are no problems apart from the mind because ideas leave not the mind which seemed to think them.

All things that seem to be "manifested in the world" are really thoughts and concepts. And thoughts and concepts never leave the mind that thought them. The ego's attempt at projecting thoughts to a seeming "outside cosmos" is delusional because everything is mind and there is therefore nothing "else" at all. This is also why all seeming illness is mental illness and has nothing to do with bodily symptoms.

Salvation or Enlightenment is therefore nothing more than escape from false concepts that have no reality or existence. This brings an end to the illusory idea that there can be an "inner" and "outer," for mind is one in forgiveness and Mind is One in Reality.

Love,
David

How to Forgive Feeling Betrayed by God

Dear David,

I feel betrayed by God. As strange as that is to say, if I'm being completely honest, that is how I feel. I'm 32 and I was raised in a Baptist church. I bought into what I was taught about God and Christ. I believed that Jesus was raised from the dead and I believed that I was forgiven for all of my sins. I asked God to come into my life and to direct my path. For doing so, I expected to have peace of mind and happiness.

The older I get, the more disenchanted I become with my own life and the hope or possibility of me finding happiness and peace of mind, I feel as though I made a "bad deal." I feel as though I have been betrayed. Even though I have tried to be the best Christian I can be, God hasn't rewarded. Worse yet, it doesn't even feel as though God is there. I can't begin to tell you how awfully lonely that feels.

I have a counselor that I see regularly and we have discussed this in some depth. He tells me that my current view of God will only lead to more anger and resentment for me and that I need to change the paradigm in which I view God and faith. I agree with this completely, but my problem is that I don't feel as though I can trust or put faith in God anymore.

I do believe that all the emptiness, loneliness, anger and resentment I feel could be resolved if only I could resolve this crisis of faith that I am experiencing. I'm reading this and I keep thinking what right do I have to feel betrayed by God? I know that I have been blessed and that there are those who are much less fortunate than I. Intellectually I know this, but in my heart I feel so hurt and I just don't know what to do or where to begin. I would sincerely appreciate any insight you could provide me. Thank you for your time.

Dear Beloved One,

Thanks for sharing what is on your heart. You are so precious and deserve to feel the Love that is buried beneath the hurt. Love is our Inheritance or Birthright.

The ego (Satan, in Christian terms) is a false identification, a mistaken identity, and the Purpose of our work with the Holy Spirit is to realize that the real Self is not the ego and remains forever the Perfect, Innocent Child of God in Spirit. The ego's feelings of betrayal run very, very deep as do the feelings of abandonment, loneliness, hurt, anger, emptiness and loss.

The world was made by error so that God would not be discovered. It is indeed a profound step to ask God to come into one's life and direct one's path. Yet, as profound as this step is, it is only the beginning. The entire cosmos was made from the belief that it is possible to be separate from God or to fall from Grace. Forgiveness is the undoing or release of the original error and all the errors that seemed to follow.

Jesus was raised from the dead to demonstrate that sin or error has no power. You have received the reminder of our Sinlessness and Perfect Innocence, the Holy Spirit, and now you are Called upon to release every spot of error to the Light of the Holy Spirit within your Heart. The ego was the error that it was possible to leave God, and feelings of betrayal, resentment and anger arise from this unconscious error. Your counselor is offering a helpful suggestion by saying that you need to change the paradigm in which you view God and faith, for such is forgiveness. God is perfect Love and Christ is perfect creation. What needs to be forgiven is the belief that God had anything to do with the time-space cosmos of duality and multiplicity, sickness, pain, suffering, and death. What God creates eternal Spirit remains eternal Spirit, and that which seems fleeting and temporal will fade and disappear.

The disillusionment you feel can be viewed in two ways. The ego would blame the feelings on its version of God, an anthropomorphic view of a "god" of human concepts and traits who is capable of betrayal and abandonment. However, the Holy Spirit ever gently reminds that God is Spirit and Identity in God is Spirit.

The Holy Spirit lovingly offers forgiveness as a replacement or Correction for dreams of anger and of pain. The mind is very powerful and the issue is never really an issue of faith or lack of faith. The central decision is *what* you put your faith in. And every decision you make is a conclusion based on everything you believe, regardless of whether or not you are fully aware of what you believe.

The ego is an unreal belief, and, while the mind invests in this belief, sin or error *appears* to have reality and existence. Who You are in Truth is far beyond the need for forgiveness, yet the illusion of false identity must be forgiven or released that True Identity may be remembered.

Be happy and glad that you are beginning to see that there is no hope of peace or happiness in the appearances and forms of this world. Happiness and peace of mind are real and are found within as Christ teaches: "The Kingdom of Heaven is within."

We are embarking together on what seems to be a journey within, and I assure you that happiness and peace of mind are inevitable and certain. I speak from the Perspective and the experience that this is the Truth right now. What is true for the One must be Totally Inclusive, for the Spirit that God creates Includes Everything. Therefore nothing is apart from this Spirit.

Forgiveness applies to that which is false. That which is forever True, Spirit, is far beyond the need for forgiveness. God does not forgive, for God has never condemned. And yet there must have been an illusion of condemnation before forgiveness was necessary. The world is in need of forgiveness as long as you believe in its reality, for a world apart from God could never be. Awakening to Truth is the dawning of the realization that it is impossible to leave the Mind of God. Such is Salvation or Enlightenment.

I am joined with you in the Great Awakening. We cannot fail to remember Identity in God, for illusions cannot veil the Truth. Please feel free to call, write or visit anytime. We shall rejoice together in God's Love, and in this experience of complete rapture there is only Joy! God knows Spirit as One and there can be no "body" that is "more" or "less" fortunate in the Perspective of the Holy Spirit. Let us give thanks to God for creating Spirit as One forever. Amen.

I Love You forever and ever,
David

From Concepts to Application to Experience

Dear David,

I have read the Course all the way through and studied bits here and there so that I can probably say I have read it through at least twice. And peace of mind still eludes me. It seems cruel to me that sometimes I feel very at ease and clear. But then that goes away and I end up going through long periods of depression. I have been practicing meditation since I was fifteen and I'm forty two right now.

My problems seem to be centered on my relationships. Every love interest or relationship ends with heartache for me. I feel like I must be totally unlovable. I'm very overweight and I just can't seem to take the weight off. But I'm not so dumb that I think that all my problems would be over if I lost weight. Peace simply eludes me. And I feel very angry at God right now. I keep thinking about the phrase in the Course that says something like, "If you really wanted to see the truth you would." Well, I really do, but I don't see it. Or "All things are echoes of the voice for God." So I think to myself, God must be awful darn cruel then. It just doesn't make sense. My last relationship was with someone I met through the Course. I just ended the relationship with him. It was clear he was losing interest. And he told me honestly it was my weight. And all this time I have been saying to myself, "I am not a body, I am free, for I am still as God created me." Well...this latest lesson that "God would have me learn," didn't exactly support that idea.

Please talk to me. Why does God or Truth elude me? I'm tired of this search. I just want truth. But I'm really tired of begging God for it. Why do I have to? I dig deeper and deeper within myself but the crap just never ends. I'd like to say, "I give up!" But I don't know how. How do I surrender? Why do people claim it's so easy? Why can't I feel peace of mind? Help Please!

Hello Beloved One,

I am so grateful you opened up and shared what is on your mind. That is always a big first step in forgiveness and inner healing. To open and share with a brother is a symbol of your willingness to hide nothing from the Holy Spirit. When progress in meditation and peace of mind seems slow and frustrating, this is always a Call to go deeper within. There is a tremendous fear of looking within, for the ego has convinced the sleeping mind that God will punish those that have "left" Heaven. The ego's world is filled with distractions and fantasy goals to offer many substitutes and diversions from the "dreaded" looking within. Christ teaches in the Course:

> To learn this course requires willingness to question every value that you hold. Not one can be kept hidden and obscure but it will jeopardize your learning. No belief is neutral. Every one has the power to dictate each decision you make. For a decision is a conclusion based on everything that you believe. T-24.in.2

> This course will be believed entirely or not at all. For it is wholly true or wholly false, and cannot be but partially believed. And you will either escape from misery entirely or not at all. T- 22.II.7:4-6

These two ideas, taken together, give some indication of the deep desire and commitment necessary to delve inward to the base of the unconscious mind if lasting peace is to be found. The Atonement, or Correction, is buried deep within under a cloud of guilt and unworthiness. The good news is that you are never alone and Help is always Given. There is a stage in the development of trust in which mighty companions appear in awareness. This is a stage of yielding to the deep desire to join in a common Purpose.

You will find that the inner doorways will open easily with just a little willingness to follow the Holy Spirit's promptings. The ego is angry and fearful of God, yet the Quiet Answer is always available to sooth and comfort the restless mind that is open to receiving

Inner Help.

When you are tempted to give in to anger and depression just remember this: Trust would settle every problem right now. I have faith in You Beloved of God. I hope to always be in contact. Know that I am always in prayer for your peace and happiness. You are never alone and isolated.

I love You!
David

What is the Meaning of Awakening Mind?

Dear David,

What is meant by the words Awakening Mind? Do you actually believe we are asleep in a dream? Sometimes awakening means to be aware of the difference between reality and illusion. As when watching a magic show or illusionist – what they do may look very real, but we are awakened to the truth that it is only a trick or illusion. I believe we are awakening from the illusion that we allowed our selves to be tricked into by the greatest illusionist/ deceiver there is – satan! We bought into satan's illusion that there is something greater than the Spirit of Love, which is God, by believing there is something else that exists that was not created by God. Such is the self or ego and so we pursue the illusion of the ego self, forgetting what is truth and what is illusion. But, as we were given the choice to believe the illusion, we also have the choice to awaken or be aware in remembrance that what we see is not reality but only illusion.

I believe the only truth is that we are part of God. I am not sure if the illusion state that we see now was created by God. Maybe it doesn't matter as long as we see the truth through illusion in the one spirit of love which overcomes all mysteries!

Hello Beloved One,

The time-space cosmos can seem very much like a dream, for it was the projection of the belief in separation. God, being perfect Love, creates forever perfect Love, and such is eternal creation. Christ is a perfect creation in the Mind of God and Christ creates forever perfectly in Love as God creates. In this sense "all that exists is Christ or from Christ."

Truth and error are not both true. Truth is true and only Truth is true. Because God/Christ/creation is true, error is false or nonexistent.

The deceived or sleeping mind seems to have forgotten God, Christ, and creation. It dreams of many parts separated by time and space, for it has forgotten the wholeness of the forgiven world that the Holy Spirit offers as well as the eternal Heaven Which is Mind Awake in God.

The Holy Spirit's Perspective of forgiveness is what you pointed to in writing: "As when watching a magic show or illusionist - what they do may look very real, but we are awakened to the truth that it is only a trick or illusion." The Holy Spirit sees the error of separation but looks past it to the Atonement or Correction. The Holy Spirit is the present reminder of what is beyond error entirely, for in the Holy Spirit is the Memory of God and Christ.

Before the deceived mind can Awaken to eternal Reality it must accept the gentle dream of nonjudgment that the Holy Spirit offers. In this forgiving dream the cosmos is seen as one whole tapestry. Distinctions, categories, increments, levels, degrees and parts have vanished entirely, for only wholeness "remains."

This perception of wholeness is itself an illusion and will not last, yet this illusion is the last illusion, for it is the gateway to the eternal.

Since God is real, the cosmos is not. Since Christ is real, satan is not.

Since eternity is real, time is not. "Perfect Love casts out fear" is a way of saying: Since Love is real, fear is not. Love and fear therefore cannot co-exist.

When fear is "experienced," Love has seemingly been blocked from awareness. Yet only Love exists and Love is ever present; so the "experience of fear" is but an illusion to be released.

When you turn a light on in a dark room the light does not battle the darkness – it is simply light. Similarly, the Light of Love shines and there can be no darkness in Light. Bring the error of darkness to the Holy Spirit's Light and see that only Light "remains." For there is only Love to behold, Beloved Child of God.

Awakening mind is simply a phrase used to represent the uncovering or release of error. Release is the Holy Spirit's Purpose for a deceived mind that believes in the "reality" of the time-space world. It is as you wrote: "the choice to awaken or be aware in remembrance that what we see is not reality but only illusion." Forgiveness sees the false as false. Forgiveness is a miracle.

From *A Course in Miracles*:

> A miracle is a correction. It does not create, nor really change at all. It merely looks on devastation, and reminds the mind that what it sees is false. It undoes error, but does not attempt to go beyond perception, nor exceed the function of forgiveness. Thus it stays within time's limits. Yet it paves the way for the return of timelessness and love's awakening, for fear must slip away under the gentle remedy it brings. W-pII.13.1

Love & Blessings always,
David

Letting Go and Trusting God

Greetings Beloved,

Follow your heart on a journey of discovery. Listen to the Voice within and do what It says, even if it sometimes doesn't make sense according to what you believe are your "personal" best interests.

Your passion to discover the Truth will guide you on and draw others along with you. The journey is about forgiving the past and remembering the Love that is ever-present. Love waits only for welcome and acceptance. When the heart is ready, the witnesses will appear. If you make ready the Altar of your mind, God will come into awareness. God is always present.

Innocence is unfettered by the laws and ways and thinking of the world. With faith to just take the next step, Life takes care of Life. Contentment and happiness come from simple nonjudgment, extending love, and letting go of the idea that you really know what anything of this world is for. The journey is simply a yielding or surrender to What Is. When you give up trying to control the direction of the wind, the feather of Serenity will gently make its way to you. You are the Restful State of Divine Mind. Bask in What You Are Deep inside.

Many Blessings dear brothers and sisters,
David

What is the Meaning of Guilt?

Dear David,

I am very big on the Course, and have dramatically changed my life because of it. However, I have a question that I have never completely understood.

Can you please elaborate on what "guilt" means in the Course. Every time I get to a section about guilt, my eyes read it, but my mind does not comprehend it. Any insight would be greatly appreciated. Thanks for all you do.

Beloved One,

The Course teaches that there are really only two emotions: love and fear. Guilt, therefore, would be a form of fear. Guilt for believing it is possible to separate from God is a deep, unconscious feeling of wrongness in the sleeping mind. Guilt follows from the unconscious belief in sin or error.

All apparent symptoms of sickness are the result of the attempt to project this unconscious guilt onto the body. As error is released, guilt is replaced in awareness by the Love that resides deeper still at the core of our Being.

Guilt, as the term is used in psychology, refers to the feeling connected to behavior that is judged to be wrong. Yet guilt is the result of false belief and is healed in forgiveness as the Course teaches it. Behavior is an effect. When the false "cause" (ego) is exposed and released completely, the experience of guilt is impossible.

Peace & Blessings,
David

Meaningful Questions

- A conversation with David

David: It's important not to judge yourself. Look at the apostles with Jesus... questions, questions, questions. He just kept talking and talking. That seems to be the way we come to clarity. I have had times of wandering and being disoriented, looking for answers and asked lots of questions in my life. Only through questioning do we come through that.

Friend 1: Is it true that questions come from the ego and that answers come from the Holy Spirit? "In you are both the question and the answer; the demand for sacrifice and the peace of God." T-15.X.9. So the question is the demand for sacrifice and the peace of God is the answer.

David: Well, I don't put all questions immediately in an ego category. Jesus simplifies it: Are you asking a real question or a pseudo-question? He says that a pseudo-question both asks and answers. It only allows for answers within the world of illusions. The way I word that is, "Which of these illusions do I want?" That is what's behind our asking as we go through the day. Even if we don't have a conscious question like, "What am I going to have for breakfast?" or "What am I going to do next?"

The real question is turning it back into, "What is it for?" That is what you are starting to ask in all the seeming situations, "What is it for?" It's a real deep question. It is not about what is on the screen. It is about, "What is the purpose of this?" And that is a very helpful question.

A closed mind will not question. It is arrogant. It thinks it knows that separation is a reality. A closed mind can even try to fool itself and ask the pseudo-questions which already have the answers built in. And then it is still not really asking a question. But a crack of opening comes when the mind starts to ask real questions in the sense of purpose. And the more it asks them, the more it opens to the light. And once it has opened up, like a flower, there are no more questions, because the answer, the light, is apparent.

We don't have to put all questions into the ego category. People have said, "I don't even want to say anything because every question that I ask is of the ego." Yet we know that coming together with a sincere intention and asking questions can be really helpful.

Friend 2: So the real question addresses the mind?

David: Yes.

Friend 2: It addresses content, not form.

David: It's not analytical. It doesn't break it apart. With Friend 2, one of her biggest things was her "wonder" questions.

Friend 2: [Chuckles]

David: She would ask questions about form; about how things worked mechanically, whether it was the computer, machines or nature.

Friend 2: Or motives... "Why do you think somebody did this?"

David: Other peoples' motives. And it got to the point where I would just go, "Another wonder question." After a while she started to understand that type of question, because it was always about the form. Then sometimes when the words would start to come out, the mouth would stop and she would say, "Oh, I guess this is just another wonder question, never mind." She didn't become dependent on having someone tell her every time she had a wonder question; she started to catch the thoughts even before they seemed to come out of the mouth.

Friend 2: There are two different contexts in which you can hold questioning. One context is that it is a sign of weakness and the other context is that it is a sign of willingness to ask a question of the mind. I can't imagine that you could come to the clarity and certainty in which all questions cease, except by questioning.

David: Yes, she would ask a question which led into another question and then another one. And it didn't take long before she asked, "Is every problem just a problem because of the belief in the separation from God?" Her questions were coming from all different angles about all sorts of problems and every time it was traced back to the "unreal cause of the unreal effects." Finally the questioning led to: "Are they all the belief in the separation from God?" It is the simplicity of salvation to see it clearly like that.

Friend 2: And it seems like you have to go through that a number of times before it starts to generalize. And when the mind can actually get to the point of generalizing, then there is the recognition that you don't have to unearth every single little concept and belief because there is really no difference. It is all one and the same.

David: That's the collapsing of time. And it's a relief, because there can be a belief that you have to spill everything. You don't have to scrutinize every little thing.

Friend 3: I have been sitting here thinking, "What is forgiveness?" I just wanted a quick answer in a nutshell. I think the Holy Spirit gave that to me a few minutes ago. I wanted to get upset about something on the screen, and forgiveness is saying, "Thank you for showing this to my mind, thank you for letting me see this part of my mind." And just remembering to stay in a state of gratitude.

David: Because you are the dreamer. From the position of the dreamer, it is total gratefulness to everything on the screen because it is just a projection, just a falsity. I don't have to change it; I don't have to fix it or strive or anything. That's what the joy is.

And that dreamer knows that the dreamer is causative. In other words, the mind is causative and not the world. I dreamed this up; it wasn't done to me as a person or as a figure on the screen. I dreamed it up. Dream-ed. That "ed," that past tense, is always important to me because I don't have to get into blame and guilt. Not, I am doing this to myself. But, I did this to myself. From this vantage point, I can watch calmly.

Sexuality –
Remembering the Focus

The spiritual journey can seem intense and difficult whenever a seeker loses sight of the focus: inner peace. The journey to Awakening is a remembrance of the Sacred Presence within through removing the blocks to the awareness of Love. The path involves steps in which the symbols of the world are retranslated from icons of hatred to reminders of love, and eventually toward a step in which all symbols are eclipsed by the Present experience of the Sacred Spirit which is One forever. The body is part of the perception of a sleeping mind that has forgotten its Divinity. Denial of the body during the Awakening process is the inappropriate use of denial, for the central focus must always remain on exposing and releasing all limiting beliefs and thoughts that obscure the Light from awareness. The focus is not what must be "given up," for this approach is the ego's interpretation and always involves the concept of sacrifice. The only question the seeker need ask about any practice, including sex, is one of purpose: What is it for?

The ego has made a world of preferences, and sexuality is part of the pyramid. These preferences are beliefs, and they make a hierarchy of illusions that the ego jealously guards and protects. The unconscious guilt from these beliefs maintains the world of distorted perception. The Spirit's forgiving Perspective, on the other hand, releases the mind to again bask in a State of Innocence and Freedom that is its natural condition. With mind training, the Spirit's Perspective grows stronger and stronger in awareness, clearing away the belief in lack that distorts and clouds desire. Without mind training, the surface of consciousness is bubbling with distorted miracle impulses that seem to express in a variety of forms, cravings, and needs.

Every distorted miracle impulse is actually a Call to remember God, but through the ego's lens of lack the impulse is perceived as something to "get" for satisfaction. The apparent satisfactions that come from making false associations of thought are fantasies of pleasure, brief and temporary, and they never truly satisfy in a lasting way. All appetites are getting mechanisms. These distortions all have their foundation in the belief in linear time, and they are always remembered or anticipated. They have nothing to do with the Divine Present.

"Sacred" sexuality, as a practice, can be thought of as spontaneous expressions of affection that are prompted from and Guided by the Spirit with the sole Purpose of undoing the belief in linear time. They are prompts that come from the willingness to listen and follow and flow with the Spirit as a reflection of the lesson: I will step back and let Spirit lead the way. Because of the shared obedience to follow the Guidance of Spirit, "sacred" sexuality is a stepping stone on the way to releasing all expectations, needs, and desires; approaching the Purity of Heart Jesus spoke of in the Sermon on the Mount. Spontaneity based in following Guidance, rather than the counterfeit impulsivity of the ego, is a way of placing the mind under the direction of the Spirit and allowing the mind to be used for miracles, which are natural expressions of love. Miracles are involuntary and thus are always under the control of Christ, and the resulting happiness and joy are unmistakable experiences of a willing mind.

Repression and indulgence are the only options offered by the ego when it comes to sexuality. The miracle offers a real alternative that brings release from the tensions associated with lack and deprivation. Miracles teach the mind that it is whole and complete, and thus the Purpose of forgiveness ultimately releases the mind from all sense of lack. When the belief in lack has been replaced by the experience of wholeness, the ego, with its defenses and games, no longer remains to haunt the mind. The mind Awakens to the Pristine Abstract Light that shines eternally in the Mind of God. Oneness has no needs and simply extends forever and ever.

Listen and follow your Intuition. This is the same Answer for any problem, difficulty or area of question. It matters not whether an issue seems to involve the body, the world or the many apparent aspects of the world, for in hearing One Voice there is no problem. Before sexuality ceases to seem to exist, rest assured that the Intuitive use of the body and world will come to take the place of the ego's uses of the body and world. The Intuitive use for the body is the decision to allow it to be used solely as a communication device. All real pleasure comes from doing God's Will. And God's Will is forever for Perfect Happiness.

How Do I Get Out of Here?

Dear David,

I've been searching for something more. If what you're saying is the way home, I virtually have to let go of every belief I've been taught, and do a complete turnaround. I must say this is just like the film, *The Matrix* – awesome. Could you tell me how do I get out of here?

Beloved One,

The experience of Awakening is truly profound. To know One Self is to be alive as Spirit. The experiences perceived through the five senses may seem real during the undoing, the release of false belief, yet the experience of the present moment is inevitable. Just as Neo seemed to be carried along step by step in The Matrix, the Awakening may seem like a process. There comes a moment in which the world is seen to be past – and this moment is the moment of Freedom. In the Present there is no process. It seems to require leaps of faith only because faith has been placed in illusion and must be withdrawn from error. The perceived world of opposites was the attempt to deny the Oneness of Reality, and as the desire for peace calls the experience of peace into awareness it is obvious that peace is without an opposite.

Here is the key: Listen within... the steps are obvious to a willing mind.

First, it must become apparent that duality is not the home of our Self, the Christ. It is therefore impossible to be content and happy in duality. All restlessness is simply the fear of Waking. The dreamer of a dream must be aware of dreaming to awaken from the dream.

The awareness that leads to Waking is forgiveness of illusion. To forgive is simply to see the false as false, and there are no exceptions to this state of mind. It is impossible to achieve partial forgiveness. Forgiveness must be experienced completely to be experienced at all.

Christ is calling you "out of the world" T-18.I.12, T-13.VI.11.3 and, as the meaning of this statement is first glimpsed, it is apparent that there is literally no way to participate in the thinking of the world and simultaneously "Know thyself." T-8.III.5 Truth and illusion have no meeting point. Perfect Love casts out fear and Light abolishes darkness.

The Guide within first leads inward toward an experience, an adventure, a discovery of the awareness of dreaming. In this state of awareness, it is always apparent that nothing real is happening in the world. The forms seem to shift and change, the dream figures seem to come and go, yet the substanceless nature of appearances, the fabric of the dream, can no longer deceive the dreamer. The matrix of the illusion of control has no attraction or allure from the Perspective that arises from thinking with God. Dream softly of a sinless world, devoid of judgment. God does not judge, for there is literally nothing to judge between. Forgiveness might be called the acceptance of a wholeness that knows no parts.

Often spiritual awakening is associated with giving up something. This false association springs from the belief in lack, which was the impossible attempt to deny wholeness. What God creates is forever whole and knows not of lack. There is no need to give up something that never existed. The illusory nature of dreams is obvious when the wish to separate has been released. Instantaneously it is evident that wholeness never went anywhere, for it is ever so. Willingness to Awaken also includes the release of the desire to get out of here, for in the discovery of wholeness there is no here nor there. It is impossible to pursue or fight to escape something without "seeming" to reinforce the belief that something other than wholeness exists. Wholeness transcends all apparent seeming.

If Christ is real the world is not. Spirit comes not into time-space. Awakening is the recognition that Spirit is real and Identity in God is changeless. The body has no meaning because Mind is One and Spirit is One and there is no gap in what is forever One. The withdrawal of faith from the illusion of meaning projected onto time/body/world and the awareness of Present Meaning is apparent as All. I am Spirit. Rejoice in this Fact! Thank You God for creating All as One in Spirit!

Following the thinking of the Holy Spirit is easy, as there is no desire for something else. Awakening is natural and only seems difficult if appearances are given value. Value no appearance and truth instantly leaps into awareness. How simple and obvious is the truth.

I Love You forever and ever, Holy One!
David

Forgiveness Equals Guiltlessness

Greetings Beloved One,

By opening the Heart and learning to trust, we learn to let go of the past and thus release the "source" of all hurt, anger, and blame. Forgiveness equals guiltlessness. We finally open to hear the gentle Voice of Love remind us over and over: "It's not your fault. What you believe you have done wrong was never real. Error has no foundation and cannot be true, since only the Truth is True."

This present moment is a shining, clean, clear, fresh, rebirth, a remembering of our eternal innocence. The seeming descent into fear was but a dream, a belief in the impossible. Only the unconscious erroneous belief, the ego, sought to place a limit on the beautiful, magnificent inner Being that yearns to shine and shine. The mind sees the inner beauty of the Divine Mind when it is ready and willing; for awareness of Love waits on welcome, not on time. When the altar of the mind is cleared of idols and desire becomes Singular, all that remains is desireless Love extending Love.

Be happy Now! For the time of Awakening is Now! Beloved One you are free and innocent because you are forever created, creating, and living in the Mind of everlasting Love! Thank You God.

Blessings forever,
David

Spirit's Relationship to the World

- A conversation with David

Friend: I intuitively sense that there is actually a relationship between form and Spirit. I think that this runs through everything. Some metaphysical thought tends to blow off form or matter, as in Christian Science: "There is no life, intelligence or substance in matter." Like matter is a bad thing, that if you are not operating in the realm of Spirit then you are not doing what you should be doing. And I do not believe that. It is, for lack of a better word, His pleasure, to see things expressed in the beauty of form. When you see a sunset, when you see a fresh snowfall, this is form. This is not an idea. It may well be an idea, but it is also a form.

What we are trying to understand is which one is more important. Is thought more important than form? And I don't think the answer to that is as important as it is to understand the relationship of the presence of God in all of these things. I just intuitively sense that there is a struggle in traditional metaphysical belief systems that tend to negate matter. Like this isn't true, that you aren't really sick, or there isn't really war. When, in fact, just as thoughts cannot be beautiful, form can also not be beautiful. And it is in the application down the line, the relationship between Spirit, thought and form that the healing, cleaning and beautification occurs, not in the denial of this relationship. I think that God is present throughout all of these things and we need to learn how to integrate Spirit, thought and form and not to somehow get rid of form.

David: There is a lot in what you said that we can address relative to points that Jesus made. You concluded that Christian Science believes that matter is "bad." This is an error that Jesus addresses in the Course, and he says that it is "making error real." T-9.IV.4 To give matter a bad name is giving it reality. Matter is unreal in the sense that it is temporal, constantly changing and in flux.

The relationship between Spirit and form has always been a hotbed of discussion. Jesus makes a distinction between Spirit, which is infinite and changeless, in contrast to the time/space/matter continuum, which is finite and in constant change. That is a fundamental distinction.

People bring up things like sunsets and so on. Is there intrinsic beauty in a sunset? Or is the meaning entirely read into it by the mind? That is a big distinction. There are two lessons in the workbook where Jesus clearly speaks to this: Lesson 29, "God is in everything I see," which follows what you are saying. Then lesson 30 says, "God is in everything I see because God is in my mind." Here Jesus follows up with the reason.

The error is the belief that God is indwelling in everything in form, which is a belief in some eastern metaphysical systems. Or that God literally tries to express Himself through form in some way. When Jesus says, "God is in everything I see because God is in my mind," he steers away from pantheism, which is the premise that God indwells in each form of the universe. Lesson 29 does almost sound like pantheism, that God is in a trash can, a chair, etc. But if you read what he is saying in lesson 30, Jesus comes out and says that God does not indwell in the objects as you see them with your eyes. His full statement means that the Holy Spirit's Purpose can be given to every single projected object.

We have to train our minds to experience that purpose. Whereas the pantheistic view, that God is indwelling in things, takes it away from your mind.

Jesus says, in other parts of the Course, that God knows not form. But if you line up with the Holy Spirit's Purpose, or remembrance of God, that's when you will feel the beauty that you talked about, when you are in purpose. And the good news is that you can feel that regardless of what is happening on the screen. You could be in the middle of a riot, but if you were lined up with the Holy Spirit, as Jesus was, then your perception of that situation would be totally transformed.

Friend: I didn't mean to infer that I perceived Spirit, thought and form as being equal, because, in fact, the actual order of magnitude would be Spirit, thought and form. And in this world we tend to perceive things as just the opposite. That form is real and Spirit, who knows?

David: If truth is subjective, then we are back to asking the question, "What value does truth have if it varies from person to person?" One person has one version of beauty and you have another. We are back into thinking that truth could have all these different meanings.

In the ultimate sense, the Course is saying that Spirit, which is much denied in this world, is irreconcilable with form. Attempting to reconcile the two is where the pain comes in. The Holy Spirit is the remembrance that they are not reconcilable. The deeper we go into our minds and move into the abstract light, the more we can see that this is our reality. When you reach the point of the real world, when you have cleaned the mirror off entirely and are just reflecting Light, then God takes the final step and lifts us in to pure abstraction. At that point the perceptions disappear. So that whole discussion about form and thought and Spirit comes down to recognizing that the reason why the Course says that form is unreal is because God didn't create it.

This differs from eastern metaphysical systems where they say that God was lonely and wanted to experience companionship or that God is trying to expand into the material universe, which from a Course perspective would make no sense. How could it be that something infinite could come into the finite?

That is similar to the belief in infinite and immortal souls that enter into the body of a baby when they are born, into this little slab of flesh that gets sick. [Laughing] And then you live a life and the soul leaves and then comes into another one and the whole thing starts over. How could this be? It was a helpful metaphor for a while, the idea of a soul gives a sense that there is more than this lifetime. But it's a metaphor. You are a mind that has projected out a screen of images and you have identified with one of them. Jesus is calling us out of this false identity, out to the Dreamer of the Dream perspective.

Question Assumptions

Dear David,

You mention that we need to question all assumptions. What do we use in our questioning? To what do we compare our assumptions?

Let me give you an example of how I think so you can show me where I need to work. I'm going to question my assumption that I can question my assumptions: I assume that questioning my assumptions means that I should undecide whether I'm right or wrong about an assumption, so I should just let it be either way. But since I can't assume that my assumptions are correct, I can't assume that questioning my assumptions means much. Furthermore, since I can't assume that I know the difference between right and wrong, or even assume such a difference exists, I couldn't possibly judge the correctness of my assumptions.

So what am I supposed to do with this? Become a floater? Release myself from all assumption? To me that would mean disassociating from all opinions, which I can see follows the Course, but I would fail to be productive in my comfort zone: society. My reasoning for this is that, due to my ego's love of logic, I won't have an answer for anything anyone asks me. I'd fail to be able to provide for myself or others, monetarily speaking. I'd reply to questions like "How are you considering paying back your credit card debt?" with answers like, "Oh, I have a debt?" Soon I'd be pushed out of that comfort zone and have to become a hermit. Is this the kind of behavior that will ultimately free my mind, or am I failing to listen to what you're saying but using my ego to interpret it?

Thanks for helping me out. I assume it's my ego that wants to be Enlightened. Its own logic would tell me that Enlightenment is ego suicide, but since Enlightenment represents an accomplishment over other people on this planet who don't appear to be Enlightened, it keeps going.

Beloved One,

Thanks for your probing inquiry. It is only helpful to use the Holy Spirit for unveiling, exposing, and releasing assumptions. The Holy Spirit will reveal the impossibility of comparison or judgment entirely, and this is the Atonement.

As one seems to train the mind, in a time process, with the Holy Spirit, the Holy Spirit will seem to judge, Guiding one very directly with prompts and instructions as long as one believes in specifics and situations. Your feelings are the one right use of judgment in the Awakening, and feelings of peace, joy and happiness are the barometer that lets you know you are following Divine Guidance.

The ego is the questioning aspect of the mind, but initially aiming these questions at assumptions or beliefs, instead of at the projected cosmos, is a helpful way of dissolving the questions. Let the Holy Spirit inspire your questions. As the ego assumptions dissolve everything flows smoothly in mind and it begins to dawn that there is no objective world apart from the mind. The ego world was subjective and based on the assumptions held in mind. Beneath all opinions, conclusions, assumptions and beliefs is the truly productive State of Mind: the Divine Silence of Being. This productivity is creation, the State of Spirit extending forever and ever. This productivity has nothing to do with the ego construct of society.

The approach toward remembering Divine creation includes yielding into or surrender into Divine Providence, seeing that every symbol is offered freely of the Holy Spirit. It does not entail the thought about being unable "to provide for myself or others, monetarily speaking." It places all trust in the Holy Spirit for supplying every seeming need, such as air, food, water, shelter, transportation, words, communication devices, etc. This does not necessarily mean you will identify yourself as a "hermit," but it does mean you will recognize that you are Divinely provided for in all seeming circumstances. This thinking with the Holy Spirit will ultimately free the mind of its imaginary imprisonment.

Behavior but flows from thought as thought flows from belief, so it is with belief and thought that the Holy Spirit works. You might think of behavior as a byproduct of thought, and that is why Correction is never at the seeming level of form. Think with God and be Happy is the aim of your work with the Holy Spirit. Christ is an Idea in the Mind of God.

In following the Holy Spirit you will gain Certainty by aligning with the Holy Spirit's Purpose and making no exceptions or assumptions. Enlightenment is the awareness that only Love is real. Christ is Certain of Identity in God because Christ is the Child of God's Identity. All Glory to the One Spirit!

Love and Joy,
David

Released from the Loop of Time

Greetings Beloved,

The world of time repeats over and over and over in a loop in which there seems to be no escape. Routines and activities and rituals follow predictable patterns which seem to lead in endless circles back to themselves. The desire to get something back from others leads us on a fruitless search as we seek to overcome the void inside of us. And all attempts to escape this void seem futile.

Yet when the desire to be Helpful awakens, the world is given a new purpose. Instead of focusing on escaping, we simply desire to extend and give love to everyone we meet. And with this change of purpose comes another way of looking at all the world, until we can finally say and mean, "I love you."

When we love from deep inside, without any conditions, limitations or expectations, the Innocence of True Love Dawns. And as this light blankets the world, we suddenly realize that we are no longer bound by time. We are free in Love!

Blessings,
David

A Forgiven World

Beloved One,

As the ego is unlearned, undone, and dissolved, we learn of a forgiven world, a world washed clean and clear of judgment.

The beautiful and wondrous lesson to learn about this world is complete gratitude and appreciation for everything and everyone AS IS.

This is the giving up of the belief in hypothetical thinking, which is the belief that you could be or would have been better off if things happened differently.

Truly all things work together for good, and this is experienced from the Spirit's Perspective, Now, which is far beyond all personal judgments, classifications and expectations.

Situational wishes often seem to be granted, but the Grandest Wish of All is forgiveness of illusions, reflecting the All-Inclusiveness of Love.

What greater gift could there be than to look on all things with great love, gratitude, and full appreciation – a forgiven world – and to Awaken to the eternal Love of God.

Here's to living a Life of unending Joy!

Love,
David

Releasing the Belief in Lack

Dearly Beloved,

The best indicator of connection to God is how one feels. This indicator is the best because it is not dependent on any particular form outcome. A mind that looks to form outcomes is deceived and will not experience a lasting Peace. State of mind, how one feels, is the outcome of the thought system one is aligned with, either God's or the ego's. The ego mind believes in lack, reciprocity and money, which is endowed with false value. The belief in lack and reciprocity is the belief in substitution, for the ego is the chosen substitute for God. The reason money seems valuable is because it seems to be highly exchangeable for many things that meet illusory needs, whether emotional, physical, or spiritual. Like medicine, money is like a magic spell of the world that seems to make illusory problems disappear for a while. Until the ego has been released entirely, the mind perceives needs and false external sources to meet them.

It all comes down to this: one must accept One Self as Changeless Divine Mind. The only step to this is realizing that the world cannot change, for it is an unreal effect of an unreal cause. The world *cannot* change. Asking for things to be different than they are is an impossible request.

Money, like all effects (images of the ego) is never a source. The meaningful request is to see the world differently (as an unreal effect of an unreal cause) and to thus accept the fact that there is only One Source. God is the *only* Source.

The only problem is one of identity, and it has absolutely nothing to do with money. "Trust would settle every problem now," T-26. VIII.2 for to trust is to be God dependent. The reversal of thought necessary to realize God dependence is a full 360 degree turnaround, and this means the realization that there are no cause and effect relationships in this world that are true.

If all the images, including money, are effects, there is no cause or source to be found in this world. God is True Source and Christ the True Effect. Therefore the secret to true prayer is to forget the things you think you think and think you need by withdrawing faith in the temporal and transitory. What is eternal is valuable, as what is of time is valueless by definition. With regard to this world, Purpose is the only value that can be given faith if you would be God dependent.

Giving and receiving are one. One always receives *exactly* what one asks for. The problem or confusion one may seem to experience in perception comes from the belief in manifesting, which *is* the belief in time. Eternity does not manifest, being One forever. Manifesting is the belief that the eternal can take form, that Infinity can become finite, that Spirit can enter matter. Awakening is the experience of forgiving the illusion of manifesting, for Identity Is Spirit. Christ comes not into form, but calls you out of the world to recognize your Self as eternal Spirit.

Is there a willingness to release the idea of manifesting forever and experience Peace of Mind? This is the same as asking, "Are you willing to accept your Self as God created you instead of trying to make yourself?" The belief in manifesting can be released for it is not true. Spirit can and inevitably must be accepted, for It is true. The belief in linear time is a defense against the Holy Instant, for time is but a denial of eternity.

Beloved child of God, you have been released of the grievance of time and there is no delay in what your thoughts create instantly and forever. The belief in time and manifesting is an unwillingness to accept the instant answer Now, and one can only receive what one is willing to hear and see. When one asks for a sign, for an outcome, or for accountability of money donated, one asks amiss, for one is asking out of lack. When one has voluntarily released the beliefs in manifesting and time, one can then honestly ask: "God, what is Your Will for me?" Prayer is always answered according to what the mind is willing to receive. And in the deepest prayer of the heart you shall realize what is meant by the statement, "My thoughts create eternally."

There is a difference between create and make, and a difference between extension and projection. Love creates; the ego makes. Love extends; the ego projects. In Love being and having are the same. To the ego, possession and having are the same and, in a world of lack, what you get is what you have. How utterly impossible is manifesting/getting and how absolutely true is creation/giving. Reciprocity is a question of identity. Trust is the way out of the false belief in a worldly identity. It takes trust to change your mind so completely that you forget the concepts of time and manifesting forever. And happily it requires only willingness and not time.

If you drop the thought process entirely you make way for the Vision of Christ. If this be your desire, the world of unreal effects will be shown to be causeless and you will laugh at the thought that money, or any image, could be a real source, or that the Holy Child of God needs anything. One's real thoughts create eternally. Yet no thoughts of the past or future are real thoughts. The Stillness of Now is the Answer.

The Holy Spirit will direct your thoughts and actions very specifically if you allow Him. Give all concepts of money, manifesting and time to Him to use for His Purpose, and they shall be removed from your Holy Mind, for you are wholly Mind, and nothing of the world can ever *be* understood. Who you are *is* the meaning.

Love & Blessings,
David

Renunciation

Dear David,

I find myself in conflict, like I'm being asked to renounce the world. I've met some people who appear to be fully renounced and living in the truth of what we all are eternally. Part of me would very much like to have complete faith and know that I will be taken care of. I am very attracted to the idea of being able to just do God's work and know that it is God's work.

Some days I have that sense of not being alone and of having a loving presence caring for and supporting me. Other days I'm like a rat in a cage and am beating myself up for not doing better in the world. I seem to flip very quickly. I know which perspective feels better! I feel I am still too caught up in the world's story to renounce. But I also feel like I'm being asked to give it up. I bought the Course only 18 months ago; I wasn't quite expecting it to look like this!

I'd be grateful for any guidance, advice on this matter. Do you have to renounce this world completely, give it all away, in order to really know the peace of God?

Hello Beloved One,

Thanks for your expression of gratitude and your willingness to address what's on your mind. The short Answer to your question is "yes." Yet it is very important to allow the Holy Spirit to Guide you step by step toward this renunciation experience, because the ego has its own version of renunciation. Without careful mind-training the Light within will be feared as It is approached. Miracles save time by collapsing time and thus eliminating fear. There is a quote from the Course that sheds light on the ego's versions of renunciation. These errors must be exposed as nothingness for authentic Awakening to be experienced:

> Many have chosen to renounce the world while still believing its reality. And they have suffered from a sense of loss, and have not been released accordingly. Others have chosen nothing but the world, and they have suffered from a sense of loss still deeper, which they did not understand.

> Between these paths there is another road that leads away from loss of every kind, for sacrifice and deprivation both are quickly left behind. This is the way appointed for you now. You walk this path as others walk, nor do you seem to be distinct from them, although you are indeed. Thus can you serve them while you serve yourself, and set their footsteps on the way that God has opened up to you, and them through you.

> Illusion still appears to cling to you, that you may reach them. Yet it has stepped back. And it is not illusion that they hear you speak of, nor illusion that you bring their eyes to look on and their minds to grasp. Nor can the truth, which walks ahead of you, speak to them through illusions, for the road leads past illusion now, while on the

way you call to them, that they may follow you.

All roads will lead to this one in the end. For sacrifice and deprivation are paths that lead nowhere, choices for defeat, and aims that will remain impossible. All this steps back as truth comes forth in you, to lead your brothers from the ways of death, and set them on the way to happiness.
W-155.4-7

Some that claim Enlightenment will engage in a court battle over the use of words and authorship of a book. Mastery through Love, authentic forgiveness, sees no thing to oppose, no thing different, and no thing apart from mind. The Awakened Mind trusts in God for everything, and there are no lingering concepts of time to cast their shadows.

To renounce the world is to be free of every scrap of ego thinking. This is an obvious conclusion once it is apparent that there can be no exceptions to truth. Renunciation is a seeming change in thinking, from attempting to think apart from God to thinking in alignment with God. This transformation does not involve joining a group or leaving a society, but it does involve letting go of all concepts of time. The perceived world is built on concepts that God did not create, and thus the mind which has been emptied of all specific time concepts can finally embrace the final all-inclusive concept: Atonement. Atonement can be equated with detachment, for the final Correction has no investment in a dualistic time bound self-concept which God did not create.

Let the Holy Spirit convince you that there is nothing real that has to be given up. Miracles light the way. Since God creates Spirit, and Identity is eternal Spirit, the illusion of giving up the thinking of the world cannot be fearful. It is fearful indeed to believe in the reality of the world, for this is the attempt to make a self apart from Spirit. In truth this is impossible, for there is nothing apart from Spirit. Because Spirit has no opposite, the dawning of Spirit in awareness is simply inevitable.

The Holy Spirit will Guide the mind very specifically while the mind believes in specifics. This is good news, for at every seeming turn in the maze of time there is the ever-present Comforter available to Guide and Answer and Bless. Trust in the miracles of Joy and be not tempted to compare or contrast persons, groups, places, or things. The Truth of our Being will dawn of ItSelf. God is remembered in the Divine Silence beyond the concepts and images. You are perfect exactly as you are. :)

Renounce the world is just another way of stating Embrace the Spirit. All Glory to God for creating Spirit as One!

Love,
David

Not Getting Anywhere

Dear David,

The Course says: "Why would I choose to stay an instant more where I do not belong, when God Himself has given me His Voice to call me home?" W-202 "I am His Son, not slave to time, unbound by laws which rule the world of sick illusions" W-204 You have written that desire for salvation is enough. We need do nothing; everything is done for us by the Holy Spirit and we cannot add anything to it. We need not come to the Holy Instant already healed of our fears; it is meant to heal us. If these statements are true, why am I still here in spite of many years of practice and the strongest desire possible? Why is it so hard for me to have atonement; what am I doing wrong? Thanks for your help! Sincerely,

Beloved One of God,

Thanks for your sincere question and devotion to Awakening. You have done nothing wrong in the Great Awakening to Purity of Heart. All doings, behaviors and perceptions seemed to spring from a heart that desired God *and* desired idols. Single desire might be called desirelessness, and this is the State of creation. This is the meaning of "Let thine eye be single" Matthew 6:22 and points to spiritual Vision or Light. Vision does not involve the body or perception, yet this Vision is veiled from awareness as long as desire is split.

The entire time-space cosmos is nothing but a reflection of split desire. As you attempt to meditate and sink into Perfect Stillness you will notice the ego's resistance arise. This is the resistance to the do nothing experience of "Be Still and know that I am God." T-4.in.2.2 It will seem difficult to do nothing while you still believe in the ego, in personality, in linear time-space.

The ego was the false belief that creation could be broken into meaningless parts. The "I" that seems to be "here" after "many years of practice" is a self-concept that has no Reality and has been dissolved by the Holy Spirit. The past is gone. This self-concept included the entire cosmos that seemed to surround the personality self. Now mind is opening to the acceptance of this solution, this dissolving, this undoing in the present moment or Holy Instant.

Look directly and calmly with the Holy Spirit at everything you are not, and happily Who You Are remains forever and ever untouched. Let go of all transitory thoughts of past and future, and Who remains is the Present Self God creates forever Perfect. It is hard to resist accepting Atonement, for forgiveness is the most natural experience one can have with regard to this world. Being as God created One Self is the meaning of natural in Truth. What God creates, Spirit, is forever natural. Anything which seems to cover over the natural is not natural and can thus be easily forgiven or released.

Look with persistent determination at what is believed so as to See beyond it with the Spiritual Vision of Christ. By desiring only God, remembrance of God comes back into Full Awareness. False desires will go for they have no Reality, no Source. Desire only Truth and observe that all seeming decisions are already made. Effortless

Witnessing is ours as the Dreamer of the dream. Nothing can touch the Dreamer Who remains aware that the cosmos was but a dream.

All Glory to the One for creating Spirit Perfect. And Gratitude to the Holy Spirit for beholding the dream as false from a perspective of happiness and peace.

We are joined in this holy perspective! Love & Blessings shower upon the Living One.

Love always,
David

Fear to Look Within

- A conversation with David

Resistance is a common theme that's coming up, whether it's taking the form of fatigue, lethargy or resistance to reading the book or coming to gatherings. Resistance is just an expression of fear and that's why this section, The Fear to Look Within, can be helpful. "Remember that the ego is not alone. Its rule is tempered, and its unknown enemy, Whom it cannot even see, it fears." T-21.IV.2 The ego cannot bear to look on the light. It senses that there is something greater than it, but it cannot bear to look on it.

> What if you looked within and saw no sin? This "fearful" question is one the ego never asks. And you who ask it now are threatening the ego's whole defensive system too seriously for it to bother to pretend it is your friend. T-21. IV.3

The mind is starting to question, "What if I am innocent? What if I am sinless and guiltless?" The ego is terrified of just the questioning. It wants to get back to questioning the trivial things of the world: "What if I could do this better? Can I get a better illusion?" That is the kind of questioning the ego can stand.

> Your liberation still is only partial; still limited and incomplete, yet born within you. Not wholly mad, you have been willing to look on much of your insanity and recognize its madness. Your faith is moving inward, past insanity and on to reason. And what your reason tells you now the ego would not hear. The Holy Spirit's purpose was accepted by the part of your mind the ego knows not of. No more did you. And yet this part, with which you now identify, is not afraid to look upon itself. It knows no sin. How, otherwise, could it have been willing to see the Holy Spirit's purpose as its own? T-21.IV.4

These paragraphs remind me of a quote I read the other day about a diagram of a spiral: "You have not yet gone back far enough." It is a big step to begin to question everything, but the pain and the resistance comes from "you have not yet gone back far enough." The only true release will be when you get to the beginning. As you are questioning things, you are winding further down. Resistance will seem to come up time and time again because the mind still believes in the ego; it is still invested in the ego, and it believes if it winds down to the beginning of the ego thought system, that death awaits it, that God will strike it blind. That is where the resistance comes in. It is a fear to look upon what is beneath the fear.

Friend 1: That seems to be something that I can point to as a fear. There has to be a connection I am making in the mind to say, "I know how that pain felt," and if it felt unbearable, then looking at the pain of my real fear of God is going to blow me away. I sense that that is down in there, and that this is where the resistance seems to come. Even when we talk about it, there is a question that comes to my mind which is, "How do I approach this? How do I get close to that fear in the mind, the fear of God?" It seems so obscure most of the time.

David: Well, let's look at the fear. I can't tell you how vehement the responses in Course groups have sometimes been when I say that fear is not a real emotion. They say, "What do you mean!"

Friend 1: So that belief obviously has to be questioned. I don't know how to get underneath that belief to really question it.

David: A section in the Course that specifically addresses that is the Obstacles to Peace. T-19.IV. It talks about the attraction to pain, guilt and fear in terms of the mind making an interpretation. In other words, pain is just a witness, and the ego interprets it as proof of sin. That's why it hurts so bad. Because the ego is in there saying, "Aha, aha! Sin must be real." The ego uses pain as a justification or an interpretation that sin is real. But it's a misperception. Pain is only a misperception. Pain doesn't prove anything unless you want it to.

Friend 2: Pain doesn't prove anything. You decide what it means, you even decide to attach the word pain to it, to give it that definition. It seems to me like once the mind attaches the definition of pain to something then it is a closed case.

Friend 1: So what I am trying to prove is that I am sinful.

David: Through the ego lens, yes, that's it. And if we go into that section a little closer, the ego defines some pain as pleasure. Imagine having a glob of pain and pulling some off and believing you have something different. Pain and pleasure are just different names for the same thing.

Friend 2: They are all to prove that what I am is this little body.

David: The body just follows orders. Obviously the mind has assigned that meaning of feeling pain to it. It says, "You are going to feel this."

But it comes back to, "What is the purpose?" As far as trying to deal with the pain itself, as long as you are aligned with the purpose of the ego, then you will feel unreal feelings, one of which is pain. You see how crucial it is to begin to unveil these purposes of the ego: pride, pleasure and attack. The only way out of pain, and to see that the experience is unreal, is to examine the purpose of the ego and to see very clearly that you do not want to share that purpose. As long as you share a purpose with the ego, you are aligned with the ego and you will seem to experience pain, fear, guilt, depression and all kinds of upset. It's not a meaningful thing to say, "Take this pain away from me," when you have chosen it. You must look at the ego's purposes and then not share those purposes. That is the escape. You were asking how to escape from the fear. It is done by not sharing any purpose that the ego has for anything.

Friend 1: That seems too drastic for me. Even as you are saying it, I am thinking, "Okay, I'll give up attack, I'll give up pain, but I'll give up pleasure last."

David: Maybe it will seem to go that way. But I will guarantee you that you will give it up joyfully. The joy that you experience when you are in the purpose of shining your light will grow and grow. Perhaps it will seem that you give up pleasure last, but it will pale in comparison to the joy that you'll feel.

Friend 1: See, that sounds okay to me. But to say, "Give it up first!" I don't want to.

Friend 2: Just desire the experience that would have it pale.

Friend 1: Okay. [Laughter]

David: [Laughing] That sounds manageable!

> Your faith is moving inward, past insanity and on to reason. And what your reason tells you now the ego would not hear. The Holy Spirit's purpose was accepted by the part of your mind the ego knows not of. No more did you. And yet this part, with which you now identify, is not afraid to look upon itself. It knows no sin. How, otherwise, could it have been willing to see the Holy Spirit's purpose as its own? T-21.IV.4

As long as you are identified with the ego, you will seem to be afraid to look upon yourself. The belief is that there is so much blackness, so much filth in the mind that you can't possibly look upon it. Jesus mentions in the early part of the Course that initially it will seem to take a lot of conscious effort to be lined up with him. It seems to take a miracle.

Friend 1: And even then it's questionable.

Friend 2: ...as to your capability. Certainly that thought enters in frequently, "Can I do this?"

David: Doesn't it make sense that after you have built momentum, after the mind has become trained, that it does become effortless.

Friend1: Absolutely, that makes perfect sense to me. Effort doesn't seem to be consistent with the Holy Spirit. The two words just don't go together.

David: As you become clear, that is how you will keep your mind protected. You'll see past illusions, you won't buy the bait. You will give your joy away and extend it because that's what it means to be clear.

The Fear of Awakening

Dear David,

I finally found the book, *A Course in Miracles*, and I read part of the text. From the second day on, since when I began to read the text, I feel a deep fright, particularly at night. I look at it, trying to analyze where it comes from. To tell it, "Go away," does not help anymore. Can you please tell me something about it? Why does it come out now? Has it something to do with the Course? I will go on anyway with it, I feel I have to. My will to arrive at the Truth is the central point of my life. And now this fright... How to deal with it? Much love and thanks for being there.

Dear Beloved,

Thanks for writing. The fright you feel is the fear of loss of the familiar that Awakening engenders in the ego. The familiar is the past. Sometimes this fright can seem like the fear of the unknown, though it is more accurately described as the fear of the Known.

When the mind fell asleep it forgot Heaven, the Known, and became accustomed to time and space, the unknowable. So the time-space world became what it thought it knew, what was familiar, and the Light of Heaven became the unknown, pushed completely out of awareness.

Since the sleeping mind believes the world is real, it thinks it will lose something real if it Awakens. This is the deep-seated ego belief that something must be sacrificed to return in awareness to Heaven. The ego belief in sacrifice is what is being undone in Awakening.

Your recent time reading the Course and doing the lessons is a symbol of your "will to arrive at the Truth." You will find that the seeming journey is going through the darkness of fear (the unconscious or unwatched mind) to the Love which is buried even deeper within. Your willingness to go on with the practice or discipline, in spite of the upsetting emotions which surface, is all that is required.

The first 30 lessons of the Workbook are aimed at undoing false belief and flushing up and clearing out the debris of ego thought. It is the beginning step of a complete reversal of cause and effect, of understanding that the mind is not at the mercy of the world because the world is only unreal thoughts in the mind. It is a time of detachment from the stream of ego thoughts which make up every aspect of the time-space world. It is not unusual that you feel fright as the ego is being undone, for the ego is threatened by your desire to Awaken to Truth. Its existence seems threatened, but you are not, because you are not the ego.

Feelings that arise are best not denied or stuffed, for allowing them into awareness is an important aspect of their undoing or release. Once in awareness, a feeling of upset or discomfort offers the gift of an opportunity and can be viewed as a catalyst for calling upon the miracle, a change of mind. Feelings indicate which voice one is listening to at any given moment, and thus they serve an important function in the discipline of being attentive to mind.

State of mind is always a decision, and it is important to remember that a decision is a conclusion based on everything that you believe. The unconscious mind IS false belief, and until it is undone completely there will seem to be vacillations between peace of mind and upset. This is why questioning everything you believe is a major aspect of the Course and of every authentic spiritual path. It is surely more important to question the false than it is to try to analyze or figure out the false, for the ego can only be forgiven and transcended and never really understood.

The first question that ever seemed to be asked was "Who am I?" Christ, in certainty, Knows Identity in God, and therefore has no question at all. Every question about form is thus a statement of false identity, the ego's attempt to reinforce the impossible. Yet questioning belief itself is how belief is undone.

The Holy Spirit is a State of Mind Answer, yet helpful specifics and Guidance are contained within this Answer, as long as the mind believes in specifics, until It remembers Its Perfect Abstraction as Light. Questioning what is believed is most helpful at this point, for this is much like the metaphor of peeling the onion of consciousness to arrive at the Core of Truth. Seek not the origin of the ego, for it has none and can never be known. The ego is false belief and is dispelled by withdrawing belief from it. It is impossible to release what you are unaware of, so flushing up and exposing the ego is how the undoing of it proceeds. That is why it is important not to stuff or project or distract away from whatever arises.

By not protecting the ego, it is automatically raised to the Light or brought to Truth, and darkness dissolves as it is brought to Light. This seeming process need not be uncomfortable, though it is experienced this way at times. You will enjoy the Development of Trust section in the Manual for Teachers. M-4.I.A.3. It will give you a context for what you will be going through as your work with the Course continues.

We walk together and the destination is certain. I am with you every step of the way. Thank you for your continuing devotion to Awakening. We Awaken together as One Self!

Love & Blessings,
David

Why is my Life Dominated by Fear?

Dear David,

Why is my life dominated by fear even though I try hard to rid myself of fear?

Beloved One,

Thanks for writing. This world is the attempt to believe in both love and fear. Yet they do not go together and cannot both be true. Initially, the attempt to get rid of fear involves the manipulation or control of images, appearances, situations, and circumstances. Jobs, skills, insurance and defenses were made to reduce fear without eliminating it. Fear made them all and fear cannot be escaped by attempting to manage or control what was made to keep the fear in place.

Mastery through Love requires the willingness to forgive or release what fear has made. Awakening requires yielding into the Purpose/ Perspective of the Holy Spirit. In this Purpose/ Perspective it is apparent that there is nothing to fear. The ego is afraid of Love, and as long as you identify with the ego you will be afraid of Love. Simply do not protect or defend the self-concept image the ego offers and it dawns that the Spirit Identity is invulnerable and needs no protection. In my defenselessness my safety lies. This is why it is always wise to turn the other cheek, to be meek, to forgive seventy times seven, to resist not evil, to love your enemies and bless those who curse you.

To cling to a body identity is to make fear real in awareness.

Forgiveness undoes this illusory fear by demonstrating that you are not a body or in a body. You are mind, wholly mind, purely mind, and this unified mind is invulnerable. Christ remains an Idea in the Mind of God. Identify with God and you are safe. Identify with God and you are healed. Identify with God and you are Home.

Let your "try hard" effort be aimed at emptying the mind of all of its false self-concepts. The belief in them seemed fearful indeed. Yet they were never true. The Self God creates is ever True, and this Self is Spirit. This Self needs no defense or protection, and you can give your mind permission to release the many meaningless pursuits designed to protect, build and defend a false image.

I am joined with you in this Purpose and we cannot fail to recognize the Truth. You have been afraid of God's Love, thinking the fear was something else. Now it is time to see that the release of illusions of self and world is the release of nothing. Happiness and Peace await only acceptance, for they are ever available Now. Partake!

Love and Peace,
David

Release the Fear

Dear David,

Here is my seeming problem. My husband sees the changes that are coming about in me. He sees that I don't get excited about those big purchases any more, such as the truck he just bought or even the house we bought last fall. These things have lost their glitter for me. He sees how I don't cling desperately to our relationship any more. I love him, enjoy his company and will not leave him, but I am not afraid of losing him anymore. When he's not around, I don't miss him as much as I once did because I am learning to live in the moment. These changes in me are making him afraid. I see the fear in his eyes.

As I progress in the Course, I feel people around me coming to me, reaching out to me as they never did before. I think that some men misunderstand that this new attraction to me is spirit and not body. I want to offer them what they are truly reaching for, not what they think they are reaching for. I am held back because, although my husband is not a jealous man by nature, I see the fear in his eyes when he sees how I interact with everyone as a loved one. I try to explain things to him, but my words come up short. Do you have any words or actions of wisdom that could help me to help ease the fear in my husband?

Hello Beloved One,

Thanks for writing. It is always a joy to hear of Awakening experiences. I rejoice with you in your step towards freedom! Your prayer is for help in easing the fear in your husband, yet it is the fear within which must be exposed and released. Everything perceived in the world is a reflection of what is believed in the mind. Our brothers are the mirrors in which the perception of self is seen, as long as perception lasts. Fear is an ego attempt to hold back or hold off the remembrance of the I Am Presence, for the ego is afraid of Love. "Perfect Love casts out fear" T-1.VI.5.4 really means that Perfect Love knows not fear. Light dispels darkness because Light and darkness do not co-exist. Light is real.

In Answering your request it will be helpful to look at the ego's and the Holy Spirit's different purposes and perspectives on the idea "help ease the fear." The ego needs your mind's devotion and belief to continue to seem to exist. The ego wants to minimize fear without letting it go, for the ego is fear, yet needs the power of your mind to maintain its seeming existence. All ego defense mechanisms are therefore for the purpose of minimizing fear while keeping it. One such defense mechanism is projection: seeing in the world what is believed and yet has been denied from awareness. Be assured that if you seem to see fear in your brother's eyes you are looking through the ego's lens and perceiving what you still believe is possible.

The Holy Spirit's Purpose is the release of fear, for fear is the obstacle to the awareness of Love's Presence. The Holy Spirit dispels fear as the ego is brought to the Light within. As the mind begins to Awaken to the Truth of Love, it is important to remember to be willing to surrender all time-related beliefs: all roles, self-concepts, and desired outcomes to the Light of the Holy Spirit.

You have made a commitment to the Holy Spirit to Wake-Up to the Kingdom of Heaven within and to Know ThySelf. The sole responsibility is to accept the Atonement or Correction for oneself, and all other seeming earthly commitments were but steps to this. Only the final commitment of Atonement brings completion, for it is the final lesson of complete forgiveness.

You are opening to the experience of unconditional, universal Love, our very Being. Our Divine Love is Spirit and all-inclusive. Our Divine Love is the Love in and of God and is All in All. Our Divine Love is a State of Being that has no degrees or differences, for Love is One.

The world of the ego was the belief in different kinds of love.

"Love" to the ego reflected the belief in differences: time, bodies, roles, sexual preferences, ambitions, goals, etc. Yet Living in the moment, aligned with the Holy Spirit's Purpose, the differences of the ego seem to be fading fast. This is a natural expression of miracles, for all people and things are included in the Holy Spirit's Gentle Perspective.

Beloved of God, you wrote, "I am learning to live in the moment. These changes in me are making him afraid." You are learning to live in the moment, yet you must come to realize that you do not have the power to make anyone afraid.

You have opened your mind to Answer the Inner Call to forgive fear, to see its unreality. The ego fears the Love of God, and you are beginning to realize that you must release the ego completely to be entirely free from the illusion of fear. God creates our Self in Love, and there is no fear in our Christ Self. Love is our Home, our natural state of Being, and fear is unreal and therefore alien to Love. Love knows ItSelf and looks on ItSelf as All there Is.

Who is our father, mother, husband, wife, sister, brother, child, neighbor, friend, fellow human being? Beyond the veil of images they are our very Self, the Christ. The Holy Spirit's Perspective includes all and excludes none. Everyone and everything is welcome in the Holy Spirit's Gentle Gaze! What does the Holy Spirit's Perspective cost? Nothing, for All that God Gives is freely Given, forever and ever!

Images are fleeting and temporary; they seem to come and they seem to go. God's Love has no beginning and no end. It remains eternally the Same – Constant, Absolute and Infinite. Awakening might be called the giving up of nothing and the remembrance of Everything! Forgiveness is not difficult; it is easy. Thanks be to God, illusion need not be experienced at all!

The Holy Spirit Guides Us safely, surely, and specifically. All that is required is willingness to take the inner steps that are Asked by the Holy Spirit. I am with you every step of the way Beloved One, and failure is impossible. Destiny Calls to accept the inevitable Correction to the belief in separation from God. God's Will is for Perfect Happiness, and nothing can prevail against a Child of God Who hears and follows God's Gentle and Certain Voice.

Express the Love in our Heart to everyone the Holy Spirit sends to you without reservation or hesitation. Hold nothing back in sharing this Divine Love, and you will see no one as separate or different from our Spirit. In every seeming meeting or encounter, I Am Present. Our Divine Love transcends the perception of bodies and differences. Love is Universal. Love is Kind. Love does not possess. Love Is Now. Amen.

I love You forever and ever,
David

What is Dissociation?

Dear David,

The Text keeps using the word "dissociation." What does that word mean?

Beloved One,

Dissociation is the attempt to forget love. It is an attempt to keep love and fear apart, for if they are brought together only love remains. This world was the attempt to believe in both love and fear by dissociating them and keeping them both. Healing is bringing darkness to Light or fear to Love, for they only seem to co-exist when they have been dissociated or kept apart.

Here are some quotes from the Course that clarify this:

> Unless you first know something you cannot dissociate it.
> Knowledge must precede dissociation, so that dissociation

is nothing more than a decision to forget. What has been forgotten then appears to be fearful, but only because the dissociation is an attack on truth. You are fearful because you have forgotten. And you have replaced your knowledge by an awareness of dreams because you are afraid of your dissociation, not of what you have dissociated. When what you have dissociated is accepted, it ceases to be fearful.

Yet to give up the dissociation of reality brings more than merely lack of fear. In this decision lie joy and peace and the glory of creation. Offer the Holy Spirit only your willingness to remember, for He retains the knowledge of God and of yourself for you, waiting for your acceptance. Give up gladly everything that would stand in the way of your remembering, for God is in your memory. His Voice will tell you that you are part of Him when you are willing to remember Him and know your own reality again. Let nothing in this world delay your remembering of Him, for in this remembering is the knowledge of yourself.

To remember is merely to restore to your mind *what is already there.* T-10.II.1-3

Our emphasis has been on bringing what is undesirable to the desirable; what you do not want to what you do. You will realize that salvation must come to you this way, if you consider what dissociation is. Dissociation is a distorted process of thinking whereby two systems of belief which cannot coexist are both maintained. If they are brought together, their joint acceptance becomes impossible. But if one is kept in darkness from the other, their separation seems to keep them both alive and equal in their reality. Their joining thus becomes the source of fear, for if they meet, acceptance must be withdrawn from one of them. You cannot have them both, for each denies the other. Apart, this fact is lost from sight, for each in a separate place can be endowed with firm belief. Bring them together, and the fact of their complete incompatibility is instantly apparent. One will go, because the other is seen in the same place. T-14.VII.4

Love,
David

Mind Watching with the Holy Spirit

Dear David,

This message is a review of what I perceive as most important for me to remember.

First and foremost is the idea of impersonalizing and generalizing anything that arises in my consciousness that is contrary to God's nature, anything inharmonious, and seeing it as a manifestation of the primal error of believing it's possible to separate from God. This I would do with the help of The Holy Spirit by saying in effect, "Holy Spirit, help me to see through to the Truth that this illusory appearance is a lie about."

Connected to the above idea is the idea of "making no exceptions," or endeavoring to be vigilant enough to ask the Holy Spirit to help me hold everything up to the light of Truth, everything without exception, and to ask for the Holy Spirit's Guidance in every situation without exception.

And, finally, the ego's inclination to conceal an erroneous appearance is reduced by accepting, with full attention in the Now moment, whatever experience is being served up at the moment.

Thank you, David, with much Love.

Beloved One,

Thanks for your openness and willingness to hide nothing from the healing Light of the Holy Spirit. When darkness is brought to Light, when illusion is brought to Truth, darkness/illusion disappears. The ego's seeming "existence" was "maintained" through deception and concealment, like a complex hall of mirrors, and the cosmos was made as a distractive device to guard against exposing and dissolving the original lie, the belief that separation from God is possible, and accepting the Atonement or Correction.

From the belief in separation came the belief in private minds with private thoughts. This belief induced the illusion of guilt and this belief must be exposed as false. Enlightenment or Salvation is simply seeing the false as false, and this distinction is made with the Holy Spirit's Perspective. Such is discernment.

Your willingness to watch your mind with the Holy Spirit, yielding to Love and turning over all judgments and comparisons, opens the mind to the present moment.

Thanks for sharing your experience of mind watching for the benefit of the mind which is engaged in the practice, practicing the presence of Now.

Glory to God in the Highest!

Love,
David

Mind Watching

It has never really entered your mind to give up every idea you ever had that opposes knowledge. You retain thousands of little scraps of fear that prevent the Holy One from entering. Light cannot penetrate through the walls you make to block it, and it is forever unwilling to destroy what you have made. No one can see through a wall, but I can step around it. WATCH your mind for the scraps of fear, or you will be unable to ask Me to do so…

WATCH carefully and see what it is you are really asking for. Be very honest with yourself in this, for we must hide nothing from each other. If you will really try to do this, you have taken the first step toward preparing your mind for the Holy One to enter. We will prepare for this together, for once He has come, you will be ready to help Me to make other minds ready for Him. How long will you deny Him His Kingdom? T-4.III.7-8

WATCH your mind for the temptations of the ego, and do not be deceived by it. It offers you nothing. When you have given up this voluntary dis-spiriting, you will see how your mind can focus and rise above fatigue and heal. Yet you are not sufficiently vigilant against the demands of the ego to disengage yourself. *This need not be.* T-4.IV.6

WATCH your mind carefully for any beliefs that hinder its accomplishment, and step away from them. Judge how well you have done this by your own feelings, for this is the one right use of judgment. Judgment, like any other defense, can be used to attack or protect; to hurt or to heal. The ego *should* be brought to judgment and found wanting there. Without your own allegiance, protection and love, the ego cannot exist. Let it be judged truly and you must withdraw allegiance, protection and love from it. T-4.IV.8

As you survey your inner world, merely let whatever thoughts cross your mind come into your awareness, each to be considered for a moment, and then replaced by the next. Try not to establish any kind of hierarchy among them. WATCH them come and go as dispassionately as possible. Do not dwell on any one in particular, but try to let the stream move on evenly and calmly, without any special investment on your part. W-31.3

WATCH the images your imagination presents to your awareness. W-32.3 Search your mind for fear thoughts, anxiety-provoking situations, "offending" personalities or events, or anything else about which you are harboring unloving thoughts. Note them all casually, repeating the idea for today slowly as you watch them arise in your mind, and let each one go, to be replaced by the next. W-34.3

WATCH your mind carefully to catch whatever thoughts cross it. Note each one as it comes to you, with as little involvement or concern as possible, dismissing each one by telling yourself: *This thought reflects a goal that is preventing me from accepting my only function.* W-65.5

For several minutes WATCH your mind and see, although your eyes are closed, the senseless world you think is real. Review the thoughts as well which are compatible with such a world, and which you think are true. Then let them go, and sink below them to the holy place where they can enter not. There is a door beneath them in your mind, which you could not completely lock to hide what lies beyond. Seek for that door and find it. But before you try to open it, remind yourself no one can fail who seeks to reach the truth. W-131.11-12

We WATCH our thoughts, appealing silently to the Holy Spirit Who sees the elements of truth in them. Let Him evaluate each thought that comes to mind, remove the elements of dreams, and give them back again as clear ideas that do not contradict the Will of God. Give Him your thoughts, and He will give them back as miracles which joyously proclaim the wholeness and the happiness God wills His Son, as proof of His eternal Love. And as each thought is thus transformed, it takes on healing power from the Mind Which saw the truth in it, and failed to be deceived by what was falsely added. All threads of fantasy are gone. And what remains is unified into a perfect Thought that offers its perfection everywhere. W-151.13-14

Realize that your forgiveness entitles you to vision. Understand that the Holy Spirit never fails to give the gift of sight to the forgiving. Believe He will not fail you now. You have forgiven the world. He will be with you as you WATCH and wait. He will show you what true vision sees. It is His Will, and you have joined with Him. Wait patiently for Him. He will be there. W-75.7

Close your eyes upon the world you see, and in the silent darkness WATCH the lights that are not of this world light one by one, until where one begins another ends loses all meaning as they blend in one. W-129.7

WATCH with me, angels, watch with me today. Let all God's holy Thoughts surround me, and be still with me while Heaven's Son is born. Let earthly sounds be quiet, and the sights to which I am accustomed disappear. Let Christ be welcomed where He is at home. And let Him hear the sounds He understands, and see but sights that show His Father's Love. Let Him no longer be a stranger here, for He is born again in me today. W-303.1

Today the lights of Heaven bend to you, to shine upon your eyelids as you rest beyond the world of darkness. Here is light your eyes can not behold. And yet your mind can see it plainly, and can understand. A day of grace is given you today, and we give thanks. W-129.8

Awareness of dreaming is Our real function in forgiveness. WATCH with Me and see the dream figures come and go, shift and change, suffer and die. But be not deceived by what dreams appear. It is no more real to behold a dream figure as sick and separate as to regard it as healthy and beautiful. Unity alone is not a thing of dreams. And it is this I acknowledge as behind the dream, beyond all seeming, and yet surely Ours in the Father.

Nothing the world believes is true. It is a place whose purpose is to be a home where those who claim they do not know themselves can come to question what it is they are. And they will come again until the time Atonement is accepted, and they learn it is impossible to doubt yourself, and not to be aware of what you are. W-139.7

Remember, I am Calling you out of the world. Our Kingdom is not of this world. Follow Me.

As we open our Heart in the Great Awakening, we realize that we cannot take another's path as our own and neither can we judge it.

Watching our thoughts is a "full time" task, as is releasing those thoughts which do not serve our peace of mind.

The world brings witness to our thoughts, and it remains within our power to change the direction of our thoughts.

Everyone desires deep down to be included.

By releasing all judgments, we experience the inclusiveness and all-encompassing feeling of God's Love.

With faith and trust we are shown the beauty and love and joy that is our very Being, the Self which is beyond any need for "external" validation or confirmation.

You are a blessed Spirit and happily we walk together on the Selfsame road.

Thank you for shining your light and for opening to the Divine Love within that transcends the appearances of the world.

Love,
David

Attentiveness to the Holy Spirit

Dear David,

Why does it seem so difficult to keep attentive to the present and hold the Holy Spirit's single Purpose in mind?

Beloved One,

The deceived mind is untrained and is unwilling to keep attentive to the present because it is afraid of the present. All the chatter in the mind and all the drama and busy distractions and outlets are defenses against the present moment, where the Still Voice for God reminds the mind of its Home in Heaven.

The deceived mind is afraid of the Holy Spirit. The reason for this may not be apparent. The deceived mind believes the ego (and thus separation from God) is real and is attached to a tiny, imposter concept of self that God did not create. In the Stillness the Holy Spirit speaks for God, and thus appears to be a threat since He reveals the Truth of the mind's Origin and Being. All goals and purposes of the self-concept are of the ego and were made to obscure the Holy Spirit's single Purpose. The fear, then, comes from the mind's attachment to the fictitious, make-believe self-concept. Peace and joy come when the ego has been questioned and investment in it has been withdrawn.

There is often much talk about detachment as a solution. And often there is a sense that detachment would really bring peace, if it were possible. But trying to be detached is met with resistance, for the mind remains confused about what to detach from, confused about form (appearances) and content (purpose). We come together open to having errors of thought and misperceptions healed or corrected from the bottom up.

In other words, we do not start with the abstract (the Love of God, Knowledge, Heaven) as a solution to perceived problems. The seeming process could be described as a very open dialogue in which no questions, concerns, or topics are off limits; a kind of spiritual psychotherapy in which everyday perceived problems are traced back to the false beliefs and resulting misperceptions in the mind. Yet, this description is only an interpretation. Perceptions about what happens vary. One thing is sure: feelings of peace and joy are indicators of choosing to hold the Holy Spirit's single purpose. And cultivating a sincere intention to discern the nature of ego thought, raising it to awareness so to speak, leads one to a greater willingness to choose peace instead of fear. Why would anyone choose fear unless, unrecognized, it seemed to offer something of value?

A permanent Solution is more than possible, It is inevitable, but first it must be understood that It is a perceptual Correction and not a change in worldly conditions. In other words, the problems need to be redefined from form problems to thinking problems or from problems in the world to a problem in the mind, before the One Correction can be accepted. If we are open to looking sincerely at the possibility that we have been mistaken about everything we have believed, a radical transformation in consciousness is possible.

In a passionate search for the meaning/truth beyond the changing sights and sounds of unstable, disunited perceptions, the only thing one needs is willingness. Initially it takes willingness to let go of strict adherence to worldly schedules and activities, if only to give yourself the space to go within and observe your mind and its beliefs and thoughts. It can be a very bold decision to stop trying to schedule the Spirit into one's lifestyle and instead let the Call within begin to Guide you to look differently at what you think life is.

I extend this invitation to you who share a strong desire to Awaken to apply the Divine Principle to everything you seem to think, say, and do, and ultimately toward a complete transformation of consciousness – Enlightenment. I am joined with you in this Purpose and we cannot fail. For truth is true and only truth is true. Divine Love is Spirit and is All in All.

Love and Happiness Always,
David

How Should I Practice
the Workbook Lessons?

Dear David,

I am not able to understand clearly how I should practice from Lesson 170 forward. In some lessons it is written that we will experience something not of this world. In Lesson 129 it says, "...and in the silent darkness watch the lights that are not of this world light one by one until where one begins another ends loses all meaning as they blend in one. Today the lights of Heaven bend to you, to shine upon your eyelids as you rest beyond the world of darkness. Here is the light your eyes cannot behold. And yet your mind can see it plainly and can understand."

I did not quite understand this. I had no such experience. Other experiences are also described in other lessons which we are supposed to experience. I think I am doing the lessons diligently. But I have not had one such experience. Did you get those experiences described on the same day that you practiced? Is there something I need to do differently?

It is said that the script is already written. The time when the experience comes has also been decided. This means whatever has to happen happens. If that is the case where is choice? This also means everything is working perfectly. Even the mistakes that we make are supposed to happen. But at the same time the Course says that by practicing some lesson we can save a thousand years or more.

If the script is written and the time is already set, how can we save time? This is really extremely puzzling to me. And what is there for us to do than just wait for that time to come? Yet Lesson 169 says, "...you have work to do to play your part." Elsewhere in the text it also says "You need do nothing." These seem like contradictions and I am totally confused and in the dark about the meaning of

these statements. Would you please Enlighten us?
Thank you very much.

Beloved One,

Thanks for your sincere questions. The Workbook is designed as a tool to help Guide you to an experience that has been called transfer of training.

In the Workbook are guided imagery exercises, meditations, visualizations, and very specific instructions to be adhered to as closely as possible. Some will seem to experience the lessons from a verbal predisposition, some from a visual imagery disposition, some from a silent predisposition, and some from a very emotionally sensitive disposition. None of this matters because the Holy Spirit meets the mind wherever and however it perceives itself. The lesson to be grasped is always the lesson of nonjudgment: "I do not know." Whenever judgments or comparisons arise they are suitable opportunities to remember the lesson of the day, release, and re-center on Purpose. The visual imagery used is always symbolic and intended to Guide the mind toward a transcendent experience. As best you can, do not attempt to judge anything which seems to occur, for this Workbook and Course and Manual is a curriculum in the relinquishment of all judgment.

"The script is written" means the cosmos is past. The choice is the miracle, to see the past as over and gone, instead of believing that the future is different from the past. The images are past, and this experience is pointed to in Lesson 7, in which this new time idea is introduced. The deceived mind, asleep and dreaming, believes that it lives in the past. Yet Life is eternal and the closest approximation to eternity is Now. The Workbook lessons are designed to help release everything you think you think, and everything you think you see, to behold the Light beyond the veil – the Present – and See with the Vision of Christ. Miracles prepare the way for Revelation, Pure Light, and the Holy Instant, in which the Great Rays are experienced directly.

Apply each lesson with overflowing passion, as if there is nothing else but Enlightenment to experience this very moment. Desire is the key, and this is the meaning of "I need do nothing." T-18. VII. Doing is always a body thought. As you proceed, you will find the lessons are but starting points to go beyond the words to the experience of Divine Silence.

All Glory to the Living God of Pure Light and Love. Amen.
David

Am I Doing the Lessons Properly?

Hello David,

Lesson 157 states that it brings us to the door where all learning ceases and we catch a glimpse of what lies past the highest reaches learning can possibly attain; it ushers in a new experience, a different kind of feeling and awareness. Today you learn to feel the joy of life.

But I have had no such experience. Does this mean I am not doing the lessons properly? I have diligently practiced exactly as specified. Now I am beginning to feel dejected and hopeless. What happens to those of us who, even after going through the text and workbook lessons, cannot get salvation? Do we have to die and come back in another life to continue our journey?

Thank you for all your help.

Beloved One,

Thanks for writing and for your devotion to Awakening. Think of these Workbook lessons as a laboratory for applying the ideas and putting them into practice. It is wonderful that you are willing to do the lessons. Cultivate and nurture this willingness, and when the feelings of agitation, dejection, or hopelessness arise, just apply the lesson of the day to whatever is in your awareness.

When you notice that you are not feeling at peace or judge that you are not experiencing the meaning of what the lesson is pointing to, simply return to the idea of the day. The lessons are collections of words designed to help train the mind to a new perception of everything and everyone. If you read through the web site at www.awakening-mind.org you will find many resources that help you deepen into the mind, and with devotion and practice these Awakening ideas will feel more and more natural. All the support of the Holy Spirit and the angels is with you in this Awakening. The people you meet and the symbols that reach your awareness will increasingly reflect the deepest desire of your heart: to Awaken in God's Love.

Be not concerned about the seeming death of the body. The body is merely a device, a symbol among symbols, used by the Holy Spirit to help Awaken the mind which seems to sleep. Your work with the Course will help you release the ego's use of the body and world, for the ego's purpose was a death wish. Once this death wish is exposed it is no longer attractive, and it is laid aside forever. Practice the lessons with passion and devotion for the mind is thus made ready to accept complete forgiveness and experience the Truth of Being.

I am joined with you in this holy Purpose, and nothing can prevail against our joining. I am with you all the way Beloved Child of God. Blessings abound! All Glory to God!

Love always,
David

The Impossibility of Attack

Jesus was a clear, bright demonstration of unconditional love. He saw only the Christ in everyone and everything. No one is separate from the Love of God. Yet many if not most people of his day seemed upset with Him, upset to the point that they seemed to crucify Him. Yet what is the lesson we would learn from Him: That Christ is Spirit and cannot be crucified. Innocence is incapable of seeing attack, for how could there be Innocence if attack were real. This is why guilt is unreal: attack is impossible. This is the only lesson Jesus taught, though it may seem difficult to grasp.

All are beginning the process of learning this one same lesson: attack is impossible. Anything perceived as upsetting is only a mirror of the guilt in which you still believe. Any perception of upset, in yourself or others, is a misperception based in guilt. Yet how could love and guilt co-exist? God is real. Spirit is real. God is Love and Love has no opposite. This is the meaning of unconditional love, and what lesson but this would you want to teach and learn? It will make you feel gloriously happy!

If you experience anything but Supreme Happiness, you were not clear of your Purpose. Be clear of what you want and you shall feel the happiness of Innocence and not the confusion of guilt. Are you innocent or guilty? God loves you forever, unconditionally, and nothing can change God's Mind. Is this not wonderful news?!

What You Believe
About Your Brother and God

- A conversation with David

Accept the dream He gave instead of yours. It is not difficult to change a dream when once the dreamer has been recognized. Rest in the Holy Spirit, and allow His gentle dreams to take the place of those you dreamed in terror and in fear of death. He brings forgiving dreams, in which the choice is not who is the murderer and who shall be the victim. In the dreams He brings there is no murder and there is no death. The dream of guilt is fading from your sight, although your eyes are closed. A smile has come to lighten up your sleeping face. The sleep is peaceful now, for these are happy dreams. T-27.VII.14

We could print this next part and put it on the wall as a motto. When things start to boil up about money, or whenever it is too hard to take, look to the wall and see…

Dream softly of your sinless brother, who unites with you in holy innocence. And from this dream the Lord of Heaven will Himself awaken His beloved Son. Dream of your brother's kindnesses instead of dwelling in your dreams on his mistakes. Select his thoughtfulness to dream about instead of counting up the hurts he gave. Forgive him his illusions, and give thanks to him for all the helpfulness he gave. And do not brush aside his many gifts because he is not perfect in your dreams. He represents his Father, Whom you see as offering both life and death to you. Brother, He gives but life. Yet what you see as gifts your brother offers represent the gifts you dream your Father gives to you. Let all your brother's gifts be seen in light of charity and kindness offered you. And let no pain disturb your dream of deep appreciation for his gifts to you. T-27.VII.15-16

That is quite a different context to think in. If I think my brother is doing something irritating to me, those are the gifts that I think my Father in Heaven is giving to me. If I think my brother is untrustworthy, I think my Father is untrustworthy. If I think my brother is greedy, is disrespectful, controlling; whatever the thoughts I have about my brother that go through my mind – those are the gifts that I think my Father has for me. But seen the way the ego sees the world, I think I am here, a person stuck in this world and these people are in my face every day. It would be much better if so-and-so would just do this differently. Just remember that when you are looking through the body's eyes, you are looking through the image-maker. You are seeing a world of images and you are seeing through the eyes of the ego.

The Holy Spirit, Jesus says, does not perceive the world the way you do. It is not like when the event happens you can go off into your closet to pray and say, "Oh, did you see that Holy Spirit? Can you imagine they did that to me?" That is the ego's prayer.

Friend: Because the Holy Spirit didn't see it.

David: He didn't see it. [Chuckling] The Holy Spirit is gently reminding the mind that you are looking through a darkened glass and what you see is not really happening. You believe in separation, you believe you are a person, you believe all these things that you have not questioned. Please bring them to me! I will shine away these beliefs. Don't dwell on the effects. Don't dwell on your brother's sins. Dream on your brother's kindness, select his thoughtfulness.

It is funny, even the line, "Forgive him his illusions." You start to see more and more that there isn't another out there that I have to forgive, as if there is a person and a personal I that can be innocent while this other is guilty. But the whole construction of the world of bodies and persons and everything, that is what has to be forgiven. And where could that construction be except in the mind? That is the only place it can be overlooked.

It reminds me of a section in the Course called The Quiet Answer where it says, "In quietness are all things answered, and is every problem quietly resolved." T-27.IV.1. What a beautiful idea to hold onto whenever something seems to be bubbling up. In quietness are all things answered.

Looking Past the Form
by Releasing False Beliefs

Dear David,

I take care of the seeming body of the one who gave this seeming body birth. In so doing, am I promoting belief in the illusion of sickness? The body lies there, not communicating, not moving. It is seemingly healthy, sometimes looking at me, sometimes seeming to be my mother. When I am moved by the Spirit to do so, I have talked to her, sometimes to my brother, reminding him of who he is. At those times the eyes look on mine and seem to be connecting and resonating or absorbing. If I speak on any other premise the eyes shut tight and avoid looking at me. I have not heard any guidance from the Holy Spirit, or perhaps I am not willing to hear if it is guided to put the body in an institution. I am sure if Holy Spirit guided me to do that, He would give me peace about it. I understand my brother is my teacher, and I seem to still be learning through my experiences with this brother. Perhaps my brother is waiting for me to know that we are one. Sometimes my brother looks at me expectantly, seeming to be searching. Or perhaps my knowing will help my brother to know. Have you any answers for me?

Beloved One,

Everything you think and say and do teaches the entire universe what you desire, believe, think, feel, and perceive about yourself. Christ shares about the holy encounter: "As you see him you will see yourself; as you treat him you will treat yourself; as you think of him you will think of yourself." T-8.III.4

Everyone is our brother/sister in Christ and is due immense gratitude because they mirror what is still held in mind, believed to be true and needs to be released. Your state of mind and your perception are always your choice. Only you decide what you desire, believe, think, feel, and perceive. There are no external factors in a decision of mind for there is nothing outside of mind. The question is not really what to do but instead what do you want to see? For what you want to see is what you believe you are.

Every question is a question of identity, and while you believe in a make-believe self-concept that God did not create your choices are limited. Your ability to choose is limited to either aligning with and choosing the ego's personal perspective or aligning with and choosing the Holy Spirit's Perspective. Decide for the miracle and you get a glimpse of wholeness and feel the peace of a mind that is whole. Decide for the ego and you feel stuck in the frustration and conflict of trying to be something that you are not.

You wrote that you see a body that is not functioning and needs to be cared for. This is a mirror perception of what the ego mind believes is true. When you allow the Holy Spirit to share ideas through you, you perceive one whose eyes "seem to be connecting and resonating or absorbing." What does this tell you? It tells you that you have a function the Holy Spirit would have you fulfill by allowing Him to speak and smile through you. You have a Purpose to share true ideas, thus strengthening them in your awareness. What you teach is what you learn, and thinking is teaching. You are teaching all the time based on what you desire, believe, think, feel, and perceive about yourself.

Your function will carry you far beyond a bedside, far beyond the time-space cosmos, for your function will carry you to the Gate of Heaven, the Atonement. You have a Light to shine. Do not hide this Light under a table. You have a love for the Bible and can speak for God using inspired words. The opportunities are many and they are waiting only on your Answering God's Calling for you. You will be a teacher of God and will seem to speak to many in the years to come. And through this function you will find the experience of the Answer you have requested, for Who You Are is the Answer that everyone who walks this world seeks. Christ is the Answer! Love is the Answer! You will be given specific instructions and direction from the Holy Spirit once you are willing to hear them. There are many answers you have received but have not heard. The

Holy Spirit is holding these answers you seek for you until you are ready to hear them. They all reside within your heart and await the readiness of mind to be heard.

I close with a quote from the Bible: "That which is born of the flesh is flesh; and that which is born of the Spirit is Spirit." John 3:6 Is your brother/mother flesh or Spirit? Remember, as you see your brother/mother you will see yourself. And remember that the way God created you is Reality: perfect, eternal, innocent, loving, Spirit which has no opposite.

Love Always,
David

Does My Brother's Pain Exist?

Dear David,

I have an issue that has kept me from progressing in my path back to God. It has come up again in my life, so I will illustrate it with the current situation.

Last night, my boyfriend of four years and I broke up. He had an unusually troubled childhood with violence and a mother who abused him and committed suicide when he was a teenager. Because of this, he is a very needy person once you get past his hard exterior. Throughout the relationship I kept believing that I could create a miracle and show him that life is not so sad and scary as he believes. At times it seemed to work, and there were some truly sacred moments. In the end, however, the ego took control, and I felt incapable of seeing past the ugliness and darkness – especially when he seemed to think I was the only bright thing in his life and clung to me for dear life.

I'm sure my friends and family will be happy that I got away from such a cynical, childish person. But now all I can think is that the things that disgusted me in the end: the dirty house, the clinging attitude and the irresponsible behavior were really just his belief in the lack of love. And sadly, it was that belief that drove me away, proving his fears. I've failed.

Many months ago, I wrote to you about my concerns about abandoning this person. You said that the falsehood is my belief that I am capable of abandoning another. I have contemplated this idea many times, and I do understand that this person is in God always, as am I, but I also cannot deny the seeming pain that he is experiencing by my pulling away from him.

Why is the seemingness of things always dismissed in the Course? If he experiences a seemingness of pain, then I don't care if it's not real – it's still cause for my concern! It seems that if I followed the Course principles, I could just go do my lessons and feel happy and loving while he rots in his own self-created hell. Or maybe his pain really doesn't exist on ANY level, and therefore I should just not give a crap about other people's suffering.

I hope you understand the issue I'm trying to get at. Or maybe this is all just ego talk, and I don't even know what I'm saying? I don't know any more. Perhaps you can see through all this better than me.

Thank you so much for your love and patience!

Beloved One,

Thanks for sharing what is on your heart. Your question about the perception of pain is a good starting point in clearing the mirror of the mind. This mirror must be cleared of false beliefs and concepts and thoughts if you are to radiate the Light that is ever Present.

Pain is always a misperception, for God has nothing to do with pain. If God is real there is no pain. If pain is real there is no God. The illusion of pain always stems from wrong-minded thinking, and this is what must be exposed and released to experience lasting peace and happiness.

Concern is another word for worry, and this emotion has nothing to do with compassion or true empathy. Concern is an emotion that is painful and arises from a desire to be right about a particular person, situation or event. One aspect of such concern is the belief that something false has already happened. Another aspect is the belief that past events caused the fear and pain. This misperception gives reality to the past and denies the Present Solution offered by the Holy Spirit.

When you pray for a miracle you are praying for a change in your perception. Even when you seem to pray for another, this is still the case. If you seem to have continuing concern for a brother after asking for a miracle, you are not allowing the miracle to be as it is. Miracles do not create or really change; they simply look calmly upon the false and see that it has no consequence. Miracles offer only Joy, and when Joy has come all pain is over now.

The concept of leaving someone behind is a strange belief, for in God's Love there is no such thing as leaving. The ego is the belief in possession, and what seems capable of being possessed also seems capable of being lost. Loss is the ego's story and originated with the belief that it is possible to separate or fall from God's eternal Love. This error seems to be acted out and repeated in human relationships, just as the past seems to repeat. The miracle Awakens the mind to the awareness that the past is over and only a blessing remains.

Pain is correctly perceived as a Call for Love, and this is always one's own Call to release the false perception of pain. Looking through a glass darkly never brings peace, happiness, love, or joy, so any seeming upset is a Call to empty the mind of false concepts and thus clean the mirror. This is the mind training that is required to accept the Atonement and remember God. Atonement is the awareness that the separation never happened. Until this Correction is accepted the world will seem real and the unreal emotions of the ego that are one with the world will seem to persist in awareness.

Let the feelings come up into awareness. Then, with deep honesty and sincerity, give the judgments, interpretations and feelings over to the Spirit. When darkness is raised to Light the darkness is gone. Do not protect the darkness, for the Spirit will not dissolve what has not been willingly offered for release. You have the Answer within but have been unwilling to let go of the ego definition of the problem. The Holy Spirit must wait until you see that you have had a perception problem based on belief in the ego. Until this point is reached the problems will seem to be projected on to brothers that seem apart from the mind. They are not. There are no problems apart from the mind. Healed perception will spring to awareness the instant the misperception is seen exactly as it is and not concealed or projected as something else.

All illness was mental illness, and all perceived pain was nothing but a faulty formulation of reality. Reality is Love, and Love is created eternally perfect. Love has no opposite. Glory to God for creating Love as One forever and ever!

Love and Blessings,
David

The Projector Metaphor

Hi David,

You wrote, "A movie projector analogy may be helpful. Inside the projector is a brilliant light. That's a great metaphor for the Holy Spirit. That brilliant light seems to pass through the film, which is filled with a lot of dark images." When one cleans up the film, the projector only projects light... Correct? In that scenario, it would seem that form ceases to exist. According to what I am reading, the perception of any form at all is an illusion, a dreamlike state that is not real. What happens to form during this cleaning up process? Does the world become more and more beautiful, or less positively and negatively charged, or what? I understand the shift from hearing a seeming attack to hearing a call for love. It's becoming a bit easier for me to hear that call for love. Is this whole healing process a progression toward being in a pure energy state?

Thanks.

Greetings Beloved One,

Your intuitive discernments are right on. Your desire for Truth is drawing It forth in awareness. Glory Be to God!

The six stages in the Development of Trust M-4.I.A.3 are a good description of what seems to occur during the "cleaning up process." The perception of form seems to undergo changes in consciousness as the illusory process is experienced in awareness. This process may be described as the relinquishment of judgment, and the world indeed seems to become more and more beautiful as it is viewed without judgment.

As you discern in your question, the relinquishment of judgment is the release of the entire spectrum of judgment, the positive through the negative. Complete forgiveness, the Atonement, is a state of mind which reflects abstract Divine Mind. Divine Mind, Mind Awake, is the One pure energy state that is reality. The forgiven world reflects eternity for a moment and then disappears. This is the meaning of "God will take this final step Himself." W-193.13.

God is eternal and creates the eternal. God's creation has no beginning, end, steps or levels, being pure Oneness. Forgiveness, the last illusion, represents a consciousness so cleared of judgment that it is ready to behold the truth of Divine Love. Judgment is not an ability which God creates, for Christ remains forever as pure Oneness in God. It is not that one ceases judging, as if judgment had really happened before, but has now stopped. Forgiveness sees illusions as one and therefore shows that judgment is forever *impossible* since there is nothing to judge between.

Forgiveness is a Perspective of Meaning, that of the Holy Spirit. As you share this Perspective, you share the Meaning of the Holy Spirit – the reminder that "I am as God created Me." W-94 The world beheld in this Perspective is indeed beautiful, for in God's Peace it is apparent "All things work together for good." T-4.V.1. In this Perspective time is simultaneous and there are no separate images and events. It is happily impossible to sequence, arrange, order or judge that which is one. This momentary Perspective is the Peace that passeth the understanding of the world.

Glory and joy to the mind emptied of concepts. Love cannot be described or explained – only Experienced. Yield to the Experience. There is nothing else.

Love,
David

Decision and Belief, Perception and Experience

- A conversation with David

In the section Specialness as a Substitute for Love we get an insight into decision and beliefs: "Beliefs will never openly attack each other because conflicting outcomes are impossible." T-24.I.2

Conflicting outcomes are impossible because the outcome is the outcome. The mind is seeing something that seems unified on the surface. That is the outcome. Everything is perceived is an outcome. For example, someone was talking about racing a sports car on a highway and the emotions he feels hitting the gas, passing one car and then being passed. You can't simultaneously be passed by someone and simultaneously be passing them. [Laughing] It's one or the other.

What one sees in the world is the outcome. But this seemingly stable singular outcome that the mind seems to be seeing is being produced by this belief system which has a number of unconscious conflicting beliefs. They are kept out of awareness; all the mind is seeing is the outcome that the beliefs are producing. So beliefs will never openly attack each other because conflicting outcomes are impossible.

> But an unrecognized belief is a decision to war in secret, where the results of conflict are kept unknown and never brought to reason, to be considered sensible or not. And many senseless outcomes have been reached, and meaningless decisions have been made and kept hidden, to become beliefs now given power to direct all subsequent decisions. T-24.I.2

So the decisions have been made and they have been kept hidden and secret. An unconscious belief is just a decision that is kept hidden.

Let's start off with the decision to separate from God. That decision has been kept hidden from awareness, been pushed out of awareness, and it's become a belief. It's like the mind has made a chain of decisions, and once it's made a decision and doesn't want to see what it's decided upon, it just pushes it out of awareness. So now you have an unconscious belief that directs all subsequent decisions. So the robotic man on the surface, who seems to be making decisions every day between all these things, is just a projection or an image, and those aren't real decisions at all. Those are just outcomes of beliefs.

Friend: From where I am, I see this whole communication thing as being at the very bottom. There is a belief that my communication has been broken off with God and that is very fearful. And of course I don't want that fear so I am going to project that out everywhere and anywhere I can. It seems simple to me that that's what's happening. But there are so many other beliefs layered on top of that core belief way at the very bottom with personhood. Is there a way to approach that belief directly or does it have to be approached indirectly through all the other beliefs that are covering it over so that it doesn't seem apparent in the moment?

David: Well, the way to approach it directly is to look at the idea that all the beliefs are really the same. They have taken an enormous variation. They seem to be specific beliefs but they are all the same.

Friend: They spring from one belief: that I have separated.

David: Yes.

Friend: That's the one belief. So it's just a matter of coming to that awareness that it's all the same?

David: That's the recognition where the release takes place. "To learn this course requires willingness to question every value that you hold." T-24.in.2. You have to question every belief. And that can seem like, wow, that's going to be a mess. It's going to be a huge undertaking to overhaul my whole mind. And the joy comes in really being able to clearly see that all the beliefs are one, kind of like the genetic code or the DNA of the ego belief system. And that is where the release takes place.

Friend: But realizing that it is all the same only happens by tracing it back to that central belief each time until I can clearly see, each and every time, that there seems to be something out here that is upsetting to me and I just keep tracing it back to the same place.

David: Another way to come at it is to say, "Why do anything?"

Friend: I've had that thought for a while! [Laughing]

David: You would do well to hang with it and use it and follow it in. That is what I did when I was on the spiritual journey before finding the Course. I believed that life had to be purposeful and that I didn't just want to do things because people told me to do them or because I learned it in a book. So I just kept questioning, "Why do anything? Why lift a finger? If there is no purpose in life, why go forward with anything else?"

So I ended up looking at all these concepts. I found out that I was doing a lot of things to please other people. I found that I was doing a lot of things because of responsibilities that I had to fulfill. But I kept questioning those. I kept going deeper and deeper into it. It's like, as you perceive yourself in the world, you are wound into it and it seems like you have to unwind out of it. That is the seeming process of questioning all the beliefs. Why work? Well, I listed things, for example about needing to eat. Also, I really wanted a relationship and I couldn't imagine having a significant other type of relationship without having finances to support that. So I had to question that too.

You have to question it all the way to being able to approach the possibility that this world is just a world of ideas. There are not real, concrete, objective things. You don't have to play the game. At one point the Course says that you just made one error but it's become multiplied, splintered and subdivided over and over.

Think of a mirror with one point pressing down on it shattering and fragmenting it into millions and trillions of pieces. The mind perceives the pieces. The mind perceives through the body's eyes and the body's ears. It sees lots of different images and hears lots of different sounds. And there seem to be more and more images multiplying.

The whole point is to pull the mind's allegiance away from those images. As long as the mind thinks that it is one image among other images, as long as there is that split, that seems to be out in the world between the subject and the object, there can be no peace, there can be no unity. It would be good to journal a belief inventory. I have done them and it has helped get in touch with some of the things I have believed in that I didn't even know I believed in.

Jesus says that all conflict comes from the belief in levels. He says that you have splintered yourself into different levels. Even to talk about mind and body would be talking about two levels.

Jesus says that right below the surface of the world that you see through the body's eyes is a ring of fear that you can't see. T-18. IX. It is like the underlying program that produces all the images: mountain ranges, oceans, trees and everything. You can't see the ring of fear with your eyes. It is analogous to the self-concept. The self-concept is made up of all these unconscious and unquestioned beliefs; the mind feels very guilty and fearful. Then there is the surface which seems to be a fairly kind, benevolent lid placed on top of this blackness. I seem like a decent person. There are a lot of people worse off than I am; I have a good education. This sugar coating that the body's eyes can see is on the top. But the underpinnings have to be questioned. So a belief inventory would be helpful to do.

Friend: Whenever I have done that, I have written stuff that I had no clue was there. Then I could see how my beliefs don't make any sense. And I can see that I have been making decisions based on that. So, guess what? When the underlying belief doesn't make sense, then what comes from it makes even less sense.

David: The robot just continues. So you see that you have to start questioning beliefs and where you perceive yourself as being. It's the thing that comes up about jobs, paying off loans or responsibilities to family and so on. You start where you perceive yourself to be and in my case I had all these things to take care of and I took the steps necessary to meet the obligations so that I wasn't trying to run away from it. As soon as I seemed to meet those lacks, those obligations and responsibilities then the questioning just continued.

Mind Overhaul

- A conversation with David

Mind is all-encompassing and it cannot be limited. Mind can seem to fall asleep and dream, but it can never be what it is not. While it seems to sleep, the only thing left for it to do is change its mind about itself and wake up. This discussion between David and some friends, centers on the change of mind that is necessary to recognize Enlightenment. It becomes evident that this requires a thorough questioning of all obstacles to the awareness of Love's presence, a mind overhaul.

Truth is within the mind. Yet there is a belief system that produces deception, a state of unawareness, which obscures the awareness of truth. We have an opportunity, in a deeply meaningful way, to come together and look calmly at the obstacles to Love and ask the Spirit to bring illumination. The mind which perceives itself as existing within a world of duality always operates from a dualistic belief system. Continually questioning this dualistic belief system is often perceived as unsettling and overwhelming; yet this questioning is necessary if one is to attain a constant state of peace.

There is just one Spirit, but there appear to be many thoughts, emotions, and perceptions that conceal awareness of Spirit. They are all temptations to forget Self and God. If faith is given to these illusions, there is no willingness to question the underlying false belief at the root of all misperception. It is very important for us to be open-minded and willing to let the Spirit help us unveil this false belief.

What I'd like to do today is talk about ideas reflected in *A Course in Miracles*, since it is a practical mind-transformation tool that can be extremely helpful in coming to clarity. It is meant to help you experience lasting inner peace. The message of the Course is that truth is within you, and that consistent peace of mind is a goal that you can and inevitably must attain. It's a peace that comes from being tuned in to that small, still Voice within, and letting go of another voice in the deceived mind, the ego, which is the voice of conflict, fear, and death. In that sense the Course can be summarized like this: there are two voices in the deceived mind, and this is a course on learning to listen only to the Voice for God and thus ending the deception.

This Voice for God could be called one's intuition or inner guide. In the Course it is called "the Holy Spirit." If you relate to these ideas from another tradition or background, you may think of this Voice as an "Inner Knowing," or "Higher Power." We want to get beyond the words, which are forms, and go deeper. We want to join in an intention to experience clarity of mind and peace of mind.

When Jesus says, "The Kingdom of Heaven is at hand," Matthew 3:2 He's really guiding one to the present moment, and to the realization that right now, this very instant, one is perfect. It's not a matter of trying to build up and improve one's self. No matter how improved the limited self seems to be, it will never be the changeless, eternal Self that God created. One must be aware of the trap of thinking that one's happiness, peace of mind, and salvation are somewhere off in the future. The linear past-future concept of time is part of the dualistic belief system that must be questioned. There is great joy and contentment in the experience of the Holy Instant, Now. God isn't dangling a carrot of eternal peace before us, saying "Here's Heaven, keep reaching ...oops, you missed again." Enlightenment is right here, right now, for the mind that is ready, open, and willing to recognize it.

Friend: If Enlightenment is so close, why does recognizing it seem like such a struggle? Why do I keep feeling guilty, anxious, and depressed? And why do I keep repeating the same behavior patterns over and over?

David: If truth is immediate and as close as one's hand, then we need to look at what is blocking truth from awareness. What is standing in the way of accepting one's perfection and one's happiness? We want to examine what blocks feelings of peace, joy and love from being experienced in sustained awareness.

The Course's teaching is that Love is all that there is and nothing else exists. God doesn't have anything to do with fear. God doesn't have anything to do with disease, suffering, anxiety, depression and all the different forms that fear seems to take. God, truth, is Spirit, and one's essence, one's true Identity is Spirit. Jesus teaches: You are the living Son of God; You are the Christ, but you've forgotten your Identity. You've fallen asleep and you're dreaming a dream in which you think you are not "in the image and likeness of your Father." Genesis 1:21. Instead you think you are in a tiny body surrounded by a vast world, and at the mercy of outside forces. It seems that you constantly have to protect the body. It seems like a struggle to survive, a struggle to keep your head above water. This false perception is founded on the belief in separation from God.

There are but two thought systems in the deceived mind. One of them is the Holy Spirit's thought system of Love. The other is the ego's thought system of fear. Trying to hold in mind two completely irreconcilable thought systems is intolerable. The deceived mind attempts to project the split out onto the screen of the world. That's how the world of duality seems to have existence. So instead of seeing the split where it is in the mind, the sleeping mind sees it in the dualities of the world: fast and slow, hot and cold, male and female, good and evil, etc. This world is an attempt to avoid seeing that the split is in one's mind. There are no problems apart from one's mind; the Solution to the problem is within one's mind and available this instant.

Friend: If nothing unreal exists, what is there?

David: God and everything that comes from God has existence. So Christ, Who is His created Son, has existence. Christ is the Thought of God. God extended His Son from Himself "in His own image and likeness," T-3.V.7. which translates to alike in thought and of a like quality. In the Course Jesus also says that the Son of God has creations and the power to create, since God gave His Son creative ability. So the Son's creations also have existence.

However, we can make a distinction between the world's definition of creation and what Jesus calls creation. The time/space cosmos, world, and the bodies that seem to inhabit the world are projections of temporary, ever-changing thought-forms that God did not create. These, then, are called miscreations. To induce the mind to give up its miscreations is the only application of creative ability that is truly meaningful. There was a time when these ego thought-forms seemed to begin, and there will seem to be a time when they will end. That time is now, if one so chooses. This ending has already happened via the Holy Spirit. The linear time/space illusion has been corrected. Accepting the Atonement or Correction for all misthought only seems to be a matter of time. It is a present choice which brings an end to all choice.

The cosmos and world of bodies are a make-believe dream that is illusory. Spirit, in contrast, is eternal and changeless. Spirit comes from Spirit in a continuous line of creation. God is Spirit; the Son of God is Spirit; the creations of the Son of God are Spirit. Spirit, however, has nothing at all to do with the world perceived through the five senses of the body, including the body itself. When the Course says nothing unreal exists, it is referring to the unreal projected time/space world of bodies, planets and galaxies. Jesus is contrasting the eternal Spirit, which is of God, with the time/space universe, which is of the ego.

Friend: Wow! When I look at the stars and I look out at the vastness of this physical universe, I see oceans, I see mountains, I see continents. The material universe seems pretty vast for something that doesn't even exist.

David: All of that is testimony to the power of the mind given to an unreal belief. In the Bible, the Genesis story says that God created Heaven and earth. In contrast, Jesus in His Course reserves the term creation for the perfect, the eternal, and the changeless. The fall of mankind refers to the world of duality within which mankind now seems to struggle for survival. The world is merely the unreal projection of an unreal belief: the ego. In other words, this puff of an idea, or this belief in separation from God, was an incredible, ridiculous idea. The cosmos/world seemed to arise as a hiding place from God for the mind that believed in the separation, having remembered not to laugh.

Again, the distinction between what has existence and what has no existence is the distinction between the eternal and the temporary. Anything that is temporary, including the tiny, mad idea and all that seemed to spring from it, does not exist. Anything that is eternal or of God does exist and has reality.

Friend: I'm still puzzled about our creations. What are they? What is it exactly that we create?

David: Jesus refers to the Son's "creations" many times in the text. Yet He never goes into a description of these creations in any specific detail except to imply that one remains unaware of them until one truly remembers one's Self as the Son of God. To try to imagine what they might be is impossible, for the imagination is still within the domain of the ego and these creations are not. Imagination involves images. Creation does not. There are no specific references as to what the creations are because they are not concrete or specific, being abstract Spirit. These creations are known when one wakes up from the dream of the world. When one is lined up with and listening to that still Voice in one's mind, when one is right-minded, that is a reflection of Life. When one is listening to the ego, when one is wrong-minded, that is death.

What the Course calls "the real world" is the experience one has when perception becomes straightened out via the Holy Spirit. The real world is the Holy Spirit's perception of the world, or the forgiven world. This is the metaphorical stepping-stone in the seeming return to God or Knowledge or creation. True perception, or the real world, leads to God or truth. When God's Son seemed to fall asleep and dream of separation, the Answer that God gave was the Holy Spirit. The Holy Spirit has a purpose for the dreaming of the world which brings with it the Vision of Christ.

In the Bible it is written: "As you sow, so shall you reap." Galatians

6:7 The way this world is set up, this translates into "whatever the mind thinks and feels and believes about itself, the world will prove or bring witness to." The ego-invested mind feels guilty, believing it actually separated from God, and therefore calls forth scripts and scenes from the world that witness to this guilt. Abuse, neglect, victimization, sickness, pain, and suffering are all, therefore, interpretations of the world that are based on the belief that one has separated from God.

A movie projector/theater analogy may be helpful here. In the projector room, inside the projector, is this glowing, brilliant, radiant light. That's a great metaphor for the Holy Spirit. That brilliant light seems to pass through the film, which is filled with a lot of dark images. We'll call those dark images "attack thoughts" or "ego thoughts." As these thoughts are projected, what seems to be produced on the screen are shadows. To the mind watching the movie, these shadows appear to have meaning. However, the only meaning the movie seems to have is given to it by the mind, which has forgotten that what it sees is just a movie. It has identified with figures on the screen and thought of itself as a person among other persons.

The world perceived through the body's eyes and heard through the body's ears is also a screen of images. The world is just the shadowy reflection of the attack thoughts in the deceived mind. If one becomes aware of these attack thoughts and is willing to let them be replaced by clear, real thoughts, one is willing to clean the film up, so to speak, and let more light shine through. When this happens, the screen is going to light up more and more. The world will reflect the light in one's mind.

As the mind begins to let go of the ego belief system of separation, it opens up to the Holy Spirit's thought system, which is the memory of God in the deceived mind. This is a thought system which reflects love and offers a completely different interpretation of the world. As the mind embraces the Holy Spirit's thoughts, the world brings forth witnesses to that love. When one accepts the Holy Spirit, the world that was once seen as a place of kill or be killed, of violence, competition, and inequality becomes full of miracles – witnesses of wholeness and completion. Only then is it possible to experience the peace, and joy of forgiveness, what Jesus calls "the real world."

Friend: What do I have to do to see the forgiven world the Holy Spirit sees?

David: One has to be willing to give up judgment, or more accurately, to see the impossibility of judgment. The reason one seems to experience pain and pleasure, sickness and health, death and life and all the variations is because of judgment. Judgment breaks apart and fragments. Use the thought of unity as a contrast. Just think of the word "unity." One. Oneness. Union. An unbroken continuity. The circle is a great symbol of unity; no beginning, no end, no duality, just one. The deceived mind looks through the body's eyes and experiences fragmentation and duality. How does one reconcile duality with unity? One doesn't, for they are not reconcilable. The Holy Spirit's function is to translate duality or misperception into healed or true perception, which is the bridge to Oneness. The Holy Spirit, an eternal creation, functioning as the memory of God in the sleeping mind, sees the thought of duality as false. Therefore, it is the Holy Spirit that is the bridge back to truth, reality, or God.

When we really start to look closely at perception, we find that no two people see exactly the same world. Within a world of duality, a world of unreality, there is no universal agreement. It seems as if some perceptions have common elements. People may seem to be able to agree, for example, on the color of the grass or the sky. Yet even these agreements are not without exceptions. When one really explores the topic of perception, it becomes more apparent that everyone sees a different world, based on subjective interpretation. That's where all the conflict comes in. Nothing in a world of subjectivity and relative perception can be completely shared. Only true ideas, ideas of God, which are not of this world, can be shared.

What is seen with the body's eyes doesn't make any sense because true meaning and happiness are beyond the body, within the mind. When perception is distorted, pain, anguish, and a host of fear-based upsets can seem to be experienced. Therefore, the attempt to reconcile what is perceived through the body's senses with peace, happiness, and joy is impossible! Peace, happiness, and joy characterize the Spirit of God which is within, within the Silence.

A first step in coming to peace of mind is bringing the many seeming problems of the world back to one's own mind, admitting that one has a perceptual problem and opening to the idea that all the competition and conflicts that seem to be happening in the world just mirror one's own conflicted mind. Only if the problem is seen to be in one's mind, can the solution, which is also in one's mind, be accepted. Let's take a look at some of the beliefs and perceptions that are held. Doing so is a big, but necessary, step on the road to release. Thoroughly questioning all beliefs, and ultimately the one belief in separation on which they are based, is the way to come to a lasting state of peace of mind.

Friend: I have a sense of what you are saying, yet I don't feel like I have an idea about how to stop criticizing and judging. It seems automatic, like a habit, and I don't know how not to do it. Can you give me any suggestions about how to begin to let go of that?

David: Yes. The Course gives a framework for laying aside judgment. The Workbook is a tool designed to undo personal judgment and make way for the one Judgment of the Holy Spirit: God's Son is guiltless, sinless, forever whole, pure and innocent. Jesus says it is not that one shouldn't judge, but that judgment is something that one is totally incapable of doing. One is like a little child trying to run the world. Jesus says that in order to judge anything accurately, one would have to be aware of an inconceivably wide range of variables, past, present, and to come. In order to judge fairly and correctly, one would have to know the consequences of one's judgment on everything and everyone. That's not the way one generally thinks of personal judgment. It is usually thought of in terms of the consequences to the personal self, family and friends.

What Jesus is saying is that a sleeping mind is incapable of judging accurately because it doesn't see the total picture. It is literally blind, for it hallucinates. The good news, though, is that the Holy Spirit is in one's mind, and the Holy Spirit does see the total picture. His Judgment is accurate. In any conceivable situation the Holy Spirit knows what is most helpful for the entire Sonship. The Holy Spirit is always the Answer, regardless of the question.

The most helpful answer I can offer you is this: use the Workbook as Jesus instructs. We can examine the metaphysics on which the Workbook is based and that can help make the lessons more meaningful to you.

From the belief in separation from God an entire thought system of separation seemed to arise. To go to the bottom of this thought system is to realize that the ego is the underlying belief that one can actually separate from God. According to logic, any statement is only as true as the premise on which it rests. The ego is the false premise. When the mind seemed to separate and fragment, it seemed to forget abstract reality and identify with a physical time/space world. This was a stark contrast to reality and also very chaotic to a mind that was accustomed to the unity of the Kingdom of Heaven. In Heaven the mind is at home and in its natural state of oneness and completion. After the so-called "fall," the mind felt so chaotic that it tried to order the illusion, to bring some sense of stability to the chaos. That's where judgment first came in. To order the illusion, to make a hierarchy of illusions, is to judge. An example would be someone entering an "out-of-control" situation, feeling fearful, and believing that if he could just get the situation in order everything would be better. Judgment attempts to bring some type of order to chaos and thus minimize fear. But by thinking that it can order its own thoughts, or think apart from God, the ego mind blocks awareness of the Christ, which thinks only with God. God orders one's real thoughts.

If you believe your own personal judgments are necessary for your survival in this world, the teaching I am sharing will seem to entail radical trust, for this world teaches that judgment is actually good and beneficial. Educational systems are based on the belief that you can learn good judgment and become a mature, functioning, adult citizen. That's what worldly education is all about. One seems to get good at judging, which is equated with knowing what things are good and what things are bad, so the good can be pursued and the bad avoided. Yet wisdom is not judgment; wisdom is seeing the impossibility of personal judgment and therefore relinquishing any attempt to continue it. Only when one has recognized something as valueless is there a desire to relinquish it. Once the impossibility of judgment is grasped, judgment is relinquished, for it ceases to hold any attraction or value.

The belief that one knows how to take care of one's self is what needs to be undone, since the deceived mind knows nothing. When one starts to let go of thinking one knows what's in one's own best interests, it seems scary to the ego. The ego is being undone and fearfully objects: "If I don't take care of me, who will?" Yet if one does not rely on the ego's voice, but trusts instead in that small, still Voice within, decisions flow from this intuitive listening and everything works out smoothly. All the effort and judging that one does in trying to maintain the tiny personality self and to survive in this world has no value. Yet, one is always in good hands with the Holy Spirit. The Holy Spirit is deserving of one's trust.

This seems to be a world where one has to fight tooth and nail at every turn. This seems to be a world where one has to have many defenses and security systems. The world teaches: make sure you lock your car doors; make sure you take your medicine. It's a web of defenses, all of which involve protection of the body and personal judgment. The world's teaching is that you must do all these things just to keep alive in this body. What is the meaning of life as related to the body? The Course is saying: You think that's your Life. But, that's not your Life at all. Your Life is Spirit. Spirit is invulnerable and needs no defense.

Friend: The other day I was saying, "If we can wake up in the morning and forget that we're male or female, republican or democrat, or whatever we think we are, and go through the day without all that baggage, judgment is a lot less. It's almost forgotten."

David: The end of judgment is indeed forgetting all concepts of duality. Obviously there aren't any democrats or republicans in Heaven. There aren't men and women in Heaven. Whenever one gets defensive about anything and is willing to just be quiet and ask for help from the Holy Spirit, insight into what is being defended comes to mind. One finds that one is always defending a false identity. For example, if I'm identified as a democrat and I perceive that someone is knocking the democrats, a defensive reaction is inevitable. Whatever concept or image one identifies with, one will defend. The only Identity that one can identify with and be totally defenseless is the Christ. The Christ is not a concept or an image, but a reality. Spirit is something that doesn't need to be defended. It just is. When one is identified with anything of this world one has made up a self-concept that is intended to take the place of Spirit, and it must be defended because it is not true. Truth needs no defense. Defense is what the belief in separation leads to. It's the belief that one can make an image of one's self, instead of just accepting one's Self as being created by God.

It seems like it could take a lot of mind training to become completely disidentified from those concepts that we were just speaking of. But it is unavoidable. The natural direction of the mind is to disidentify from those concepts, to learn true forgiveness, and to finally remember God.

Friend: I'm really curious to get a picture of how you live your life. I mean what's the difference between judgment and priority? How did you end up here today without any judgment? How does that happen for you?

David: Every time one comes to a branching of the road, in the worldly sense, it seems as if one has to go either one way or the other. It seems as if there's a judgment involved. Which way should I go? From the time/space perspective, at every single junction of the road, the Holy Spirit knows which way one needs to go. One need only listen! The Holy Spirit appears to be evaluative as long as the mind believes that it is in the maze of time/space. Yet the last judgment one need make is that it is impossible to judge anything. God doesn't make judgments. There is nothing to judge between in Oneness. God knows only what is. But, as long as the mind believes that it is in a maze of duality, the Holy Spirit seems to guide it out of duality. So, if I apply this to the question you asked about me ending up here today, the answer is simply that I listen. I don't have any goals other than staying tuned in to the Holy Spirit and being at peace. Without worldly goals that spring from false self-concepts, there are no perceived separate interests or any future ambitions or past regrets. One can truly trust and listen and follow. This master switch is complete forgiveness, the Atonement, or the reversal of all ego thinking!

Friend: I have to go back to work today and do some computer work and some other things before tomorrow morning. I'd rather stay right here. You talk about intuition and Spirit leading you. Now how do I do that?

David: The Holy Spirit starts from where and what the mind believes it is. Suppose you believe you're a woman who has a particular job, and tonight that looks like having to do work at a computer. Let's suppose that this scenario is all just a motion picture of a belief system that you have, and that this is simply the way that you perceive yourself at this moment. The Holy Spirit doesn't try to yank this web of beliefs apart. The Holy Spirit will use those things you believe in to help you realize that you are much more than the self-concepts. This discussion, for example, is bringing witness to your mind's desire to wake up and remember your reality as the Son of God. All one has to have is the willingness, and the Holy Spirit will undo the false self-concepts and replace them with forgiveness. Start with this prayer: "Abide with me, Holy Spirit. Guide me in what to say and do and where to go." If you welcome and trust Him, you will experience immediate results.

Friend: I'm having some trouble with the description of duality and that the problem is our perception. I work in a business where I have to see things exactly as they are happening, not as I might like them to happen. So the problem for me is to understand how to get to that place you're talking about.

David: It certainly seems that when one has identified for example as an employee in a business, that there are external constraints and restrictions to abide by. For example, let's say one is identified as a manager. As a manager, one seemingly has to hold other people accountable for doing certain things. A manager monitors and evaluates employees, directs them, conducts performance reviews, and so forth. Every manager also has a boss whose job is to make sure the manager is accountable. What one must do is look closely and go deeper into the belief system that is producing the faulty perception, that is producing the scenario I have just described. One must be willing to examine what one's priorities are, what is most important in one's life. Is peace of mind one's only priority?

I've had to take a good look at everything I believed, turn inward for strength and support, and realize with certainty that the Holy Spirit is my only Boss and forgiveness my only function. One may say, "How practical is that? What do you do when you have two bosses, if you have the Holy Spirit and your employer telling you two different things?" Again, the Holy Spirit meets the mind where it believes it is. He works with the mind, helping it to exchange accepted self-concepts for the more expansive self-concepts that approach true forgiveness.

As you lay aside judgment and change your mind about the world, what happens on the screen of the world will be a symbolic representation of that mind shift and of your perception of relationships. So really we're back to just saying, "Okay, Holy Spirit, work with me right now where I believe I am and help me loosen my mind from these false beliefs. Help me let go of the ego and my perception will be healed." Trust in the Holy Spirit for everything and He will take care of you in ways you can't even envision.

Friend: Could you speak about relationships? The Course talks about special and holy relationships. Can you briefly describe what they are?

David: Relationships seem to be a difficult undertaking in this world. They seem to be a mixture of love and hate, attraction and repulsion, joy and misery. Jesus refers to special love and special hate relationships as destructive, selfish, possessive, and exclusive. These are ego-based relationships that are songs of praise to their maker. Holy relationship, on the other hand, is a metaphor for a relationship that has been given over to the Holy Spirit for His purpose of forgiveness. Holy relationship is a healed relationship that reflects wholeness and completion.

Beyond all metaphors, one might say that the only real relationship is one of Spirit, of God and creation, of Father and Son. As the only real relationship is given by God, the holy relationship is learned of the Holy Spirit. As the scarcity principle is undone by the Holy Spirit, the sense of lack, inadequacy, weakness, and incompletion that is typical of the special relationship is replaced in the holy relationship by joining, extension, appreciation, and acceptance.

I like to speak of the special relationship in the past tense, for as with everything of the ego, it is history. If we recall the metaphysics we have covered today, the sleeping mind became so terrified of the light that it attempted to hide from God in a world of form. Believing it had torn itself from Heaven, it attempted to set up a body-world self as its new identity. It attempted to forget about its Identity as Spirit. As it became identified as a body, it was shaky because, though it had tried to forget the light, deep down it knew that it was making this world up and that God could and must be remembered. Being uncertain and afraid to go back to the light, it looked for an external solution – other bodies with which it could join to find happiness and completion. That was how the so-called "co-dependency" of special relationships began.

As soon as the mind believed it was out on the screen of the world, it sought outside itself to alleviate the guilt, fear, loneliness and emptiness it felt within. It looked for other bodies to be its friends and companions. Associations with the right people, the sleeping mind's God-substitutes, took on great importance. The whole world became one giant special relationship, because everything that the mind associated with on the screen was set up to be a God-substitute. And the reason why special love and special hate relationships are never completely satisfying and never bring lasting peace and happiness is because there can never be a substitute for the Love of God.

The holy relationship can only be experienced now as a reflection of the Love of God. It is analogous to the real world, complete forgiveness, or healed perception that I spoke of earlier. As one realizes the impossibility of personal judgment, one also realizes the impossibility of special relationships of any kind. Holy relationship, then, is not personal in the sense of bodies relating to one another. It is symbolic of a universal wholeness, a state of mind that can only give of its complete perfection. The concept of getting something in return for something else is utterly meaningless in the present moment. Right now, there is only rest, contentment, and fulfillment.

Friend: I'd like to bring up a particular relationship I'm having trouble with. I realize that this one person keeps reflecting something back to me. I perceive this person as controlling and really manipulative. I buy into it and then feel guilty. I really don't think I can go on with this any longer. It is dangerous for me to hang around this kind of control. It doesn't do me any good and it doesn't help this person either. So what's going on in my mind?

David: A control issue is always an expression of what the Course calls "the authority problem." If one takes a sampling of human behavior, there appear to be a variety of control issues. There seem to be control issues with parents, children, spouses, boyfriends, girlfriends, teachers, politicians and employers. Yet it is the sleeping mind that has the one central control issue or the one central authority problem. This authority problem is the basis of all seeming control issues between people or between people and the system.

The authority problem is a question of authorship. The central question is: "Was I authored by God or am I the author of myself?"

The sleeping mind believes that it has separated from God and has made up a self and a world. It thinks it is the author of its own identity, the author of reality. Until the Correction for this basic error is accepted, this problem is believed by the sleeping mind to be a battle with God. But a battle of this magnitude is too terrifying to keep in awareness and is therefore denied from awareness. The problem seems to be projected onto the screen of the world and thus appears to be where it is not, between persons or between persons and institutions. These are, therefore, make-believe conflicts. There are no control issues in the world, though that's where they seem to be experienced. The ego is the control issue and the ego is a belief in the mind. Again we come back to the main idea: There are no problems apart from one's mind.

Friend: So when I talk to this person again, what's supposed to happen? Am I not supposed to see any controlling behavior?

David: You will see what you believe. Just be willing to examine the belief in control. You need to go beyond the level of behavior. You may look at someone and seem to judge from their behavior that they are controlling. That is not the level at which the mirroring we are speaking of takes place. The mirroring is at the mind level. One has to believe in the concept of control before one can see it in the world or in a person. Control is just a concept made up by the ego. A sure way to retain a concept is to project it out and see it in the world instead of seeing it as a made-up concept in one's mind.

God is not controlling. God is not manipulative. Yet as long as one projects responsibility for making up the idea of control, one will believe that control is possible. One must question the false belief in one's mind, the ego, and allow it to be raised to the light.

Friend: What would you say about deceit as opposed to control or manipulation? Probably the person that I was the most angry with in my entire life was a very deceitful person. He lied whenever it suited him and I think he hurt many people that way. When I was dealing with him I wasn't just imagining those falsehoods, was I?

David: The same line of reasoning can be applied to deceit. The reason deceit of any kind seems to provoke anger is because all deceit is a reminder of the deceit in one's own mind. To believe in the ego is deception. One who perceives one's self as existing in this world has fabricated a self, and that is deceitful. To believe that one could actually separate from God is the most basic and the only deception. But that's too terrifying to keep in awareness, so it's denied from awareness and the deceit is projected onto the world and onto persons.

Anger could not really be because of a relationship with a "deceitful person," but comes from projecting the guilt inherent in believing one has separated from God. You can see that upset of any degree or variety can be traced back to that one error. And only the one Correction, the Atonement, will bring eternal peace and happiness and an end to anger forever!

Friend: What about practical advice? I want something to go with right now, something I can take with me as I go forth from here. How can I move more towards tuning into the Spirit and allowing my mind to wake up to reality?

David: Everyone in this room can look at one's self and say "Hey, I've learned some skills and abilities." Each of us has the capacity to learn and has seemingly developed abilities through life experiences, education, or perhaps skills training. Jesus meets the mind wherever it believes it is. These skills and abilities will be used in the Plan of the Atonement. The Holy Spirit can use whatever the deceived mind has learned for His purpose.

Let's examine this closely. When we consider learning in the context of this world, we may think of learning mental and motor skills, skills in reading, in writing, and so on. The key thing that one needs to get clear about is the purpose that skills and abilities serve. The ego wants to use these abilities to reinforce the separation and maintain the body identity. The ego wants to maintain itself. One needs to get clear on the Holy Spirit's use for these abilities. The practical question is: "Am I willing to be shown the Holy Spirit's use for my body, mental skills, and physical skills?"

All skills and abilities that are used to prop up the little self-concept, in the pursuit of fame or bodily convenience are used for ego goals i.e. more, better, faster. The ego is counseling one to use one's skills and abilities to become a better person. Instead, use those skills and abilities to let go of the body identity and to extend love to your brothers. Use them to share the ideas of the Holy Spirit. Use your skills and abilities to change your perception of yourself and remember that you are a mind and not a body.

The most practical thing one can ever ask about anything is: "What is this for?" For example, I liked the idea of freedom. I wanted to be free. But I discovered that my definition of freedom was way off the mark. I had defined it as doing what I wanted to do, wherever and whenever I wanted to do it. Freedom of the body was the basis of that definition. The Course teaches that true freedom has nothing to do with the body and everything to do with the mind. It has everything to do with listening to the Holy Spirit and following the Holy Spirit's guidance.

Again, it really all comes down to purpose. We can call purpose the "level of mind" or "causation." Purpose is content. Form, the level of the body, is essentially irrelevant. The ego attempts to raise up form as important i.e., how the body looks, how old or young the body is, etc. These images are merely overlays, just concepts that cover over the awareness of Spirit, and their importance naturally diminishes as one starts to follow the Holy Spirit's purpose. They become less and less noticed. One ceases judging how people look or what kind of car they drive. How does form stack up when it comes to tuning in to Spirit? It doesn't! When one really gets into purpose and intention, all the specific details leave consciousness and fade from awareness.

Friend: I'm glad you're bringing this up because I feel that following the Spirit can look no particular way. Trying to model my life after anyone else's life or trying to choose appropriate behaviors is not it, because that would be placing an emphasis on form. It's the purpose that's important, and the form just follows. It's about the transformation that takes place in the mind. Then, if the form changes, it changes because of the change that has occurred in the mind, not because I have addressed the form and tried to change the behavior or how things look.

David: Yes. Indeed, the only thing one can choose to change is the way one thinks. To try to change the behavior will not solve anything. The only way that one can solve misperception once and for all is to look calmly and directly at all false thoughts, see their unreality, and look beyond them to one's real thoughts.

If one chooses to think with the Holy Spirit, one perceives everything as either love or a call for love. So, for example, if your child is screaming or your spouse starts yelling at you, the situation is simply perceived as a call for love. It is as if your brother were saying: "Please teach me that this isn't who I really am. I'm asking you to remind me who I really am." The Holy Spirit sees it that way. But through the ego's lens, the situation gets perceived as an attack. Can you see that once you perceive attack, a defensive reaction is unavoidable? So really the key is seeing that attack is impossible. It doesn't do any good to think, "Gosh, I'm being attacked" and then try to control the behavior to appear defenseless. To try to correct the error at the form level never works.

Friend: I guess I'm confused, because to me it doesn't seem loving to say that we must leave the physical world behind, neglect it, and not take care of it to become Spirit. So I guess I'm confused and I thought that maybe you could help me understand that better.

David: The world and body have no reality. Reality is Spirit. Can one be open to seeing that while attributing a negative value to the body or world one is making the projection seem real, as more than neutral or nothing?

The flip side of this error, which is the same trap, is valuing the body/world, glorifying it for what it seems to offer, or raising it up in importance in any way. Indulgence of the senses or fame, etc., doesn't bring lasting peace and happiness because they reinforce the bodily identity and one is not a body. Trying to solve an inner feeling of lack by indulging in food or any pleasures of the world, is to make the error seem real by thinking the body is valuable and desirable. It is certainly esteemed as more than neutral or nothing. Denying the body or indulging the body is not the truth that will set one free.

Miracles are shifts in perception that witness to the mind that it is much more than a body. As I have shared, this is a Course in changing one's mind about the world and not a Course in trying to change the form and hoping that one's mind will follow. This is a Course in learning that there is a higher purpose for the body and the world: the Holy Spirit's purpose of forgiveness. Again, the body itself is neither good nor bad. The Holy Spirit uses the body solely for communication, to speak for God through it. To learn true forgiveness is to give up the ego's uses for the body, which could be summarized as pride, pleasure, and attack. To allow one's body to be used by the Holy Spirit as an instrument of healing is to allow distorted perception to be corrected.

Friend: I would like you to address the concept that what I see in front of me "is only a projection of my own mind." So essentially there's no one out there? If I still perceive a negative trait in another, it means I still harbor that thought in my own mind and have not yet released it and therefore still see it.

David: Yes. Every thought is either projected or extended. Attack thoughts are projected. Real thoughts are extended. The perceived world is just a representation of thoughts. Attack thoughts are kept out of awareness and then seen in the world as if they were external or independent of their maker – one's own mind.

Friend: I don't know; there's something else. I just really want to look deeper into this. I guess there's an aspect that I'm not understanding or I wouldn't have brought it up. So wherever you want to go with that would be great.

David: Everyone, deep within, wants to be free of attack thoughts, free of judgment. In fact, that is the only freedom. The process of relinquishing judgment may seem to be difficult. It really isn't once the value of nonjudgment is grasped by the mind. To the ego, the relinquishment of judgment is perceived as personally insulting. Giving up judgment is often interpreted by the ego like this: "Hey, I am a competent, mature person. I have learned lots of very useful judgments about the world. I cannot be completely wrong about all of it." One is told in some of the early Workbook lessons that one's mind is filled with meaningless thoughts. The key is to have faith in the Holy Spirit's undoing of the ego and not to perceive the lessons as humiliating, which would be the ego's interpretation. Start with a sense of true humility and true humbleness and say, "Okay, I want to start with an admission. I want to start with the admission that my mind is filled with a lot of thoughts that don't come from my Father in Heaven." It's starting to see that one really does need a mind overhaul, a complete change of mind about one's self and the world.

The early lessons help loosen the mind from the way one currently thinks and perceives. The later lessons in the Course are wonderful affirmations of the truth. These are reflections of real thoughts. These are the thoughts that one thinks with God. But these real thoughts are buried in the mind underneath all the judgments and attack thoughts, which need to be brought into awareness and then released.

Friend: The key thing I'm hearing is the need to be aware of all attack thoughts, to watch my mind, and be willing to release them to the Holy Spirit. That's how I get free from them. But how do I become aware of unconscious attack thoughts?

David: Just relax and let them come up into awareness. The ego seems to take myriads of forms on the surface. As a fragmenting thought, the ego seems to fragment again and again. But it has one common characteristic by which it can always be identified. The single, faulty premise behind the ego belief system, regardless of the many forms it takes, is the belief that there is a real cause other than God and that ideas can leave their source. This is the belief that there are causes in the world, apart from the mind, and that one is at the mercy of them. If one can understand the impossibility of this premise, then the ego is out of business.

The ego is identifiable, regardless of its many different forms. By consistently mind-watching with the Holy Spirit and noticing one's thoughts, ego thinking is seen as unreal instead of fearful. Once one can calmly discern ego thoughts, seeing them for what they are, immediately they are released. As soon as one can see the false as false, a belief as just a belief, then one is no longer at its mercy. At an "advanced" state of mind training, one can prevent ego thoughts from even entering the mind at all.

The key to discernment, the master switch, is the simple recognition that only the mind is causative and that the mind cannot create beyond itself. All miscreation, the time/space cosmos, is the unreal effect of an unreal cause. The seeming reversal of cause and effect is the basis of the ego. The characteristic of this insane reversal is the belief that there's something causative in the time/space cosmos, on the screen of the world. In simple terms, it is the belief that something of the world can give or take away one's peace of mind.

The ego is saying you, as a body, need to find a peaceful environment to live in. The ego is saying that if you, as a body, have good medical insurance that you have peace of mind. The ego is saying that if you, as a body, find the right partner, the perfect mate, then you will have happiness. The ego is basically saying that if you, as a body, just get the right pieces of the puzzle, if you get the script to come out just the way you want it to, you'll be happy and peaceful. What a scam! How long will one play that game before seeing that there's no cheese at the end of that tunnel. Seeking the right mate, the right job, the right place to live, the right climate is truly a wild goose chase. That kind of seeking attempts to bring about peace of mind and happiness by changing the form instead of accepting the Holy Spirit's purpose. One can never find lasting happiness and peace in the world. Accept this, but do not stop with this. The Holy Spirit will lead one to happy dreams, and on to waking from the dream entirely.

Whether one seems to get what one thinks is desirable in form or feels deprived of something in form, the Holy Spirit gently reminds: You are Mind, wholly Mind, and purely Mind. What you think you did, separate from God, has been undone. You have everything because you are everything. To accept this fact is to hit the master switch.

Friend: I knew that I had to be here today, but I didn't know why. This discussion has been very meaningful to me. It puts everything in a different light. Anger was destroying me and everyone around me. I am so grateful to have a new way to look at it. Thank God there's another way! Hearing you talk, David, dispels a lot of fear. I can now welcome working with the Holy Spirit. Thank you.

Stillness

The Silent Joy
Quiet nights and quiet days
Quiet walks on quiet ways
Floating with the Inner Force that guides us

Quiet thoughts and quiet scenes
Quiet words and quiet dreams
Soaring in a Sky of Love
Beyond the world and so together.

We shall live Eternally
In a state of Revelry
Away from all the earthly cares that bound us

The world seemed so unfinished
Until I found You in it

And all at once the happiness I knew
Is now a quiet time of loving You.

Blessings,
David

The Frustration of Pretending to be Human

Dear David,

I have a question if you should be so kind to answer. A while back a voice seemed to tell me things and my life has never been the same.

The first message was, "If you are busy pretending you are something you are not, you will never know who you really are." I kept asking what was real, looking around and saying, "Is this real?" And the voice within me would say no, that it was an illusion, here today, gone tomorrow, now you see it now you don't.

One day I was sitting on my bed, when I found a presence of peace, as if a light was around me and my questions were answered. After being told many things were not real, I asked, "Then, What Is Real?" The room seemed to fill with light coming from inside me. The moment was full of a sense of absoluteness, and it said, "I am He and there is no other." Somewhere on the inside of me, that resonated. I called the entity Spirit.

For months it seemed the only thing real to me, and I couldn't keep from telling everyone, "We are One. There is no other," as it resounded inside of me, even though I couldn't explain it beyond that. The event set me on a spiritual journey searching through religions to find that surety that I had experienced. The "spirit" continued talking to me, but it was not until I began studying the Course that I started getting the same message.

Since then I have had no interest in anything except searching for the "truth." Yet it is hard for me to get out of the vicious circle of thinking I should get busy with this or that, dreading it, and feeling guilty. I could make myself raise my family and keep my home clean, but I have a difficult time wanting to do anything.

In my shop, when I have an arrangement to create for someone, I put it off to the last minute. But once I get started, I just do it, as if I am not doing it. I am always surprised that it turns out to be more wonderful than the customer dreamed. I seem to have no judgment of it at all. All I know is that it is finished and I can do no more. I thought of making my granddaughter a dress but now have no desire to do it. It seems to have no purpose. When I get like that, I seem paralyzed about everything, even studying the Course. But I cannot seem to let go of thinking of the things waiting for me to do. I ask the Holy Spirit to give me a function but find it hard to be at peace. "Shoulds" have echoed in my head all my life. All truly does seem to be vanity, to serve no purpose. Everything I would do seems to serve this illusion I want to escape. Help! What do I forgive to find release? How do I return to peace?

Beloved One,

Thanks for pouring out your stream of thoughts and for your willingness to forgive and Awaken. It is wonderful! You have heard the Voice for God reminding you of the illusory nature of the world. With *A Course in Miracles* you have a tool to train your mind to hear *only* the Holy Spirit's Voice and release the ego's voice of doubt forever. In using and practicing the lessons of the Course you will be forgiving the belief in separation, the belief in time-space, the belief in a linear sequence of separate events. You will experience many miracles which will collapse time and leave your mind at peace. You will grasp and experience the Holy Spirit's Purpose, which is the replacement for the ego's "purpose" of death, guilt, fear, and separation.

You first glimpse the new Purpose of forgiveness, of seeing the illusory nature of the cosmos, yet until the ego's purpose is completely unlearned or undone you will seem to wander. It can seem during this wandering that the world will have no purpose at all. You see that the roadways of the world lead nowhere. As the mind approaches this point everything will seem pointless, yet beyond this point of utter meaninglessness is the Light of the Holy Spirit. As you join with this Light, the Light will shine through you and radiate to everything and everyone. The Holy Spirit shines through you, shining away every scrap of darkness, and this experience is one of effortless Ease. There is no struggle or conflict in being shone through. It is as though you are transparent, for there are no personal goals or agendas to intrude.

The Holy Spirit Guides surely. In every seeming situation the judgment of the Holy Spirit directs. This is judgment through you rather than by you, and under the Holy Spirit's judgment there is never any loss to anyone. In the Holy Spirit's Purpose there are never any commands or demands, only suggestions and instructions and reminders. You can seem to resist the Holy Spirit's Call, yet delay is always temporary and Atonement or Correction is inevitable. That is why this is a required course. Forgiveness is unavoidable, and though there seem to be many forms and pathways for coming to forgiveness, in content they are all the same. Forgiveness simply sees the false as false, and quietly rests in peace.

The voice of "shoulds" is the ego. These guilt-ridden expectations arise from a false sense of self, a self-concept that God did not create. This concept was make-believe, for it sought to replace the Self God created in eternal Perfection. All frustration arises in consciousness from pretending to be human, and all human roles are constructs that perpetuate this pretense of identity. In the Present, free from the distortions of the past, you are free in Spirit as God created you.

Forgiveness offers you an expansive self-concept in which everyone and everything is included, a Perspective that leads to Waking from the dream and remembering Christ and God. You will discover that Christ is Reality and not a concept at all. Make believe self-concepts need defense only because they are shaky, unstable, and unreal.

Spirit is always defenseless for in truth there is nothing real that can be threatened and nothing unreal that exists. Herein lies the Peace of God.

Forgiveness is giving up nothing to accept Everything. Mind is unified, and peace and wholeness go together.

You have asked: "What do I forgive to find release? How do I return to peace?" To forgive the belief in time-space is to say to God: "Show me eternity!" To forgive the belief in separation is to say to God: "Show me the union of eternity." The Holy Spirit will convince you that time is unreal and eternity is real if you will let Him. Nothing is asked of you in truth, for You are already and forever perfect, whole, and complete as God created You. Forgiveness opens the way to remember this Truth.

Love & Blessings,
David

Purpose Determines Perception

In any situation it is most important to ask "What is this for, what is my purpose here?" For the situation will be perceived according to the purpose that was set in advance. Awakening means releasing judgment and not trying to judge the motives of self or others. I learned that being attentive to one's mind was a full-time practice and required the utmost attentiveness and vigilance when beginning to discipline the mind.

A favorite ego distraction was judging the motives of others or focusing on specific behaviors and attempting to make some body or some thing right or wrong.

The Solution: Do not think of everything in the world in terms of right and wrong. Rather than seeking to judge form, the important question to ask is: "Am I in my right mind – aligned with Love – or in my wrong mind, aligned with fear?" For where I am coming from on the inside determines what I perceive on the outside, until the belief in inside/outside dissolves completely.

The Holy Spirit always reminds to look inward to beliefs and thoughts, for Correction can only occur in the mind.

I offer the following: "As a mind thinketh, so it is."

Remember this: The thoughts I offer are from my Source, and it is my Source that gives me my Being. I am an Idea in the Mind of God, and happily Ideas leave not their Source. This is true for everyOne as One Mind, for there are no exceptions in Absolute Truth.

Blessings always,
David

Perceive the Body
or Behold the Spirit

Dear David,

I have been grieving because a relationship came to an end and yet I did not really lose anything. I was thinking I would like to meet a spiritual man who could rock 'n roll dance, which I love. Lo and behold I have met a lovely spiritual man who is a rock 'n roll dancer. He has a beautiful heart and soul, but when I met him I found his appearance and the way he talked unattractive. Not the content of his communication, but the sound of his voice. I enjoy his company but find it hard to accept his weasely physical appearance. So I told him I didn't want a romantic relationship; I just wanted us to be friends. I need to see that a weasel can be a beautiful man and I need to stop my lousy thoughts. It is so hard!

This is all ego stuff. Deep in my heart I know I've worked hard on relationship in the Course and have attracted a heart-opening partner. Last night I got upset and suggested we end our contact. He just stayed calm and peaceful and we talked it through. He is patient, understanding and recognizes that I am fearful because of past hurts. I am not used to receiving such blessings from a man. I know I have created this man in my life and don't want to sabotage it. My ego is trying hard to sabotage this. Do you have any suggestions that might help me?

Beloved One,

You are doing well recognizing in each circumstance that your own thoughts and judgments are being mirrored back to you. It helps to keep in mind that people aren't really people, they are thoughts. As you heal your mind and release thoughts that no longer serve you, people in your life may seem to change or disappear. The world is a world of ideas, an out-picturing of beliefs.

Each experience you have of sadness, loss or grief is the result of thoughts projected out onto people. By tracing your thoughts inward you are able to get down to your beliefs and beneath your beliefs to your desires. By meditating in a state of enquiry, you can ask yourself "what do I really believe is true" regarding a certain situation. When your desire is split, when you desire anything other than God, you are on the ego's playing field and your thoughts, emotions and perceptions will reflect back to you your split desire – your desire for something other than God – which cannot possibly bring you Love.

Each moment you choose to perceive your brother as a body or to behold the spirit. This relationship seems to be the perfect opportunity for you to practice beholding the spirit and allowing the Holy Spirit to Guide you in an experience of holy relationship in which judgment and fear of love can come up for release. Regarding sexuality/romance, simply follow your prompts in every moment, allowing yourself the time to tune in and check that each step feels right. Rather than drawing conclusions or setting rules and boundaries, or trying to define the relationship in worldly terms, allow the Holy Spirit to Guide you gently, moment by moment, in an intuitive way that feels right for you. Each moment is fresh and new, an opportunity to release expectations of yourself and your brother. The past is gone, including the very recent past. You are free to be Who you are in every moment.

Communicate openly with your friend about the purpose of your relationship, about your commitment to God and to healing. When the purpose is opening to Real Love and releasing fear, and when you hold it out front together, you pave the way for trust to develop. When you are clear about purpose you can quickly dismiss the ego when you sense pressure or fear taking things personally. Treat your relationship like a new flower opening it's petals in the warm sunshine. It is in need of gentle nurturing and tender care – all that is required is Given of God. You do not have to figure out how to make the sun shine and the rain fall. Remember always to put God first, then enjoy!

With love,
David

Dear David,

Thank you for replying to my call for help. I still struggle to understand the concept of there being no people out there, only my thoughts. However, I reflected on your words people may seem to change or disappear. Yes, my friend is a miracle in my life because I am changing my mind about what I deserve. For too long I carried a deep-seated belief that I was not worthy of the best and that relationships meant rejection and pain. God wants me to express love and let go of fear (ego). Thank you so much and I will remember to ask the Holy Spirit to guide me in every moment as to what needs to happen. I will remember to hold the relationship as a way to opening to real love and releasing fear.

From Partnership to Divine Relationship

Greetings Holy One,

It seems that relationship in this world involves partnership. And the concept of partnership is a mirror of the unconscious belief in incompletion or lack. Reciprocity always involves giving to get, and this ego belief is dissolved in the Light of giving as God Gives, unconditionally and everlastingly.

Learning to give in the fullest sense will draw one out of a sense of having a separate will apart from God's Will. As long as one holds on to a self-concept or image, one must want to get something outside of One Self, and must believe it is possible to do so. The opportunity with a partner, indeed with anybody you meet or even think about each day, is to learn how to give totally, completely, without distinctions or conditions of any kind.

Think of it like this. A partner is calling on the Sacred. Listen carefully to the Spirit, for what your partner is asking for is what you are asking for. And what you give to your partner, you give to yourself. This is the path of devotion. In devoting yourself to one goal, forgiveness, you lose all sense of separate interests and separate selves. No request is too large or small in this Perspective. You can only join in this Perspective, the Perspective of the dreamer – never in the dream. Love does not oppose. There is nothing fight, defend against or be right about. And devotion requires trust, for trust in the Spirit dissolves all doubt.

By learning to give without distinctions, you will learn to experience your Self as beyond situations, as Everywhere and Everything! All that you need do is trust, step back, and not interfere with an Experience that comes directly from God. True Giving will reveal Itself as You.

Relationship is not personal. The only real Relationship is creation and Creator. Relationship is not between persons, for thought-form associations deny the only real Relationship of Spirit. You cannot experience what True Relationship is until you have first realized the impossibility of the attempt to make past associations take the place of Reality. Reality and God are always in eternal Relationship and direct communication or Communion.

All concepts of relationship must give way to forgiveness, seeing the false as false, and understanding that thought-forms cannot be meaningfully associated, ordered, or arranged. A hierarchy of relationships is meaningless, for Love is One and of Divine origin. Time is simultaneous, not linear and sequential. Forgiveness does not attempt to change the past to compensate for a feeling of lack, guilt, or incompletion. It sees the past as over and gone. By seeing that the world is just a picture, the mind is freed from attempting the impossible and can recognize Itself as Changeless Mind! The awareness that illusions are one opens the way for the Recognition that Mind is One! This is the realization that Love is All there Is!

Thank You God for Divine Relationship which inspires forever and ever! Many blessings cascade upon You Holy One. Our Relationship is intimate and eternal and Divinely Content.

Love,
David

Holy Relationship Shifts Away From the Personal

Beloved One,

Greetings of Peace. A friend recently asked me to share more personal miracle shifts from my journey so she could relate to the ideas I share. The Spirit uses parables, and people smile and nod in recognition of the Divine Principle that glimmers beyond the stories. Abstraction is the natural condition of the Mind and the parables are very specific examples that serve to point to a State of Mind that experiences nothing as special and perceives everything in the cosmos as a happy dream and a reflection of God's Love.

I experience God's Love as universal and expansive and unlimited. God's Love is literally beyond definition of any kind. The Holy Spirit uses lots of examples and metaphors to point to the present moment, which is the presence of God's Love. The examples are witnesses that God's Love is not dependent on form or specifics at all and that the Holy Spirit can use any symbols to help the sleeping mind recognize this pristine and tranquil moment.

Holy relationship is not between people. It is very simply the Purpose of acceptance and non-judgment held firmly and surely in mind. It looks, waits, watches and judges not. It does not seek to change the world, for holy relationship is the symbol of a forgiven world. The Purpose is equally applicable to every person, place, thing, situation, and event. The Purpose is the understanding that there are no real differences possible in unified awareness. Love is all-inclusive because Love is One. Love is friendly because everyone is a friend in the experience of extending Love. The cosmos of time and space was made to hide Love and push Love out of awareness, so examples of Love in action are extremely helpful in Awakening to Love's Presence, Which is ever-Present.

Here are some specific examples that point to holy relationship or what I refer to as Holy Union. "X" and "Y" are symbols. They are symbols which represent two people. Holy relationship is not between "X" and "Y". The symbols of people are used by the Holy Spirit to point toward Divine Love. The symbols are never the actual experience of Love, for representations of Love merely reflect the belief that Love and symbols are the same. Love is God's Will and has no object. Never mistake a symbol for anything Real, for symbols are temporary and Reality is eternal.

The holy relationship can be described as loving, trusting, open, honest, kind, free, spontaneous, present, affectionate, nonjudgmental, inclusive, happy, joyful, peaceful, extending, communicating, healing, and wonderful!

The holy relationship is not romantic, sexual, possessive, exclusive, time-based, judgmental, controlling, fearful, angry, guilty, jealous, comparative, insane or sick in any way. The holy relationship is therefore unlike any and all interpersonal relationships that seem to be so very common and natural in this world, which have been based on separation and individuality.

Holy relationship is shared purpose, and only the Holy Spirit's purpose can truly be extended or shared. The attempt to share ego concepts and beliefs is therefore the attempt to share nothing, and nothing cannot be shared because only Love is capable of being extended or shared. Love simply extends and shares, Being what It Is.

What form does holy relationship take? It takes whatever form is Helpful to demonstrate the lesson that form is meaningless and Love is All Meaning, that Love is Content and not form of any kind. Love is a State of Mind and cannot be reduced to objects in linear time. In Holy Union there is no past and there is no future. In this world, saying "Our relationship has no future," means that a relationship has come to an end, but under the Holy Spirit's guidance these same words take on a very different Meaning – a Present Meaning. Live for the moment, for Now is truly Everything. This is the key to Happiness not of this world, Happiness that comes from God.

In the Course Jesus teaches that minds are joined and bodies cannot join. Jesus also teaches, "The Holy Spirit's purpose lies safe in your relationship... for the Holy Spirit has set His temple there." T-20.VI.7 The relationship is thus the loving attitude you share and cannot be defined in terms of bodies. Bodies seem to come and go, and thus relationships that are defined by bodies are temporary. The attitude of Love is everlasting, and this can only be experienced when all body thoughts have been released to the Holy Spirit.

How is this done? Let the Holy Spirit tell you where and when to bestow miracles, and let Jesus perform them through your mind. Feel the Joy of Purpose as you step back and let the Holy Spirit lead the way. Do not attempt to tell the Holy Spirit who needs miracles and where and when, for only by receiving the miracles first can you be directed and instructed by the Holy Spirit.

The desires of the ego fade, grow dim and disappear in holy relationship. The desires for bodily comforts and conveniences, preferences, appetites, and the countless distractions of the ego become more and more peripheral in awareness. And then in the Holy Instant they are gone, and the mind rests in Peace at last.

Holy relationship is so vast that it feels very abstract, for all scraps of the personal are washed away in the river of Love. The river sees no special bodies and no couples. For the river flows into an eternal ocean that is completely abstract. The memories of time-space fade, grow dim and disappear in Oneness.

People always seem to be very interested in the script. The feeling of Love inside one's heart has nothing to do with the script. Form is eclipsed by Content, and this experience renders the form irrelevant. Such is the Mysticism of Love. For the mind that comes to a Single desire, creation is revealed as What Is. Let our Beloved holy relationship lead the way. Let all symbols merge in a forgiven world, and welcome the disappearance of the cosmic universe. The Universe of Spirit is All, and nothing unreal exists. Herein lies the Peace of God.

In eternal Love,
David

Intimacy, Peace and Freedom

Intimacy, peace, and freedom. Deep down, that's what everyone wants and searches for. And where are they to be found? Who among us has not sought for them in the physical? Who among us has not associated intimacy with the closeness of bodies, or peace of mind with a special place, or freedom with money or mobility? True intimacy, peace of mind, and freedom transcend the physical. As one outgrows the physical concepts and definitions, one can more clearly understand that holding in mind the Spirit's single Purpose, One that is not of this world, is how true intimacy, peace, and freedom are found.

Initially, this seems abstract and quite a stretch. Holding to such a purpose requires tremendous discipline of the mind, or mind training, and relinquishment of all other purposes. This seems, to the untrained mind, to be very difficult only because the untrained mind believes in the reality of the physical as surely as it believes that separate purposes are necessary to meet different levels of need. Perceiving separate levels of need is a very basic error, and it leads to searching for solutions within these separate levels. Eventually the false concept of levels of need must be questioned for the mind to recognize its natural state of intimacy, peace, and freedom. The problem of separation is in the mind, not the world, for there are no problems apart from mind. Mind, in Reality, is not private and separate.

The present moment is the focal point for Awakening. It is the point of power. Desiring to be happy is to live in the moment and go with the Universal Flow. It is not the choice of forms or behaviors, of reading this or watching a TV show that will bring peace. It is not in the doings. Purpose/perspective is the real choice, and that is why discernment is important. It is the purpose you give or the meaning you assign to reading this or watching the TV show that will bring you peace or upset. There is no inherent purpose in any form. The mind always finds what it desires deep inside.

Why does it seem difficult to keep attentive to the present and hold the Spirit's single Purpose in mind? The deceived mind is untrained and is unwilling to keep attentive to the present because it is afraid of the present. All the chatter in the mind and all the drama and busy distractions and outlets are defenses against the present moment, where Stillness is. The deceived mind is afraid of the Spirit. All goals and purposes of the self-concept are of the ego and were made to obscure the Spirit's single Purpose. The fear, then, comes from the mind's attachment to the self-concept.

There is often talk about detachment as a solution. And there is a sense that detachment would bring peace, if it were possible. But trying to be detached is met with resistance, for the mind remains confused about what to detach from, confused about form (appearances) and content (purpose). Excuses are offered. The old thought patterns and resulting behaviors remain. One is left talking about or trying to completely forget about detachment. My friends, one must understand the nature of attachment very clearly before one can be detached and at peace. To hold to the Spirit's single Purpose, one must be able to discern the nature of ego thought, regardless of form.

This is the Purpose we desire to experience and share together. We invite the Spirit to make clear to us our naturally loving thoughts and experiences. This is our ongoing invitation to the Spirit. We bring a sincere intention, a willingness to go deep into the Heart of God. We show up open to the Spirit and eager to be shown our own Holiness!

This experience could be described as a very open sharing of expressions of love in which no questions, concerns, or topics are off limits. One thing is sure: feelings of peace and joy are indicators of choosing to hold the Spirit's single Purpose in mind. And cultivating a sincere intention to discern the nature of ego thought and to happily let it go leads one to a greater willingness to choose peace instead of fear. For why would anyone choose fear unless, unrecognized, it seemed to offer something of value?

Once the ego is exposed as nothing of value and all belief is withdrawn from it, it merely ceases to seem to be. For only Spirit remains, and Spirit is now, forever, and always! Yeah for the Great Awakening! We are remembering the Truth of our very Being – eternal, changeless, infinite, and perfect. And all are blessed in the remembering of our Oneness.

The Impossible Belief in Illness

Illness is an error in thought, and all thoughts err which follow the erroneous belief that a body can be ill or well, dead or alive. Death is the belief that separation from God, from the One, from the All is possible. Illness and death are the same illusion, for each would deny the Totality, the All-inclusiveness, and the eternal Everything that is Life. All Life is Spirit, and this world is nothing more than the belief that there can be something other than Spirit. The body is a neutral instrument and cannot in Truth be endowed with the attributes or characteristics of illness or wellness, death or life.

As a false belief, illness/death can only be forgiven or released. Death is not an evil victimizer or a blessing, but instead an impossibility. Seeing this is Joy! There is no death! I have realized that sickness and death were arrogant thoughts, for they would deny the Omnipotence, Omniscience, and Omnipresence of the Source of All Life. In the Presence of the Source of All Life is only Holiness.

Metaphysicians claim that sickness and death are decisions, but I ask you: "What choice is that?" You are Called to be the Living Proof that there is no death. If anyone could be sick or die, there is no God. Yet if God is Love, there is only Love and nothing but Love. There is no compromise or middle ground to be found in this. When you turn on a light in a dark room, the dark is no more. The darkness and light do not battle for what outcome will occur

– when Light has come there is no darkness. Similarly Life and death, Wellness and illness cannot co-exist. What is Real and what appears to be its opposite cannot both be true if Truth is true and only Truth is true.

In my Heart there is great Happiness and Joy! I see that the belief in illusions was the error that the Spirit has Corrected, and Divine Mind happily has no opposite. And if Correction is indeed a decision, an acceptance of what is really true, what could be more worthy in your mind of your devotion and full attention? For as you think, so shall the world represent that thinking. Will you hop on the train of thoughts of the world, or observe their nothingness from on high with the angels? Will you sing the dirge of illusions or the happy song of eternal gratitude? Every moment of every day, this is the question the sleeping ones face. Will you cover over the living moment of Life with the past/future business of the world, or surrender to the Life that You are forevermore?

Pain is a wrong-minded perception. Who in their right Mind could see anything but Love? Question everything that appears to be not Love, and what never was will surely disappear from your experience. Empty consciousness of all apparent thoughts of nothingness, and the Everything-ness and All-ness of Being remains!

I love You Holy One! I rejoice with the angels that Oneness remains ItSelf, far beyond the belief in opposites. For what could come to separate Whom God created as One forever? There is only Love, and duality was but a dream, welcome Now to Mind Awake! In Gratitude.

Releasing the Death Wish Forever

Dear David,

What would you say to someone who wants to end their life?

Beloved One,

There is no ending to life. One that ends this life simply transitions. Life cannot end. The transition that you see as death is not an end to the mind. Some memories may fade, but the core that is the mind continues on. The pain and suffering that is believed within the mind accompanies the mind into the transition, so one does not find escape through transition.

One who is contemplating ending their life is suffering from loneliness. This suffering may seem to take different forms, and the person may not realize that the pain is the pain of loneliness, but that is the basis of all pain. The one who considers ending his or her life may agonize over mistakes, lost opportunities or addictions (guilt), suffer from self-loathing or live in fear of what seems to be happening or seems to be coming in the future. But if the one who is contemplating ending their life can see for even a moment beyond the pain that tortures him or her, that one will see that the real pain comes from feeling alone within the suffering. What this one seeks above all else is love. And one cannot find love by ending one's life. But that one will also not remove his or herself from love through the act of ending one's life. For each one is love, but has lost the awareness of love through the belief in loneliness.

What each one must come to realize is that one is never alone. To be alone is literally impossible. Until a person is ready to learn that lesson, he or she will suffer from the symptoms of loneliness.

And so to one that is willing to end life, you can say, "I love you. I will always love you. And I can help you, if you will accept my help.

You are never alone."

The one you say that to may be willing to accept the love you offer and they may not. Each one will choose his or her lessons. This is why you must realize that this lesson is also your own. For right now, as you sit feeling sad or afraid for the one that is contemplating ending his or her life, you are also suffering from loneliness. For you have not learned that you cannot be alone and your brother cannot be alone. You have not accepted our Oneness as the only fact that Is. And so I say to you, "I love you. I will always love you. And I can help you, if you will accept my help. You are never alone."

The world you live in is an illusion. Nothing is as it seems. Place your faith with Me; put your heart in My Hands. Sit within the stillness and be willing to know that I Am here. Nothing can ever be lost when you accept the truth of My Reality. For that truth is eternal and inclusive and whole.

Let the one who is contemplating ending his or her life know that you love him or her, and you be willing to accept My Love as Your Love. There is no other answer to any question. To accept My Love as Your Love is to accept the Truth as it is.

Love,
David

Stuck in Hatred and Not Seeing

Dear David,

I seem to want to hate this person. I try the lessons and nothing works. I feel frustrated and stuck. What can I do?

Dear Beloved One

Thanks for writing and sharing what is surfacing in your mind.

Hatred is the ego's emotion in wanting to be right about the belief in separation from God and dictating how God must react to this insane belief. The ego is furious that God will not grant reality to a nonexistent puff of an idea that wants to rule the eternal Child of an eternally Loving God. The emotion can and will be released the instant the ego is no longer valued and taken as one's identity.

The ego uses the unreturned love of the special relationship to attempt to justify the anger until the deeper hatred at God and fear of God is exposed. But in looking deeper the original error is uncovered and the ineffectiveness of the special relationship becomes acute in awareness.

Give your mind the permission to let the seeming beast rear its head. You will go past these feelings and be free of them. Simply do not attempt to protect or project them, and they will dissolve.

Surrender every scrap of control, every attempt to manipulate the world and fix your brothers and sisters, and where is the hatred? Hatred has vanished along with the belief that something needed to be controlled or manipulated or fixed. Only acceptance is Asked, that Christ may recognize Christ. And for this it is only necessary that the last illusion be accepted: forgiveness of what never happened in Reality. Forgive illusions and hatred has vanished. Yet to forgive, it must be recognized that illusions are one, for there is no partial forgiveness in Atonement. Either forgiveness is complete or illusions are believed to be real.

Lesson 23 says, "I can escape the world I see by giving up attack thoughts." This is the only way out of fear that works because there is an admission/acknowledgement of specific attack thoughts and an active desire to dismiss them.

Aside from letting the anger come up for release, and taking a close look at your thoughts and beliefs and desires that are down there in the mind, the serenity prayer is a very helpful tool for coming back to sanity:

God grant me the serenity to accept the things I cannot change; courage to change the things I can; and wisdom to know the difference.

I am joined with you in right-mindedness, and thus is hatred impossible. Blessings of Love.

Eternally,
David

Message from the Holy Spirit

Come unto Me, My children, once again, without such twisted thoughts upon your hearts. You still are holy with the Holiness which fathered you in perfect sinlessness, and still surrounds you with the Arms of peace. Dream now of healing. Then arise and lay all dreaming down forever. You are he your Father loves, who never left his home, nor wandered in a savage world with feet that bleed, and with a heavy heart made hard against the love that is the truth in you. Give all your dreams to Christ and let Him be your Guide to healing, leading you in prayer beyond the sorry reaches of the world.

He comes for Me and speaks My Word to you. I would recall My weary Son to Me from dreams of malice to the sweet embrace of everlasting Love and perfect peace. My Arms are open to the Son I love, who does not understand that he is healed, and that his prayers have never ceased to sing his joyful thanks in unison with all creation, in the holiness of Love. Be still an instant. Underneath the sounds of harsh and bitter striving and defeat there is a Voice that speaks to you of Me. Hear this an instant and you will be healed. Hear this an instant and you have been saved.

Help Me to wake My children from the dream of retribution and a little life beset with fear, that ends so soon it might as well have never been. Let Me instead remind you of eternity, in which your joy grows greater as your love extends along with Mine beyond infinity, where time and distance have no meaning. While you wait in sorrow Heaven's melody is incomplete, because your song is part of the eternal harmony of love. Without you is creation unfulfilled. Return to Me Who never left My Son. Listen, My child, your Father calls to you. Do not refuse to hear the Call for Love. Do not deny to Christ what is His Own. Heaven is here and Heaven is your home.

Creation leans across the bars of time to lift the heavy burden from the world. Lift up your hearts to greet its advent. See the shadows fade away in gentleness; the thorns fall softly from the bleeding brow of him who is the holy Son of God. How lovely are you, child of Holiness! How like to Me! How lovingly I hold you in My Heart and in My Arms. How dear is every gift to Me that you have made, who healed My Son and took him from the cross. Arise and let My thanks be given you. And with My gratitude will come the gift first of forgiveness, then eternal peace.

So now return your holy voice to Me. The song of prayer is silent without you. The universe is waiting your release because it is its own. Be kind to it and to yourself, and then be kind to Me. I ask but this; that you be comforted and live no more in terror and in pain. Do not abandon Love. Remember this; whatever you may think about yourself, whatever you may think about the world, your Father needs you and will call to you until you come to Him in peace at last.

Song of Prayer - 3.IV.6-10

You are My Son, and I do not forget the secret place in which I still abide, knowing you will remember. Come, My Son, open your heart and let Me shine on you, and on the world through you. You are My light and dwelling place. You speak for Me to those who have forgotten. Call them now to Me, My Son, remember now for all the world. I call in love, as you will answer Me, for this is the only language that we know. Remember love, so near you cannot fail to touch its heart because it beats in you.

Do not forget. Do not forget, My Child. Open the door before the hidden place, and let Me blaze upon a world made glad in sudden ecstasy. I come, I come. Behold Me. I am here, for I am You, in Christ, for Christ, My Own beloved Son, the glory of the infinite, the joy of Heaven and the holy peace on earth, returned to Christ and from His hand to Me. Say now Amen, My Son, for it is done. The secret place is open now at last. Forget all things except My changeless Love. Forget all things except that I am here.

Accepting the Atonement for Yourself, Part 1

- A conversation with David

Atonement is a total commitment. The ego doesn't know what commitment is. It is impulsive like a child that doesn't have a parent, because it really *doesn't*. It is a frantic fearful thought with no sense of stability. The Holy Spirit is the answer in the mind, the bringer of the Atonement, that puts the Atonement principle into action for the mind that has fallen asleep.

The Atonement is so tranquil it just looks and judges not. It is just a state of pure stillness. But in order to open your mind to accept the Atonement you have to be ready and willing for something completely different than anything you've known in this world.

The Course is a tool for your mind to use. The first part of this whole plan of awakening and accepting the Atonement is to let Jesus and the Holy Spirit get your attention.

You have to be ready for the Course. I've traveled around the world many times and I hear the same stories. Some people have used the course-book as a doorstop or to put their plants on, and then one day, they go "Hmmm, I think I am supposed to read this book." At some point it gets your attention.

Once Jesus has your attention, you have to be willing to open up for miracles. You need to be convinced that there is another way of looking at the world. You shouldn't be concerned or feel pressured about this because it is the job of Holy Spirit and Jesus to convince you. You just have to have a little bit of willingness.

Through many, many miracles, you prepare your mind for the Atonement. When you are practicing the Course you have a miracle, then the ego seems to come back. The Atonement, however, is a principle that takes you to a state of certainty of who you are. For example, in Workbook Lesson 139 "I will accept Atonement for myself," the first sentence is "Here is the end of choice." How relaxing a state of mind must be where there is no decision to be made. You just rest in being Who you are.

To give you a little background on me, I got the Course delivered to my lap in 1986. When it came into my life I said, "Oh my God, this is my escape from fear and doubt and misery." I felt an immediate recognition with it. I studied it for an average of eight hours a day for the first two and a half years. It was like I was drowning and someone threw me a life raft and said, "Grab hold!" That is how I felt when I found the Course. I felt like this was the answer to an unspoken prayer. After immersing my mind so deeply for a couple of years, a Voice started to speak to me very clearly in my mind and started to guide me very specifically. "Call so-and-so." "Go here, go there." "You forgot your keys, go back." It was like a little bird on my shoulder chirping away, like having a miniature Jesus. That sped up my Awakening and the whole point of this is to save time.

When I went to my first conference, I was introduced as, "a walking Course In Miracles Encyclopedia." There is nothing like getting introduced as an encyclopedia to spur you on. I could quote verses and tell you what page number and so on, but I didn't want to be an encyclopedia – I wanted the experience. That launched me deeper into the experience of listening to the Holy Spirit, following the Holy Spirit, and feeling the joy of being in tune with the Holy Spirit.

You should do the workbook lessons with such anticipation that every day you expect to wake up. You expect that lesson to be the One. Instead of thinking in your mind, well, I've got 365 lessons and if I don't get it now I can go back and do it again. That only buys into the sense of time. I just expected to wake up. I would go, "Ah, another day, another lesson!" And I would give everything I had to that lesson.

To go for an experience that will end your doubting, that takes you beyond theories and concepts, is what Atonement is about. It is your sole responsibility. It may seem like you have many responsibilities in this world, but I can assure you, that as you keep allowing the Holy Spirit to guide you, you keep coming back to, "Oh. But I just have one responsibility. Just to accept the Atonement. And I need to be guided very carefully by the Holy Spirit." It is not about abdicating responsibilities. It is about letting Holy Spirit handle what is going on in your mind with integrity.

You will not be asked to lie, break promises or cut and run. You are going to be asked to follow so clearly, so loyally, that all things are handled through you by the Holy Spirit. There are still things that you face every day but Holy Spirit handles them. Some of you remember in the Bible, Jesus said, "Be like the lilies in the field," and "Seek ye first the Kingdom of Heaven."

In the Course, Jesus is saying, "Once you have accepted His plan as the one function you would fulfill, there will be nothing else the Holy Spirit will not arrange for you without your effort. Holy Spirit will go before you, making straight your path, and leaving in your way no stones to trip on, no obstacles to bar your way." T-20.IV.8 When you accept your function, everything in this world is completely orchestrated for you. You literally live a life that has no problems: no personal problems, no societal problems, no health issues, no financial issues, no relationship issues; that is what salvation is. That is what Enlightenment is. It is realizing as we study in Lesson 80, "Let me recognize that my problems have been solved."

For me it has been an experience of listening and following to the point that I felt a merge taking place, an integration in my mind. There is no longer a leader and a follower; there is no longer a guide and one who is being guided. The personality, the mask of being human, just starts to dissolve away. You feel yourself as the living presence of God, as the living Christ, as the I *Am* presence.

You must be clear that in order to consistently experience this you can make no exceptions to the miracle. That is what the workbook is about, making no exceptions. Go through your day willing to make no decisions by yourself, willing to let every decision be made by Holy Spirit through you. "If I make no decisions by myself, this is the day that will be given me." T-30.I.4:2

It is like Lesson 135 where Jesus says, "A healed mind does not plan. It carries out the plans that it receives through listening to wisdom that is not its own... If there are plans to make, you will be told of them." That is the feeling. "Oh, you want me to do this? Okay." It is given, but there is no sense of pressure in it. You flow in that Divine Flow and you keep your integrity. If the Holy Spirit gives you a plan or a prompt, you follow through.

It is in the present moment you start to understand what the Course means when it says, "Atonement might be equated with total escape from the past and total lack of interest in the future." M-24.6. Isn't that a lovely phrase? You can just let that wash over you. "Total escape from the past and total lack of interest in the future." That takes away the stress of trying to figure things out, of having to work out your salvation. It sounds a lot like Grace, "Total escape from the past and total lack of interest in the future."

This is very practical. This is safe. This is sure. You can have confidence in this. Be certain that this is not being gullible, not being airy-fairy, not being Pollyanna. It is lightness. There is no sense of trying to convince anybody of anything. You don't have to proselytize. There is no need to try to force something; you are not trying to change anyone's mind. You are trying to let your mind be guided and changed by Holy Spirit. You aren't trying to change anybody else. And when you allow this to occur, it brings you into a sense of relaxation and joy.

Jesus is orchestrating our lives. I read in the Course that Jesus was saying, "When you perform a miracle, I will arrange both time and space to adjust to it." T-2.V.A.11.3 Arrange both time and space for me? Wow! That sounds really interesting. They never taught us that in school.

That's a change from being a human being stuck in time like a fly stuck on fly paper. The miracle worker is in control of time, because Jesus says I will perform miracles through you if you will let me. You don't have to be perfectly clear. If you were perfectly clear, there would be no need for miracles in the first place. But just for an instant, you need to be fearless. Just for an instant, relax, and trust in my readiness, Jesus says. Don't worry about your readiness, trust in Mine. I will perform the miracles through you. But they cannot be performed in a state of doubt or fear because doubt and fear block what's there.

Over the years I've had to change from a person who was very quiet and shy. I was voted most shy in my senior class and listed that way in the yearbook. Nobody thought I'd ever go around the world and talk about God and things they tell you never to talk about in public. And I thought, "Oh boy, Moses stuttered and now here we go. I get to go around the world and talk about God."

Miracles are involuntary. It is not like you have to consciously control what you are going to say and whom you are going to talk to. You can see that I have no script up here. I am enjoying the talk along with you, as always. I am listening to what the Holy Spirit has to say as if for the first time, because it always feels that way.

When you are a miracle worker, time and space are orchestrated for you. Let me give you an example. I get invitations all around the world. I was invited to Cali, Colombia, and had not been on many trips overseas. On my way there I had a layover in Miami, Florida. When I got down there the airport looked like an evacuation area. There was a hurricane coming right into Miami and people were trying to get out of Florida to get back to their homelands in South America. Babies were crying and it was very crowded with people all over the place. I was supposed to meet Susana, a friend and translator who had flown all the way from the Canary Islands.

When I got to Miami I just kept looking around for her in this sea of people before we found each other and got on the plane. As soon as the plane was in the air, they announced that they had shut down the entire Greater Miami airport. So, Jesus had actually held off a hurricane until we were in the air!

You don't usually think about yourself as so important that a hurricane gets put on hold. I tell you that example because I'm not fooling when I tell you that Jesus says I will control time and space if you will perform miracles. I was traveling to Colombia to let the Holy Spirit speak through me. Your mind can move mountains and stop hurricanes. It is so powerful that there is nothing in this world, in this entire cosmos that is more powerful than your mind. You have dominion over the entire cosmos when you are a miracle worker.

Some of you know what is going on in Venezuela with Chavez. When I there I was on television twice and did eight radio interviews while the military was in a state of alertness for an impending invasion from the United States to take over the oil fields. I was talking about miracles and love and sharing and healing while the military was doing war maneuvers. I did not fear for my life because I do not identify with the body. I feel invulnerable. So I go wherever the Holy Spirit would have me go. When you are performing miracles, remember the line in the Bible, "If God is with us, who can be against us?" Romans 8:31

Isn't this a *great* profession that we're being called to? If you are in your state of miracle mindedness and state of readiness, then nothing can be against you because everything is being used for good. All things work together for good, the Bible says, and the Course says. It feels good to feel invulnerable. It feels good to feel powerful. And Jesus says in the Course, all power is given you in Heaven and earth. All power is of God.

If you follow the ego you can believe in manifesting. You can say that you manifest your soul mate and your yacht. Some of you have seen the movie, *The Secret*. The mind is very powerful. We are not trying to diminish the power of the mind, but all power is of God, because God is the creator. So power is of the Spirit. Even when you seem to be able to manipulate the dream and have the dream come out in a certain way, that is just a step along the way. Who could be content with such small things when the Kingdom of Heaven is your inheritance, when eternity is your inheritance?

That is why it has gotten to the point in my life where peace of mind is no small gift. I live in such a state of peace and happiness and joy that I get invitations to talk on Enlightenment with people that are into Bhagavad-Gita and other traditions. The Course is near and dear to my heart, but now my experience has gone beyond it. It is just joining everywhere I go.

I'm going to read you a few sentences from Lesson 139 and to me this is really great. This is what makes it all worthwhile. This is what Jesus said, "We have a mission here. We did not come to reinforce the madness that we once believed. Let us not forget the goal that we accepted. It is more than just our happiness alone we came to gain." It is more than our happiness alone we came to gain. What is coming next?

"What we accept as what we are proclaims what everyone must be along with us." Everyone must be along with us... Do you realize the implications of that sentence? What we proclaim for ourselves is what everyone must be along with us. We're not talking about gurus who've got it, and devotees who grovel and say, "I want to get what he has got." If you accept the Atonement, then everyone goes with you! Everyone has to be Enlightened if you are Enlightened. Do you see the implications of this? Do you see how this old game of "I've got it and you don't," isn't going to fly with this Course? If you are Enlightened, everyone that you perceive is Enlightened. You must treat everyone with the same Enlightenment that you experience. If you are love, everyone is love.

Are there exceptions? No.

"It is therefore in my power to change every mind along with mine." W-54 What that means is when you allow your mind to be changed, every mind is changed. Listen to that sentence, "I can change all minds along with mine." It must be that there is only one mind that needs to accept the Atonement. Not six billion, just one. And the one, of course, is your own.

It isn't about trying to get Mom and Dad to accept the Atonement. Some of us have tried. We know how that feels. All you are doing when you accept the Atonement is you are allowing a transformation in which you realize that everything is connected and we all share one mind.

It doesn't matter what angle you come at it from. Some of you have heard of the movies *What the Bleep Do We Know?* and *Down the Rabbit Hole*. People all over the world love movies. In all of the countries I've gone to, everyone says, "Hollywood, Hollywood!" So I bring Hollywood with me. I have *What the Bleep Do We Know?* in my pocket, or *The Matrix, The Truman Show, Eternal Sunshine of the Spotless Mind* – all the greats. I even wrote the *Movie Watchers Guide to Enlightenment.* Everybody loves movies.

People that are joining in at my movie gatherings have all of a sudden big smiles on their faces. They are grinning from ear to ear with twinkling eyes. If I am in a big auditorium with people that I've never met, we're all totally in love by the end of the movie because we all share the same parable. We are all watching a parable of awakening. In *The Matrix,* it says "You are the One." It doesn't matter what language you translate that into, everyone is like, "Ooo, yeah, I could live with that." It is so precious to let the Spirit pour through you in a language that can reach everyone in a meaningful way. It can't just fly over everyone's head.

On the many gatherings I did in Colombia more than 90 percent of the participants were women. Their macho men and husbands were not so interested in oneness, seemingly. After two weeks I was talking to women who had accepted the Atonement. I asked them what they most wanted. They said, "I wish I could communicate this with my boyfriend or with my husband. That would be the most important thing to me. More than anything else, I want to share this with my partner." Their boyfriends and husbands couldn't stand Jesus talk but they were interested in science. So they rented a theater, invited their husbands and I showed *What the Bleep Do We Know?* You should have seen the looks afterwards! I was kissed by 48 women. They were so happy looking at their partner saying, "That is what I've been trying to tell you for the last 20 years!" All they needed was that little bridge, and the Holy Spirit gives that little bridge, so the gap disappears and we're joined.

When I first started sharing the message of the Course I was guided to people who had spent many, many years studying it. The Holy Spirit said "Everyone you'll meet will give you a nugget of gold. Everywhere you go you will receive a gift, a recognition. You are going to have a miracle showing you the way back to the Kingdom of Heaven." We have such intimate connections! It is like you have known people forever even when meeting them for the first time. It is an interesting quality with Course in Miracles students and teachers. Expecting a gift, a jewel helped me to join with everyone

I met.

It wasn't just with Course students; I invited the Jehovah Witnesses into my house. My family used to go run and hide in the back of the house, saying, "Oh, my God, he's opening the door; they are in the living room!" I would join with them on Jesus. They adore Jesus so that was our nugget. When I went to Temple Square, Mormons would come up to me and say, "I love Jesus, I gave my life over to him and I am so happy." And I said, "I know exactly what you mean!"

You simply join in what you have in common. There is no time to pick things apart when you are there to join, to feel the connection and to see that there is no gap. That is really what the Course is about. You train your mind so completely to join that you reach a state that Jesus emphasizes in the Song of Prayer; *"Do not see error."* What a state!

As you work with the Course you first you spot the error, either in yourself or someone else. You are quick to spot it. Then you say, "Help. Help me get back into my right mind." I say, "You spot it, you got it. You perceive it, you believe it."

The more you purify, by allowing the Holy Spirit to purify your heart, the more it is like the Beatitudes in the Bible, "Blessed are the pure of heart, for they shall see God." This Course is leading to a state of such purity that you don't see error.

Mr. Magoo's physical eyes don't work too well in the cartoon, but he can walk across the highway and go wherever he wants. He is so happy. He is the kind of role model you start to open up to when you are working with the Course. It is kind of humbling, actually, when Mr. Magoo becomes your role model. You start to have fun with it and relax with it, taking it as a compliment when someone comes up to you saying you are "kind of out of it." On the Magoo meter, you are getting pretty high score! But remember, you are safe. In the Course Jesus says salvation comes with the realization "I do not know the thing I am, and therefore do not know what I am doing, where I am, or how to look upon the world or on myself." T-31.V.17. You are invulnerable, so you can relax with it. You aren't being carried off to be adrift and end up sleeping in the streets.

Some of you know from Eckhart Tolle that a park bench may be part of your journey. We've all had those thoughts, but it isn't your end point. You end up with a state of being the dreamer of a lucid dream you are aware you are dreaming. Jesus says that's what the function of God's teachers is: "awareness of dreaming." M-12.6. Remember, if you are the dreamer of the dream, the dream can't hurt you. And you are dreaming it. You aren't in someone else's dream. Some of you have worked in jobs where it seemed like the boss had a pretty strong dream going on, but the Course trains your mind to turn this belief around and see the empowerment in "*You are the dreamer of the world of dreams. No other cause it has, nor ever will.*" T-27.VII.13.

I am saying that Atonement, Enlightenment, is very, very practical.

You go through many phases with the Course. In the Teacher's Manual Jesus talks about teachers and students. He comes right out at the beginning and says that there is no difference between the teacher and the student; it is all the same, you are just teaching yourself even if you think you are apart from the learner or the teacher.

Years ago when I started to become very happy people showed up saying, "I'm your student." But there isn't really a role of being a teacher or a student. You start to realize that teaching and learning are really equated with thinking. You are thinking either with the ego or with Christ and teaching all the time. You start to pay very close attention to your thoughts, and you learn to hand over unloving thoughts, attack thoughts, to the Holy Spirit. You start to realize that you don't want to freeze down into a role. Because if you for example have the role as teacher of the Course, and someone appears and steals your role, you react. And if you react you are identified with an illusion.

Like Buddhism, this is a Course in emptying your mind of everything you think you think and think you know. It does so in a very systematic way. It prepares you to be still and open-minded.

A tranquil mind is not a small gift.

Meditation, for example, starts out with practice. You do have to be vigilant for God and His Kingdom. You do have to work at training your mind to jump off the thought trains, as they say in Buddhism, or to sink beneath the leaves and let the leaves flow over you.

But there comes a point when your life becomes a living meditation. You can be singing *Zip A Dee Doo Dah* and be in meditation. You can be walking or eating; your eyes can be opened or closed. There can be someone screaming and you realize that you can't be interrupted. (If all things work together for good, what would an interruption even be? It wouldn't exist.) I am talking about a state of mind that has no distractions. You realize that meditation doesn't have anything to do with posture or breathing. Those things can be helpful at the beginning but Atonement is independent of the body and independent of time.

The Holy Spirit uses everything in form to reach the state of Atonement.

Special relationships are the core of co-dependency, of reciprocity. Special relationships are interactive, there is bargaining going on: "I give to them, but they better give back to me, or else!" "There are many fish in the sea and I can find another if you don't reciprocate." "I'll take the garbage out this week, but next week, it's your turn." The ego *is* reciprocity.

If you study the lives of the mystics and saints like Mother Theresa or Saint Francis, you learn they are always giving, extending, radiating, and not looking for anything to come back. They are just in the joy of the giving. In Saint Francis' prayer he says, "I want to love instead of to be loved." It is about simply *extending the love*. Why? Because giving and receiving are the same. If you are extending the love, guess who feels whole and complete? You do. Mother Theresa would do the simplest things for everyone she met, because she was seeing Christ in everyone. It is very simple, it is just extending the love.

It became very apparent to me at the beginning of my journey that Jesus was speaking to me and saying the same thing he told the Apostles 2000 years ago. "Freely you have received, now freely give." Be very generous with miracles. Shine the light. Take time for everyone who comes into your awareness. Treat everyone with love, care and compassion. When you meet anyone, you are really meeting yourself. When you think of anyone, you are really thinking of yourself. The way you treat everyone is the way you treat yourself and you need to be in the mode of not expecting to get things back. I said, "Jesus, that sounds good, but I think it is practical to ask for things and have some expectations." And He said again, "Freely you have received, now freely give." I was told very specifically, "You will never charge money for anything. You will never charge a penny for anything. Nothing you write, nothing you say, no counseling, no talks, and no gatherings. Freely you have received, now freely give."

The more I got into this, the more I realized that I was freeing my mind of expectations, because love makes no demands. If you trust that the Holy Spirit will meet your needs, whatever you believe they are, then you are trusting in Divine Love to meet all your needs. You aren't putting that on your brothers and sisters.

Think of how wars are fought over territorial disputes. Or think of how children fight over a bigger piece of pie, or neighbors fight over locating a fence. We get into a state of ego, of personalities and defenses. It seems as if you have to fight and protect yourself, but this self that you think needs protection isn't your Self.

It is really about trust. In the beginning I didn't know how it was going to work. But Jesus said, "Trust me. Go forth and do this." That has continued for the last 16 years. I have watched how the Holy Spirit has orchestrated and taken care of everything. He says that it won't be done by your own efforts. "He will go before you making straight your path and leaving in your way no stones to trip on and no obstacles to bar your way." T-20.IV.8. It is almost like a fairy tale. So is it to have such trust in Spirit. You are being led to such a state of God-dependence that you can just relax. You can relax in your function, relax in your vocation, and relax in your purpose.

A healed mind is relieved of the belief that it must plan; you can go your way rejoicing and trusting that everything is working out for your own good; you can truly relax. You don't have expectations that people should act differently. You don't believe they should give you this or that. You are in a state of giving. It is very practical. When I have fully given my mind over to Spirit, I have been rewarded with the certainty that all things are working together for good. It is a state of non-judgment.

Friend: I want to ask about trust. What has been your experience with trust when it comes to people with terminal illnesses, with people who are dying?

David: In the 1990s I was visiting a student of mine in Michigan. I was taken to a man in a Catholic community diagnosed with a terminal illness. He was on his deathbed. My student said "Let's get Mikey to do it!" like the commercial. He said "Let's take David to the dying man's house and see what happens, maybe we'll see a Lazarus kind of thing!"

I prepared prayerfully. It was a very somber scene in the world's perception and the grieving had begun. The man was lying on the couch and his sister was there. I went in, sat down and went into prayer. I always trust that the Holy Spirit will speak through me. After I prayed for several minutes, all of these words started pouring through me. I started speaking and sharing, and ideas from the Course in Miracles came out. The sister, who was Catholic, was getting nervous. She said, "I feel very uncomfortable with whatever is happening here. You and your friends are going to have to leave." But the dying man on the couch raised his arm up and said, *"No! Let him continue!"*

It turned out that the dying man had been a student of the Course. He said, "I want to hear what this man has to say. I studied this Course and there were things that I had difficulty accepting. I feel that the Holy Spirit is speaking to me now." The whole situation turned. I tell this story because we need to have trust in the Holy Spirit and not prejudge the situations where we will be called on to speak.

I had another situation with a man who was seemingly diagnosed with the advanced stages of cancer. We had such a powerful Holy encounter that his eyes were twinkling when I left; we had joined so deeply in purpose that he realized he had a choice. He wasn't interested in wasting time waiting to die; he was interested in praying and reading metaphysical materials.

You realize that everything is the result of a decision. The belief in sickness and death is a decision. You will come to a state of such trust that you will see that there is no death. In fact, Jesus says in Lesson 163, "There is no death. The Son of God is free." What you do is bring that attitude, you bring the joy to everyone.

My Grandmother Lillian lived to be about 99 years old and I was asked to speak at her funeral. All my life we'd had these deep talks about God and she would say, "I just don't believe that God would send anybody to hell. I just don't believe it." I'd say, "Me neither." She was such a loving woman that I could never do anything wrong in her eyes. It was a symbol of unconditional love to me.

I got to her funeral and was praying. She was in my mind and what I heard was, "I want to speak at my own funeral." I thought, "Okay, this is going to be interesting. I've heard of ventriloquism, but to show up at your own funeral..." They already had a minister who had done most of the service. I got up and Lillian just came pouring through me. People were touched and starting crying because she had touched so many lives. Whatever was said, people recognized her. The whole place was crying.

I spoke for five minutes and it was a celebration. There was not a shred of grief in it. She really didn't believe in death and she was letting everybody know it! "Now that you are all here, now that you can't see me anymore, I've got some good news for you. There is no death." At the cemetery there were all these flowers that everyone had sent, and I said, "Take these flowers. Take them with you and celebrate this day. This is a day of joy and celebration. Remember Lillian for who she really is. She lives in your heart forever."

This is what I mean by not believing in terminal illness or in death itself. In the world, a funeral can be a very somber thing and grief seems almost natural. But when you reach a state of forgiveness, of "Be of good cheer, I have overcome the world," you can be truly helpful.

Another example of forgiving terminal illness is when I trained to be a hospice volunteer with a minister. We went to Wendy's to have a frosty and he told me he had been diagnosed with leukemia. It had spread through the blood system and he had only so long to live. I prayed and I looked him in the eye and said, "Is there someone in your life, a dear one, a loved one that you are not on speaking terms with?" He was shocked. He said, "Oh my God, how did you know about my sister? I haven't talked to her in years, we had a big falling out!"

I said to him, "Your problem is not leukemia; it is the grievance you are holding in your mind against your sister. That's where you have to do the work. Don't worry about what the doctor says or how long you have to live." I gave him the assignment to go home and call his sister.

Two weeks later he said, "You are not going to believe what

happened. I went home and I called my sister. We laughed, we cried, and we put the rift behind us! Then I went in for more tests and the doctors couldn't find a trace of leukemia. They were astounded." I told my friend that doctors try the best they can but they don't realize that healing is in the mind and not the body. He was so happy.

When I began working in the hospice ward, the doctors and nurses were feeling heavy. They said when the families came in and everyone broke down in heavy grief, they felt like they were right there in Vietnam on the front line. But the more I was there, the more they asked, "What is it with you? You waltz around like you are Fred Astaire, dancing in hospice! Would you let us in on the secret of why you are so happy?" I told them, "Life is real. Life is eternal. It is beyond the body."

Sometimes patients who were in a comatose state would perk up when I walked into the room and suddenly start talking about some grievances. I would always tell them that they were loved and innocent, and that they didn't do anything wrong, they did a great job. I said "go to the light, you are the light." The next day I'd come in and hear that patient so-and-so had moved on.

You start realizing that you aren't trying to save the body, you just want to share innocence. You are giving yourself the same gift you are giving others. You are perfectly innocent. You didn't do anything wrong. That is what the healing is. The body is just a temporary vehicle that you use. It is just like a pencil; you can use it. But your Life is the Resurrection in the mind. When it comes to something like terminal illness, there is a great line in the Course that helps save me every time I get caught. Jesus says, "The mind was sick that thought the body could be sick." T-28.II.11.

What Jesus did was to simply resurrect His mind. Everyone familiar with the Jesus story. Thirty years of public ministry, a crucifixion, and a resurrection scene. But what they never told us, the preachers and the ministers, was that the resurrection occurred before the crucifixion. When Jesus was at the river Jordon, with John, he walked out and told John to baptize him and John said, "No, you should baptize me, you're the One." Jesus told him, "No, baptize me." John baptized Jesus and a dove flew down and landed on Jesus' head. A Voice spoke and said, "This is my beloved Son in Whom I am well pleased." After that Jesus started to go around talking to people in a very different tone, he didn't speak like a human being any more. "Before Abraham was, I Am." "I am the way, the truth, and the life. No one comes to the Father but through me." Jesus' mind was resurrected before his public ministry. And that little skit at the end of his earth life was nothing more than an example of defenselessness with each character playing their part. There was no betrayal. It was just a bunch of characters acting out a skit to demonstrate innocence and sinlessness. Jesus was telling the Apostles exactly what was going to happen before it would happen. "When the temple is torn down it will be rebuilt in three days." He knew exactly what the script meant.

Friend: The Course has taken me from a place of loss to a very happy place. But Jesus seems to say it is time to let go of romance and sexual pleasure. It just doesn't seem right because I really like girls. This isn't a Course that wants to take away the little bit that we have, is it?

David: The ego is the mind's belief in lack. It is like a prism and when light comes into a prism, it splinters into all those colors. Similarly, when the miracle impulse comes beaming into your mind, it goes through the filter of the ego. The impulse comes out as what Jesus calls a "misdirected miracle impulse." T-1.VII.1

Any impulse is really a call home to God. When you feel an attraction to a woman, it is really God calling. Think of it as God dialing your number and saying, "It is time to come home." When that miracle impulse comes through the ego, which is the belief in lack, it comes out on the surface of the consciousness as a craving. That is why all appetites involve getting. It doesn't really matter whether you are hungry, thirsty, horny, or restless.

The Holy Spirit is such a gentle presence. He says, "I know you believe in lack. That's okay. We have a Course here with a workbook and mind training program to work on this thing. Nothing will be taken away from you; you need to experience miracles; you need to learn to listen and follow. You need to call so and so, hug and comfort him or her, wipe their tears, be a translucent instrument for God's love." The more you do that, the more you will be filled up within from miracle impulses. You are going to be a miracle worker.

St. Francis and his band of merry men took the vow of celibacy. You might have seen the beautiful movie *Brother Sun, Sister Moon* where Giacondo is having lustful thoughts for a woman and St Francis hears him say "I can't do it, I'll ruin everything." And St. Francis says to him that everyone is trying to open up and love God to their capacity. He says "if celibacy feels like a distraction to loving God, then be fruitful and multiply." "But with a wife," Francis adds as he goes off.

In other words, you need to trust the Holy Spirit for everything. The Holy Spirit is not going to give you a pathway that seems like deprivation and sacrifice, you would quit listening to the Holy Spirit if you start feeling that. You have to be given a carefully developed curriculum, step by step, to build your confidence in miracle working.

What Jesus says in the Course is that "all real pleasure comes from doing God's Will." As we open up to that, we grow in confidence; we grow in spirit. People look at my life and say, "You trusted the Holy Spirit and you have no job, no girlfriend, no money, no house, and no car to call your own. How does that feel?" I can honestly say that when you are in a state of joy there is no feeling of sacrifice. And what is this joy going to cost you? nothing of real value. But you have to let the Holy Spirit convince you. I had to let the Holy Spirit convince me.

So there are no set rules with sex or with anything; no "do's" and "don'ts." You will be guided by the Holy Spirit for the situation where your mind is at. That guidance is just for you. There is no standard answer to anything.

Accepting the Atonement for Yourself, Part 2

- A conversation with David

Sometimes people ask me about feeling anxious and afraid when they are feeling off and don't know where they are off. They were having a happy day and all of a sudden clouds just rolled in and the happy day went out the window.

The Course teaches, "I am responsible for what I see. I choose the feelings I experience, and I decide upon the goal I would achieve. And everything that seems to happen to me I ask for, and receive as I have asked." T-21.II.2. That's pretty airtight. It is breaking away from victimization. You want to get to a point where you can claim Christ control of your mind instead of ego control. You reclaim your inheritance, and that means to think with Christ and to think with God.

There are two categories of error students often make. The first category is *metaphysical errors*. An example of a metaphysical error is the belief that you are in the world, but you're really at home in Heaven and the world is your dreaming of exile. You made it up, and you forgot that you did.

For example, when doing Lesson 48, "There is nothing to fear." You might think, "I've got that mortgage payment due on Friday. Uh oh, how much money is in my bank account?" You realize that you have fears coming up and you have to look at what they are. That is where the metaphysics can help you out. When you get in a real bind, whenever you start to feel afraid or jealous or angry or envious, or just raging, it is good to have these workbook lessons in mind to help pop you out of it. I call it 5, 6, 7 and 8.

5. I am never upset for the reason I think.
6. I'm upset because I see something that is not there.
7. I see only the past.
8. My mind is preoccupied with past thoughts.

When you put those together in a cause-and-effect relationship, you say to yourself: Oh, I'm upset because my mind is preoccupied with past thoughts. I'm living in the past and still rehashing this instant of terror, the unholy instant when the separation seemed to occur. I'm just replaying it here and the ego is projecting out a scenario so I can point the finger and go, "Oh, I'm upset because I don't have the mortgage payment and might lose my house."

Those kinds of things seem very real in this world. That is why you need Lesson 5, 6, 7 and 8 – to release the mind from the false cause-and-effect relationship of thinking the world is doing it to you and you are at the world's mercy. It seems as if you are at the mercy of the dream, and you're not.

The second category of error is *transfer-of-training errors*. Those errors occur when you are making exceptions, when you are practicing the lessons, and the ego wants to make an exception for whatever reason.

An example of this exception: You start doing Lesson 1, "Nothing I see means anything. You let your eyes move around the room and glance on all the familiar objects, this chair does not mean anything, this couch does not mean anything..." Sometimes when getting to a certain point, maybe looking at a picture of mother, you say, "I'll skip over that one." That's an exception. You just made an exception. Jesus says whatever your eyes land on, it doesn't mean anything. It is a practice to undo the specialness of thinking there are certain images in this world that are more important than others. People say, "I can forgive the roaches, but my mother? Do you know what she did to me?" Here is where we talk about the transfer of training.

Ken Wapnick told a great story years ago. He once visited a church to talk about metaphysics. The nuns were studying the Course and practicing Lesson 1, letting their eyes move across the sanctuary, "These pews do not mean anything, this stained glass window does not mean anything..." They got to the Eucharist and said, "Of course we'll skip that. We can't say that the body of Christ doesn't mean anything." But Jesus actually says in the Course that he can't share his body with you, he can only share his mind. He would say that seeing the meaninglessness of the body is a good application of the Course; do it with the Eucharist too. When you've been raised with a system that sees that body as sacred, it takes an undoing of the belief that there is anything sacred in form. Everything in form is part of the forgiveness lesson.

The mind, in the full awareness of the Atonement, knows that the separation never happened. During all the years I have been traveling I've always heard the same questions, "How did the impossible occur? To whom did the impossible occur?" I call them the top questions. "Actually, it is a statement, an assumption underneath the question "How did the impossible occur?" The assumption is that it did happen! Of course the ego likes that assumption. But the very assumption is something we have to learn to release. No theology will get you out of this. An experience will come that will end your doubting, the experience of Atonement. Atonement is the full awareness that the separation never happened. In this respect, the Course is a launching pad where you get ready to take off in a rocket and up in orbit where you have no sense of gravity. It is designed to help you get up into Being-ness, into your Perfection, where you are happy and free.

One metaphysical error is to try to spiritualize matter, to try to take anything in form and make it special or spiritual. You have probably heard, "Go to India and bathe in the sacred river Ganges." Catholics believe in baptism with holy water; water blessed by a priest. Both of those are metaphysical errors; trying to make something sacred in form when only your mind is sacred. The ego wants you to believe that there are certain things that are sacred in form so you will cling to them.

Another error results if you see anything in form as being causative. Images are unreal effects of an unreal cause, the ego. The Course teaches that God didn't create this world. God creates in Spirit. Jesus is saying the image of the cosmos is the graven image, drawn like a veil over the face of Christ to cover the Light. I've had three experiences in my life where the three dimensionality just collapsed and blazing light started streaming through, almost like in a movie theater when the film burns and the light just pours through and everything goes into a flash of light. The perceptual world is just a thin little veil; there is nothing solid at all. But when you believe in the ego, the mountains seem solid. Jesus says, "You... believe you walk in sanity with feet on solid ground," T-23.II.13. and from the ego's perception of the body, the ground does seem to be solid. You have to be so thorough in realizing that your mind is causative, that the world is unreal images made from unreal cause. That is what the ego is. And that is the image that has to be released and forgiven.

There is a real Cause – God. God is the creator, the prime creator. God has creative ability and so has Christ. Christ is a co-creator because he can create in Spirit, his creations are pure Spirit. Christ is not an image maker.

Every comparison that is ever made is made by ego. Comparison must be an ego device, for love makes none. When say to yourself, "How do I improve?" there is an "I" that you believe in, and an "ideal self" that you believe in. You are trying to go from one illusion, a limited self, to another version of a limited self. You have to watch very carefully with the metaphysics. The power of positive thinking is unrecognized error because in this world both positive and negative are ego. Compliments and criticisms are both of the ego. One of them seems to puff the ego up and the other seems to rip the ego down. Remember, *the ego* isn't real. So all this puffing up and ripping down doesn't do much for non-judgment. To reach a state of non-judgment is literally a transcending of the positive and the negative.

The Course is a radically different thought system. Many of us have been trained to be positive, but you need to let go of the belief that you have the ability to judge, to break apart and sort good or bad. You can't eat from the tree of good and evil. They are two sides of the same coin. That is why you use discernment to open up to forgiveness. Forgiveness does nothing. It looks, it waits, it watches and it does nothing. You just observe the thoughts with complete detachment.

The ego got in and judged and distorted Jesus' message – that's how original Christianity got distorted. Even now scholars compare various gospels and scriptures. There are even different versions of the Course: The JCIM version, the Hugh Lynn Cayce version, the Urtext version, etc. (The words that were taken out of the Urtext version and out of the Hugh Lynn Cayce version were taken out by Jesus for good reason). The ego is laughing, "Ha, ha. Hooked 'em again!" *Don't lose sight of the goal: forgiveness.* Comparison is an ego device. If the ego can get you confused it is happy. The ego is trying to prolong its seeming existence in your mind. We don't want this. Slice right through this ego distraction to shorten time. Let the Holy Spirit be discerning for you so that you don't get distracted. Jesus says in the Teacher's Manual that the Course is not controversial, but that if you seek for controversy, you will find it.

The ego is very sneaky. It tries to make controversies to make you lose your peace of mind and start taking sides. Listen, if you hear yourself saying or thinking, "In my humble opinion..." stop right there. There are no humble opinions! If you have *any* opinions there is no humility and no real humbleness.

Atonement is the awareness that the separation never happened. A state of miracle-mindedness is a state of non-judgment and it is simply seeing the false as false. Your eyes are still reporting a world to you and you don't have to deny what your body's eyes seem to see. Jesus says, "Let's practice with what your body's eyes seem to see. Don't get freaked out because of what you seem to perceive. We are going to work with your mind. Projection makes perception. We're going to learn to release attack thoughts."

When you release these attack thoughts, there is nothing left to project. You don't have the guilt left in your mind anymore and therefore you see the world differently. You see a forgiven world shown to you by the Holy Spirit. If you start to see glimmering lights, don't freak out. That means vision is coming! You are getting ready to see with the vision of Christ. The Course even says you will see light around familiar objects, so you should really be happy when that happens.

The ego says you have to *do* lots of things to get salvation. You've heard of it in the Bible, "salvation through works." You need to be able to release this idea of salvation through works and open to Grace and open to willingness, open the desire to have that experience come into your awareness. There is a line in the Course that says, "Truth is restored to you through your desire, as it was lost to you through your desire for something else." T-20.VIII.1.

Let's look at a line about the Holy Instant. "You cannot prepare for it without placing it in the future." T-18.VII.4. Think of all the spiritualities that advocate meditating so many hours a day, meditating in a certain posture, using a particular breath, using a particular mantra. They are all aimed at *future* Enlightenment. Sneaky, sneaky, sneaky. There are millions of people doing all different kinds of rituals every day and they have this unconscious thought in their mind that doing this is going to get them there if they just do it well enough.

Let's get back to the simple teachings of the Course where we started: Don't spiritualize matter. Every time you are upset, use Lessons 5, 6, 7, 8: I am never upset for the reason I think; I am upset because I see something that is not there; I see only the past, but only because my mind is preoccupied with past thoughts. I need to release those past thoughts. In fact, that is Lesson 23, "I can escape from the world I see by giving up attack thoughts." Jesus laid it out. We're going for the fast track.

You can read another thing about Atonement in the I Need Do Nothing section. T-18.VII. Jesus talks about meditation, contemplation and fighting against sin. He calls them "tedious and very time consuming." See also the subsection, The Immediacy of Salvation: "Be not content with future happiness. It has no meaning, and is not your just reward. For you have cause for freedom *now*." T-26. VIII.9.

In a book that has 365 lessons Jesus is saying Now. Now is the only time that there is. You see it throughout the Course. So you know that this is a pretty powerful tool. If you've got eyes to see and ears to hear, get ready. Expect to wake up. This is straight from the Master. The Master is speaking directly to your mind saying you can do this. In fact, it is inevitable. You can't even mess this up. God's will is guaranteed. Salvation is guaranteed by God.

In the I Need Do Nothing section, Jesus also says, "Your way will be different, not in purpose but in means. A holy relationship is a means of saving time. One instant spent together with your brother restores the universe to both of you." T-18.VII.5

Friend: I've been on that section for a week. The first paragraph says it is your one responsibility for just an instant to realize that you are not a body. Would you say that has to do with the Holy Instant or just with forgiveness?

David: It is the Holy Instant. It is not in the future; that is why you can't prepare for it, because it is not a future event. Jesus says, "At no single instant does the body exist at all. It is always remembered or anticipated, but never experienced just *now*. Only its past and future make it seem real." T-18.VII.3

And the Manual says,

"The emphasis of this course always remains the same; – it is at this moment that complete salvation is offered you, and it is at this moment that you can accept it. This is still your one responsibility. Atonement might be equated with total escape from the past and total lack of interest in the future. Heaven is here. There is nowhere else. Heaven is now. There is no other time." M-24.6

Do you see the commonality between these teachings? This is why we are talking about holy relationship as a means of saving time. So what is a holy relationship? Jesus says, "You and your brother are together." That is how He defines the holy relationship. It gets kind of simple. What He is really saying is that we share the same mind. You and your brother together is not about bodies being together. Minds are joined, whether or not the bodies seem to join.

Jesus is talking about the singularity of mind. That is really also what quantum physics is pointing at. Advaita Vedanta and all non-dualistic paths throughout history, including the Course, are practicing letting go of time and opening to the Holy Instant. That is very practical.

Now, let's take one more look at error. As long as you believe you are a human being, a subject, and that there is an objective world outside your mind, then you will take things personally. Whether it is a mosquito that seems to bite you or somebody cuts you off on the highway, if you see it through that ego lens of subjectivity, you will take it personally. So, to accept Atonement is really to say, "I was mistaken about this whole subject-object thing. I was misperceiving. I was seeing the world through a distorted lens." The body's eyes do not see and the body's ears do not hear. They are told by the mind what to see and hear. Just like the mind tells the body what to feel. That's pretty radical. We are used to the experience of a sore throat or a headache described as if the body is feeling. People say, "I can't go to work because I have a headache." The false belief is: "My body is telling me how I am feeling and I have no alternative but to accept what it is telling me." Sometimes people will say, "Listen to your body. You are storing all your tension in your shoulders," and things like that. But the body doesn't store anything. The body is a projection. It is the mind that tells the body what to feel. These are transfer-of-training errors, tricks of the ego. You have to come back to the thoughts. What thoughts are you clinging to? Are you clogging up the mind and blocking the light in your mind?

Friend: The way I understand it is that maybe it is possible to have a physical universe in the future that is not dualistic. I'd like to hear your take on that.

David: Thank you. Yes. A universe that is not dualistic is inevitable. Because a universe that is non-dualistic would have to be whole. Some people have referred to this as the *big picture*. Instead of this tunnel vision of subject-object split, there's got to be a higher way of looking at the world with your Higher Power. Quantum physics calls it the observer. If you can get back far enough in the mind to be the observer you will see that everything is interconnected. That is beautiful. That is seeing One thing. And that's what Jesus is calling the *forgiven world*, the real world, true perception.

There are a lot of spiritualities that say if we pray, if we work on our consciousness, and if we purify our awareness, we can change the future. The future has already happened. It's gone. It's over. It's done. That's why you can't change it.

It's like watching the movie *Gone with the Wind* twenty-five times and when Rhett Butler says "Frankly, my dear, I don't give a damn," you say, "Oh you did it again! But I'm going to watch it again Rhett. I'm going to give you one more try!"

That's basically what we're talking about when trying to change the future. That is really deep. The Course's promise of "a future unlike the past" if you forgive is a metaphorical stepping-stone. The future is already over.

Friend: I know the Course says the script is already written. Does that mean that all my thoughts are scripted as well? Like when I choose forgiveness as opposed to listening to my ego, is that something that is outside of my control as well? If I got distracted again and I get angry, and I forgive and release it, was that going to happen anyway?

David: Very good question. "The script is written." W-158.4. The key word in that statement is the last word, written, which is past tense. The script is past. What happened in time is over. It is like watching *Gone with the Wind*. It is *not* an interactive thing. You can tell Rhett not to say that line, but it keeps playing. It is in the script.

The Course is leading you to what Jesus calls a purified form T-5.V.7. or a purified version of the past, which is the forgiven world. This is the same as letting go of all the meaning that the ego has written upon the world. The Holy Spirit will bless it. He says, "...think of yourself as completely at peace with everyone and everything, safe in a world that protects you and loves you, and that you love in return." W-68.6 This is a whole different way of looking at the world.

You start to get into difficulty when you try to analyze "the script is written." That can be a real mind bender. Think of it this way: time is simultaneous; it is not linear. The problem comes if you see your life as a linear story. If you saw the movie *The Secret* you might wonder "Can I rewrite the script? Can I manifest?" The clarity comes when seeing that you have to forgive the past. You have to let it go. What that means is that you have to realize that time is simultaneous when you forgive.

Time is not like a string of spaghetti, like a time line with past, present, future. What happens if you turn the spaghetti on its side and look right down the edge of it? What does it turn in to? A point, a point instead of a line! Time is simultaneous.

When you get back to Heaven, it's not like you sit around in a little group in a 12-step program and tell your war stories. "Oh, remember those lifetimes..." You don't have war stories in abstract love. It is just Divine love, everything is love. The ladder is going to disappear. But you do have to follow the ideas of the Course. You have to allow yourself to keep opening and following those symbols that Jesus teaches you. They will jump off the page. After reading it for 10 years you look at a sentence and it goes "Wham!" and leaps off the page because your mind is ready for that experience at that moment. Course students are funny because they read a paragraph and get into these big intellectual discussions about what it means, and after 20 minutes they read the next paragraph and say, "Oh."

Friend: There was a group of people here and they loved me. Two of them were going off for coffee, and one lady was so happy to see me she wanted me to go along for coffee. The other one didn't want me to go for coffee. What is that about? I didn't know how to interpret that, and I didn't want to take it personally. It is about not feeling included. I would like to talk about that. Is it just a body thing or is my mind filled with errors?

David: Thank you. This is about practical application. What it comes down to is that the power of sight, the power of interpretation is always our own. It goes back to that quote I was sharing: "I am responsible for what I see." I choose what I see. I'm unaffected, not an effect of images. You start to realize the value of getting clear on what your purpose is and what you are called to. It comes down to the Holy Spirit prompting you to go to that coffee shop or not. It comes down to the simplicity of that, but the ego tries to make it much more complicated. The ego tries to analyze the motives of others.

Jesus actually says in the text, "Analyzing the motives of others is hazardous to you." T-12.I.1. Because you can't do it without involving the ego. And you are trying to let go of the ego. So you don't want to invoke or activate the ego, you want to release it. I would recommend reading from Lesson 133, "I will not value what is valueless," where Jesus says, "Each choice you make brings everything to you or nothing." W-133.5.3 He is not talking about whether to go to the coffee shop or not. He is talking about purpose. He is talking about the real alternative. When you can see the alternatives for what they really are, it is a simple choice. We have to expose the ego. The ego wants to make guilt attractive so you'll be lured into temptation. Purpose is what the purification is about.

Friend: I chose not to go to coffee with them. I wanted to hear you. So Holy Spirit had me come here. They said that it was a manipulation. I didn't like hearing that. Where did that come from?

David: Remember that if someone speaks a word to you, the power of interpretation comes back to your own mind. People can tell you anything and everything. But the power of interpretation is your own. You always have the power to join the Holy Spirit.

I am honored that we have Jesus and Holy Spirit guiding us so surely toward an inevitable Atonement, inevitable Awakening.

Spiritual Communities

Beloved One,

Often I am asked what it is like to live in spiritual community, and I say that it is truly a State of Mind and nothing else. Through the ego's lens there appear to be bodies that come and go, details and logistics that seem to require care and attention. But from a healed Perspective everything is like a smooth, free flowing Dance.

Spiritual community is all about the attitude of Communion with God. It is about devotion and reverence and willingness, and everything Flows in the miracle.

EveryOne wants to feel connected and loved, and to have a feeling of belongingness and wholeness. Every day, every hour, every minute, even every moment, there are many, many opportunities to give, to extend that which is All Value and Meaning. The Holy Spirit gives whatever seems to be needed at any given moment. The Love radiates to everyOne and everything in the universe. There is a deep feeling of acceptance and all-inclusiveness in the miracle. Many times people ask: "How will this play out in form?" The form, whatever it appears to be, must be perceived from the Flow, from the miracle's Perspective, to be experienced as whole.

Jesus taught: "Freely you have received, now freely give." This statement is symbolic of our shared Purpose of learning to give as God Gives. How does this unfold in a practical way? It is very simple. We live simple, devotional lives, trusting completely on Divine Providence. This means we are supported entirely by donations and love offerings, and all support is seen as Given by the Holy Spirit / God. All offerings are accepted with deep gratitude and used to continue the work of the Holy Spirit in shining the Light and sharing the message of Christ throughout the world. This community is of the heart and wholly inclusive. There is nothing special about bodies coming together in form, but the symbol can be used in a very helpful and supportive way, in addition to being an acceleration for healing, thus undoing the ego.

The ego is afraid of commitment and so coming together with a devotion to Purpose, a commitment to exposing and releasing the ego, is a very helpful step towards accepting the Atonement. Atonement is a total commitment. Regarding living in community, the Purpose must come first and be held in mind at all times, for then form flows naturally in Divine Ease.

To lead with the form is to lose sight of the Purpose, since leading with the form involves focusing on the needs of the body and ego preferences. With Purpose out front there are no perceived problems, for problems only seem to arise when Purpose has been forgotten. Enlightenment is the undoing of the make believe self concept of the ego, of pride, of preferences, of possession, and of ownership. The Holy Spirit takes us gently by the hand, leading us step by step as we deepen in our trust, and deepen in our commitment to hearing only the Voice for God. Thus we release the mistaken belief that anyone could be sustained by any Source other than God.

Seventeen years ago I took Jesus up on it. And Jesus showed me the reality of Divine Providence. Suddenly a whole new world appeared in awareness with a sense of fearlessness, a joy in following the inner prompts, and a rejoicing in every symbol of coming Home. After several years of living and traveling in this way I began to meet friends who wanted to share more time being around me, asking their questions and closely observing the way I lived my life to gain insight into the principles and teachings I held dear. These friends and I began living in spiritual community, and though the names and faces have seemed to change throughout the decade that would follow, this deep feeling of community has remained with me ever since.

Now I experience this community feeling always and in all ways in my heart, whether the body of David seems stationary or in motion, alone or in a small group or among hundreds of people. The Purpose I was Called to extend has stabilized my perception of the world, and a feeling of sameness pervades everything and everyone I look upon. It is very much like a lucid dream that is very happy and calm. The serenity comes from being aware of the dreaming and not taking any of the signs and symbols personally, as if they were actual things existing in and of themselves. The unshakable peace comes from a detachment from appearances and an unswerving dedication to shared Purpose that is continuous.

Everything that seems to come into my awareness I see as Given from the Holy Spirit and Jesus. Being Source-dependent has dissolved away all sense of lack, and thus my attention is never drawn to the images of the world for the purpose of getting anything. The images are freed from past egoic intentions and therefore free Now to be used by the Spirit to inspire, bless and comfort in the Plan of Awakening.

There is no question or curiosity about the timing of events and no need to figure out the meaning of the world. There is no one and nothing of the world to fix or change. Being Present allows all things to be exactly as they are. Seeming plans, logistics and details are Given as they are necessary and helpful, though there is never an emphasis on future outcomes or goals. All that is Given comes safely and surely, and each seeming step feels obvious and natural.

Every encounter I have is a chance to get to know me in the truest sense. What I am always teaching is that there are no private thoughts and no private minds. So the experience that I have when we gather together is of our sameness. We share the same Spirit. This is a feeling more than a group of concepts. It's still always an adventure for me to meet my Self over and over in many delightful ways. I like the spontaneity of the encounters. I like the sense of innocence that we experience together. I always share in gatherings that there is nothing off limits. This offers a sense of openness that enables everyone to express whatever they're feeling in the moment. This is how we know ourselves. We take the lid off all our feelings and emotions. We bare our soul, and we realize we are not judged for baring our soul. People who I've met along the way feel like they can talk to me and unburden their soul no matter how shameful they feel about it.

Our sole Purpose is Awakening, which is the undoing of the ego, and so we are guided by the Holy Spirit within, and we never lead with the form. Jesus teaches that nothing the world believes is true and that every belief held in the mind must be questioned and undone, in order to be shown what reality is. It is not of this world. Living in Purpose is abstract, it involves being highly intuitive and it involves a deep devotion to mind training.

Although it can be helpful for those new to mind training to have some structure to come together to discuss what is coming up to be healed and released, structure dissolves the deeper one goes into Mysticism. Jesus teaches that no two people see the same world, which is why there is no universal agreement upon anything. The only solid foundation is a deep, shared Purpose with trust and willingness to unlearn all concepts, including those of family, authority, work, life-style, time, and use of resources.

We live as Jesus did, traveling where invited without expectations of reciprocity. We are not interested in growing or building anything. Purpose is a full time devotion and it can look different for everyone. With unfolding Peace House communities in the United States, Sweden, Belgium, and Australia it is important to realize that there is no central authority or unifying structure with any of them. The Spirit directs the way and each seeming spiritual community unfolds through intuitive Guidance received by the founders and the participants. I am always happy to offer teaching-learning resources and materials for these communities, disbursed freely and on a donation basis.

I received the following Guide to Spiritual Practice with Awakening Mind from the Holy Spirit:

1. Volunteers - Awakening Mind does not involve the concept of membership and therefore relies entirely upon volunteers for every aspect of the ministry. Volunteers receive no financial compensation and no perks or tangible rewards for their devotion to Awakening. The benefits given and received are entirely Spiritual and always purely and simply a State of Mind.

2. Non-profit - Awakening Mind is completely non-profit. The purpose for the ministry is experiencing present Inner Peace through forgiveness and thus there is no incentive to grow larger or attain money or power or possessions or property. Present peace is content with the present moment and therefore unconcerned with the past or future.

3. Intuitive - Awakening Mind encourages everyone to develop intuitive listening to their Inner Guide and to trust and depend upon this Guidance for decisions in everyday living. How one feels is a barometer for discerning that which is intuitively helpful, and peace is its own reward.

4. Divine Providence - Awakening Mind nurtures the

awareness and experience that trust would settle every problem now. Trust in the Holy Spirit and Christ is the means given by God to answer every seeming problem that arises in perception. Friends in the ministry are always referred and directed to the voice for God within and toward the recognition that God is the creator, source and provider.

5. Non-judgment - All comparisons, opinions and assumptions naturally give way to Intuitive Guidance as a practical Alternative to conflict. Guidance is always respected and following Inner Guidance is always encouraged. The outcome of listening to and following the Holy Spirit and Christ is always peace, love, happiness, freedom, and joy. There need not be any exceptions to trusting Inner Guidance and living a life of integrity, honesty and harmony.

6. Generosity - To give is to receive. Awakening Mind honors the Divine Law of Love. Freely you have received, now freely give. Giving is an attitude that extends Love and continuously receives and experiences Love extending. Love knows no lack or scarcity or deprivation. Love is an Abundant State of Mind that is whole and completely Shared.

7. No private thoughts - Awakening Mind is the experience of Union, a Unified Mind in which there is no secret kept apart from Spirit. Everything is openly revealed in the Light of Truth. Love has nothing to hide and is forever openly revealed exactly As It Is. Only the Thoughts of God can be shared, and there is nothing else to share.

8. No people pleasing - Awakening Mind advocates always following Inner Guidance and accepting complete responsibility for one's state of mind. Conformity to external authority or unconscious beliefs is never authentic

or helpful on the spiritual journey. The laws of the land need not be broken if one follows the Inner Guidance of the Holy Spirit, and impeccable integrity is the certain outcome of yielding to the Holy Spirit for all decisions. "Holy Spirit, decide for God for me" is our constant prayer of gratitude, and it is very practical. This yielding to the Spirit offers immediate results.

9. No control over the world - With total responsibility for one's state of mind also comes the realization that there is nothing to control in this world. The Observer is One with everything and now all things are perfect exactly As Is. Atonement is a state of perfect Acceptance. Such is the happy dream of forgiveness, the forgiven world.

10. Peaceful Experience - Awakening Mind is an experience that transcends all specific concepts. Divine Silence simply Is. Simply do this: Be still, and lay aside all thoughts of what you are and what God is; all concepts you have learned about the world; all images you hold about yourself. Empty your mind of everything it thinks is either true or false, or good or bad, of every thought it judges worthy, and all the ideas of which it is ashamed. Hold onto nothing. Do not bring with you one thought the past has taught, nor one belief you ever learned before from anything. Forget this world, forget this course, and come with wholly empty hands unto your God.

I hope to meet with you and rejoice together in the Love of God as obstacles to Love are exposed and removed. Thanks be to God for leading everyone Home.

In Love & Gratitude Always,
David

Advanced Teachings

Introduction

The call to awaken comes from deep within. It is the invitation to an adventure like none the world has ever offered. The following dialogues have the awakening of the mind as their primary focus. These dialogues are representative of this purpose. These are a few of many dialogues David has engaged in, with the intention of uncovering beliefs that seem to obstruct the awareness of love's presence. They extend both clarity and depth. The discussions include nondualistic metaphysics and often resembled a kind of spiritual psychotherapy in which everyday problems and issues are traced back to the false belief system in the mind, where correction is then possible by accepting a healing thought – a miracle. Although David's gatherings have taken different forms: talks, classes, workshops, weekend retreats, counseling, and longer intensives, the purpose has remained unchanged – to learn true forgiveness and recognize the state of Enlightenment.

To teach that one can recognize truth as all there is and awaken now, is simply to reflect clarity in mind. This is a living experience and presence more than just the presentation of ideas.

We recognize that awakening is not a casual endeavor, but one that demands a deliberate and uncompromising commitment. The depth of discussion reflects our willingness to question all our assumptions directly and immediately. It may be considered radical or extreme, and from the world's view it is. Total transformation of the mind is approached with devotion and a burning desire that comes from within. This is our unified goal and purpose.

The time has come to awaken. The time for words and concepts is almost over. Now we seek direct experience of God's Love. We gladly lay aside techniques, repetitions and rituals that we may come to meet God in the Silence of our hearts. What we thought we knew of God was a mistake. And so we come this time with empty hands and open arms, aware that we do not know the way to God, yet certain that God will show us the way.

As we look around we see that mighty companions have gathered beside us for this final ascent to God. A friend's a friend forever in the Lord. The welcome never ends in the face of Christ. The Holy Relationship has come upon us and we are filled with joy and gratitude. The witnesses to the happy dream are seen everywhere, in every direction we look, and at all times. The blanket of peace has spread across the face of earth. Tranquility is flowing to its corners.

There is nothing left to do but celebrate, rejoice, bless, and heal. All the trinkets of the world that once caught our eye are valueless before the vastness of this present experience. All ambition and striving for future goals has vanished. All curiosity about the world and its ways has ended. We rest in a stillness so deep and so unfathomable that time drifts by without its touch upon us. We listen. We hear. We rejoice.

This book is merely a collection of words. Of itself it is nothing. May its words be a reflection of the Inspiration within you, the Call to awaken and be glad. May you be speeded on your way to peace, joy, and eternal happiness. And may you experience that which we cannot speak of, but that which is yours for the asking.

Opening to the Experience
of Real Relationship

- A conversation with David

Friend: My intention is to take a deeper, closer look at the meaning of relationship. I feel like I don't know what real relationship is. Deep down I feel that real relationship is being in Union with God, but that is beyond my experience. So everything I have believed about relationship has not brought me to the experience I have yearned for. I truly want to know the experience of real relationship.

David: It's a good starting point to admit that you don't know what real relationship is. You can say the words "Union with God," though you speak of a collection of words that are not your experience. You are stating your intention to come to the experience of real relationship. What have you thought relationship is in your life?

Friend: I think of relationship as a harmonious experience of connectedness between two persons.

David: Let's start out by looking at what your experiences have been. You have experienced disillusionment. In every attempt that you have put forth to be in the connectedness, to be in a harmonious relationship, you have been disillusioned. Marriage, family relationships, friendships, employment relationships, etc. have all been unsuccessful in meeting your desire for a consistent harmony and an experience of lasting connectedness.

Friend: Yes, disillusioned in marriage and I have at some time or another been disillusioned in all of my relationships because I have not found the lasting happiness, harmony and the lasting feeling of connectedness.

David: The beginning point in dissolving the disillusionment and dissatisfaction you experience is to see how you define relationship. Are you aware of all of the unconscious assumptions and definitions you hold about the concepts of relationship in your mind? Do you have any idea of the hold these concepts exert on your experiences of this world? So, first we must take a look at how you have defined relationship, for your experiences of the world result from your beliefs and concepts and thoughts about yourself and the world.

Friend: I'm not defining it now I notice, or at least not consciously. I'm so much more aware that I don't know what it is, instead of thinking that I do know what it is.

David: If you seem to experience disillusionment, be assured that you firmly believe that you "know" what is not true. Disillusionment is not an experience of True Knowing, Wisdom, and Understanding. We are together going to discover and release the false belief of attempting to know and figure out the world and the cosmos, or, in this case, the meaning of relationship in this world. Let us start this journey together with whatever comes to mind right now.

Friend: Well relationship seems to be between persons. And I guess a characteristic of a so called "good" relationship would be open communication, a willingness to talk things out. It is a willingness to put your feelings and thoughts out on the table and work things through. And that probably results in changing some form component, a change of circumstances. That change is supposed to help the situation and to make a difference or bring about a solution to the problems. And lots of problems arise in a relationship, so there is a great need for open communication.

David: You say "problems arise in a relationship," so you've defined the problems as something wrong within the relationship as you perceive it.

Friend: Yes.

David: And in defining the problems as "within the relationship," you also believe that something needs to change "in the relationship" in order for there to be a solution to the problems, for there to be the experience of connectedness and harmony that you yearn for. You believe that a change in form is necessary for there to be a feeling of connectedness.

Friend: Yes. For example: "We're not speaking to each other enough, or we're not sharing enough activities, or we're not spending enough time together." Problems in relationships are always along those lines of thought.

David: So the problem, as you see it, is defined in terms of form and the solution to the problem is defined that way too. Did those definitions and that method of problem solving ever work for you? Did you find the lasting happiness and harmony you sought for in that perception of relationship?

Friend: No, no, no! [Laughter]

David: [Smiling] Did you give it a sufficient number of attempts?

Friend: Yes, over and over. The frustration was that the willingness was there to talk things out, but we didn't have a clue on how to do that. I think we wanted to find a solution, but we didn't know how to talk about it. We just didn't know how to work it out. It's like we were missing the boat in finding the problem and so we were missing the boat in solving the problem. So the problem was never solved. It was very circular. At best we'd arrive at a temporary solution that made things seem to feel better for awhile. But the solution never lasted because the same problem or a related problem always recurred.

I think another characteristic in my mind of a good relationship had to do with some longevity built up over time. Shared history, and shared pain and joy and struggles were all part of building a good relationship. It was a combination of the up side and down side, all of it. Longevity made the relationship seem stronger even though there were many ups and downs.

David: And what happened to that notion?

Friend: At some point longevity made no difference at all. That wasn't the cementing factor in the relationship. It seemed to crumble in spite of many years of being together.

David: Well this is a good start then, in seeing the disillusionment of defining relationship in a certain way and looking for solutions to problems in a certain way. It is seeing the disillusionment of the pattern of trying to use relationships to solve a perceived inner lack, an emptiness that was unresolved. It is a pattern of looking to forms and situations and outcomes to resolve the feelings of emptiness or lack of connection and intimacy. We are together on the verge of learning that forms and outcomes and situations are the past, so when I want to fix somebody, when I want to change somebody, when I want a situation to change, a behavior to change, I am actually hoping to change the past to resolve an inner conflict. The belief is that a change in form is a real change and will really resolve the conflict.

Friend: How do you mean that looking for a change in behavior in the other person or in myself, or wanting a change in the situation, is attempting to change the past?

David: Well everything is truly perfect As Is right now, yet feelings of emptiness, feelings of lack of connection, and feelings of lack of intimacy are all only symptoms of the belief that things would be better off if they were different than they are. The world of images is the past, and the desire to change the images is the desire to change the past. This is a reflection of the belief that one can only find what one seeks if something changes in form. It is the demand that the past be different instead of opening to the healing idea that only a change of mind is necessary to resolve the apparent conflict. This change of mind can only occur in the present, and can only offer the awareness that the past is gone.

Friend: How do I come to that awareness, that the past is gone?

David: It is essential to begin to realize that the resolution of all conflict is within the mind. You have to be willing to look within your mind before we can really get at the problem or recognize the Solution. The apparent problem is resolved as it is brought to the inner Solution, and that is why everything is truly perfect As Is right now. The inner Solution knows no opposite.

Our discussion must necessarily include metaphysics or a willingness to go beyond the physical, beyond what is perceived with the five senses. We must be willing to open to the Truth of our very Being in God. Only in the present, this very instant, the living moment, is there true freedom and release.

Friend: OK. I am willing to look at this very deeply. I truly want to find peace that lasts and an Intimacy that is Constant. I am willing to do whatever it takes. What are some basic metaphysics that we need to explore? It seems that you are implying that I have a lot of unconscious beliefs and assumptions that I need to question. Is this the case?

David: We must question all that has been believed to be true. We must from the outset not hold any belief to be sacred or beyond question, for *we cannot experience what is beyond the physical unless we are willing to question all that we have believed to be true.* Do you understand the direction our discussion must take?

Friend: Yes, I see the direction we are moving in. We are looking at very basic questions, questioning the very nature of reality, the very nature of what is real. It is asking those questions: "What is God? Who am I? What is the meaning of life?"

David: Indeed! Let us be direct and straightforward. Awakening to Truth is the simple realization that God is real and that Love is real, and that there is no opposite to a Loving God. Divine Mind, being One with God, is created to be a creator. Spirit, being and creating in the likeness of God, is Spirit. As God is Spirit, so is All creation. So the natural State of the Mind is pure creativity. Creation is the extension of God. And being One with God is to extend as God extends. This is what Jesus refers to as the Kingdom of Heaven.

Perception, as a sharp contrast, is a distortion of creative ability. And projection makes perception. In other words, there appear to be illusory thoughts in mind that weren't created by God and that seem to be projected or to go out apart from the Mind of God. In truth this is impossible, for Ideas leave not their Source, and What God creates as One is One forever. Miscreation is projection and this is always a distortion of Reality. All perception is unreal in that sense because it has no divine origin. Perception was made instead of created, and therefore cannot be real.

So in very basic terms, Mind was created to be a creator, not a perceiver. Perception is the wish to be some thing that You, as Spirit, are not. This wish seems to have taken form. So the entire perceptual world of time/space/matter is an illusion. The nothingness of illusion pertains to all matter, all time, and all space, for what seems to be linear time-space is a distortion of Reality and but masquerades as an opposite to eternity. This apparent cosmos of galaxies and stars and creatures is the belief that it is possible for there to be some thing other than God, other than eternal Love.

With the belief in separation from God, the sleeping mind became identified with a body and a cosmos surrounding the body as its new home. The body is seen as the subject, which then perceives a world and a cosmos with other bodies as the object. There is something to perceive with, a body and five senses, and something that is perceived, a world and a cosmos, and all that's involved in perception.

If we examine this in a time sense, all the forms, all the projected idol image thought forms, are the past. In other words, the ego seemed to happen in the unholy instant, in the past where the mind seemed deceived and confused and forgot its True Reality. The projected world is just a shadow or an out-picturing of the false idea that is the past. So, when we talk about personal relationships and bring our discussion back to the context of relationships, we could accurately say that all personal relationships are the past. The grievances that are held always involve the body self-concept and behavior, for example, "You said you would do this and you didn't. You aren't the same as when I first married you." Money issues, sexual concerns, jealousy, envy, and all other so-called relationship problems, no matter how you define the situation, are body based. They are based on the belief in the reality of the past. The deceived mind is trying to use the past to resolve the guilt and conflict that it feels, i.e. "I'm lacking and there's something that can make up for that lack, there's something in the world to complete me, and there's a way that things can work out that will make me happy and fill the void I feel inside."

Friend: So you're talking about the belief in separation when you say "using the past to resolve the guilt and conflict?"

David: Yes. The belief in separation gets played out in form in such a way that the out-picturing of the belief seems to be a perceptual world in which persons, places, events, and things are still here and still happening, though in reality they are already over. They are all the past. What seems to be still occurring reflects the belief in separation in mind, the belief that one is lacking something, that one is not already whole and complete.

In other words, the cosmos was made to be like a movie screen or a giant distractive device, a dream where pseudo problems and pseudo salvation could be worked out. The world is a dream of images, a vast magic show which the ego holds out as a substitute to eternal Reality. The ego is trying to convince the sleeping mind that happiness can be found on the movie screen – in the dream. Every attempt to get relationship, defined in form terms, to work out is an attempt to find happiness and love where they are not. This is a prime example of "looking for love in all the wrong places." Yet this blind seeking applies to all form, for Love is Spirit and not limited to form of any kind. And the sleeping mind which seems to have forgotten its Identity as Spirit appears to be dreaming of a world of unreality, though it knows not it is dreaming.

Relationships which are defined in terms of form are always defined in terms of persons. Believing its self to be a person, the sleeping mind has dissociated the Light of Truth and has forgotten "I am Spirit, I am eternal, I am changeless." Focused on and identified with a fragment (person), as opposed to or in contrast to other fragments (persons), the sleeping mind perceives everyone as a separate person with a separate mind and separate characteristics. There is an apparent ongoing push and pull, a repulsion and attraction in these so called form relationships, and there is an underlying friction which seems to exist between these so called fragments (persons). Each one seems to be a fragment with a life of their own, and each one seems to be unique and different from the others.

The world teaches: "Even in the best of relationships, you've got to take the good with the bad, because after all no one is perfect." In this world perfection is illusive, for there never was a perfect person or a perfect family or a perfect marriage or a perfect relationship. Yet when we go much deeper into the lack of connectedness we can begin to see that the way relationship is defined is the problem. It is an erroneous concept of relationship that blocks real relationship from awareness. The world's concept of relationship includes the concept of persons with private minds, thoughts, bodies, needs, wants, and personal interests. Therefore interpersonal relationships are seen through the lens of lack; i.e., fulfilling needs, mutual psychological and sensory gratification, reciprocity, etc.

Friend: Yes, my happiness is in meeting your needs and having my needs met by you, is a common belief, a common hope in relationships.

David: The sleeping mind believes that it is a person, that it has real needs, that it is lacking in certain ways, and that it takes other people to help meet those needs and fulfill those lacks. When one looks at the world on a larger scale there seems to be interdependence apparent in the way the world is set up, e.g., supply and demand, the food chain, the ecological system, and also psychological dependencies. The idea of interdependence is that there is a chain of dependence of one person or thing upon another person or other people and things. The belief system of the world relies on this dependence for its existence. The ego belief system, on which all of this is based, is what has to be questioned if we're to get down to the bottom of the false concept of relationship and discover the meaning of real relationship.

There is a lot of talk about intimacy, connectedness and harmony. In love songs lyrics speak of forever and everlasting, and certainly the ideal of enduring, everlasting, harmonious, continuous relationship sounds good. Yet those terms don't describe what is perceived as interpersonal relationship in this world. For even in the best relationships, when they seem to be sustained, it is still perceived that death of the body or splitting up and moving on cuts the relationship short of the ideal.

Friend: Is this perceived "cutting short of the ideal" all because the relationship is defined in terms of the body?

David: Yes. Bodies seem to join and to separate, but True Union is eternal. Loss is the belief in separation, which is symbolized by a limited body identity. All definitions of relationship that involve the body are based in loss, yet in real relationship, of the Spirit, there is no concept of loss. Even the seemingly more advanced relationship concepts, i.e. twin flames or soul mates are based on an assumption that relationship involves bodies, that there is a person in the world for everyone that is a true love. The unconscious belief is that there's some kind of wholeness which is accessible when those two people come together that is otherwise not available. Yet True Wholeness is the ever accessible Divine Mind which transcends the belief in separation and the body entirely. Wholeness is the experience of the living moment.

The Soul is Spirit and is not limited or contained in any way. The Soul is not in a body, nor are there separate souls, for the Soul is One. There are not separate souls seeking to return to the One, there is only the One. The concept that Destiny is fulfilled when two souls meet each other rests on the concept of separation. The relationship would be dependent upon the meeting of souls, dependent upon finding that lost soul mate or that twin flame. There's still a dependency on time-space and form in this artificial construction of relationship. The Mind is infinitely One in Reality, but in the deceived state of mind asleep there appear to be separate persons, separate bodies, and each separate person or body seems to have a separate mind associated with it. So the properties of the body have been assigned to the Mind/Soul, and the Mind/Soul is then seen as fragmented. In this sleeping state of mind, relationship is therefore defined in terms of persons. We seem to have one person with a body, mind, and soul and another person with a body, mind, and soul, and they may seem to have some commonalities, some shared interests and goals, some of the same likes and dislikes.

Friend: And the more the better. [Laughter]

David: Yes, according to the world, the more the better. Intuitively, common ground can be a symbol of Oneness, yet the more the better implies that there will be differences, that everybody is a unique and separate individual, and that no two people are completely alike. In the world's perspective there may seem to be common ground in terms of values, priorities, and even in terms of physical or sexual compatibility.

Friend: Or even lifestyle.

David: Yes. Social class, status, and many different things seem to be common ground in terms of the world. These are all ingredients in the world's view which go into the making of a good relationship. Yet we come full circle to the point that you began with, that you don't know real relationship. And the reason you don't know real relationship is because what the world calls relationship is not real relationship at all. Being false, it is a farce. It appears to hold out the promises of happiness and harmony. The ideal to live happily ever after in a particular form is illusory, and as one goes through experiences of this world the ideal seems to be shattered over and over and over again. The illusory form never lasts, for what was made temporal can never be eternal. There is no substitute for the eternal Love of God.

The deceived mind looks to form, to the past, to fill the void it feels. The deceived mind has denied the perfection of this very instant, and attempts to change the form until it finds the ideal, the perfect form of happiness. This is looking for Love where It can never be found. This is looking for eternity in time-space. Yet time can never take the place of eternity, nor can the finite replace the Infinite. And concepts of self can never take the place of the Self God created One forever as Spirit.

Friend: I'm feeling like I want to be more in touch with those self-concepts, whatever they are. I am not sure about what I believe and what I am clinging to and trying to make real.

David: It takes willingness and attentiveness to examine beliefs closely. You begin by just noticing the thoughts that seem to fill your consciousness and you will gain some idea of how body-related they are. As you give your attention to the Purpose of forgiveness, you begin asking in every situation: "What is this for? What does this bring me?" Is this pursuit bringing me security and connectedness and peace and harmony? If I know where I'm going to be staying, who I'm going to be with, and what I'm going to be doing in the future, what does this really bring me? Has there ever been a lasting peace and security in knowing the past or attempting to figure out the future? What self-concept has ever brought you a lasting experience of connectedness?

Friend: Are you suggesting that anytime I notice that I think there's a form that will provide me with peace, happiness, and security is an exposure of my self-concept?

David: Yes.

Friend: Can you expand on that idea? I'm not seeing the connection real clearly.

David: Well, in the ultimate sense, the entire cosmos makes up the self-concept. In its deceived or sleeping state, the mind seems to select or zoom in on particular things that it wants to identify with; that it thinks will bring it security and happiness. It has forgotten desireless Oneness and is dreaming a world of false desire. In the dreaming of the world this so-called selection can appear to have enormous variation. The sleeping mind seems to take on the forms of the world: a body identity, partnership, money, power, fame, and romance, just to name some of them.

Friend: Then love, as I have experienced it in this world, is still part of the deception, the condition of sleep and dreams?

David: If you mean by love romance, sexual attraction and mutual gratification, yes they are all experiences of the self-concept. Anything that seems to exist in form, in and of itself apart from the rest of the cosmos, is the self-concept. Divine Mind is completely abstract. An idol is an illusion of a specific form, and God knows not form. Idols are believed to offer a satisfaction and happiness that will substitute for the Abstract Love of God, and the game of the deceived mind is the pursuit of these things. Seek and do not find is the game of the world. So opening to the State of Mind which transcends the self-concept is truly a miracle. You begin by watching your mind so you can start to notice the attachment to the things of the world. Then you sink beneath those thoughts to the Divine Light within. Meditation is an emptying of the contents of consciousness. There is a Silence within in which the world disappears completely.

Friend: I can tell by thinking along that line of thought, that I must still believe that there's this perfect mix of Mind and body (Laughter). Maybe I think it's 95% Mind and 5% body, but as long as I think that there's even a tiny percent of anything but Divine Mind, it's a joke; isn't it?

David: Yes. There is no Life, Truth, Substance, or Intelligence in matter. There is no Mind in matter. Divine Mind is Abstract, yet the concepts of time, space and the body are concrete or specific. Forgiveness is unlearning the belief that there is Mind in matter. It is seeing that matter is causeless or without a source. The sleeping mind, under the Spirit's Guidance, is unlearning the belief that an Idea of God can leave its eternal source and have existence in time-space apart from it. It is unlearning the belief that spirit can leave Spirit and enter into time/space/matter. The sleeping mind is thus unlearning everything it has learned about material existence. Such is forgiveness.

The world is the attempt to combine the body and the Mind. Yet the truth is that body and Mind are not reconcilable. Divine Mind is completely, wholly, totally Mind. There can be no compromise in Absolute Truth.

The Truth is true and has no opposite. The Truth is what Is, absolute and eternal and changelessly perfect. So what is practical in realizing the Truth? To forgive is practical, and to forgive is to expose the false as false by watching the mind and releasing thoughts and beliefs that have no basis in Reality.

It is important not to despair when you begin to uncover and expose illusions, when you begin to attentively watch the thoughts of consciousness. It is important not to be discouraged as erroneous thoughts surface, but to be very grateful that such thoughts are not real thoughts. Seeing their unreality is the true release. Such is healing.

The only reason to be so attentive and alert in mind watching and to want to release erroneous thoughts is that they cover over the Divine Light in awareness. Opening to the Light within is opening to a Higher Purpose.

Friend: Do you at some point feel a certainty about relationships? As the mind is riveted on a Higher Purpose is there a certainty of Union with God in relationship? I haven't equated Purpose with relationship and I think I don't know what Higher Purpose and relationship really mean.

David: This is why we are looking at all this deliberately, directly, and slowly, step by step, precept by precept, assumption by assumption. You will discover that every question is really a question of identity and is based on what you believe to be true about yourself and the cosmos. A sleeping, deceived mind is unclear about everything and knows nothing, for it has denied its Self and God, and its Self and God can only be known. Clarity is instantaneous; it's not something that takes time to realize. Removing the blocks or obstacles to clarity is the task at hand.

Friend: You don't have to think about clarity, right?

David: Clarity is not something that requires analysis or synthesis. Analysis and synthesis are erroneous streams of thought about the past and future. Clarity is Now. It is not something that is put together or built upon or arrived at in the future. Clarity is this moment.

Friend: It's here in a flash?

David: Yes. If you are clear now, then awareness is clear now and there are no false assumptions believed real. If you seem to feel lost or unclear, there are beliefs and assumptions that seem to block the Light within, the Light of Understanding.

Friend: I don't know what questions to ask. I don't know where I'm not clear.

David: Let's keep our discussion very simple. Look at how you are feeling now. Look directly at what you are feeling in this moment.

Friend: I don't know... kind of, just kind of limbo.

David: What does that feel like?

Friend: Kind of suspended or in between.

David: In between... the belief in duality to look at and release. Suspended... something behind and something ahead ...something to move toward and something to move away from. What is this something that you believe is out in front of you, out in the future? If you believe and feel as if you are in between, you must believe you are in between something and something else.

Friend: I think I feel as if I am in between what I once defined as relationship and what is actually an experience of real relationship, between what I thought I knew and didn't, and what I don't yet think I fully know.

David: Since we are not concerned with finding meaning or understanding in illusions of the past, let us turn our attention again to the experience of real relationship, which you have labeled "what

I don't yet think I fully know." An experience of real relationship, when would that experience be, what time could it be but now?

Friend: [Laughter] I know the words "It is now," but I don't know if I really know the experience. I'm still not sure about the present moment that you speak of. Maybe there isn't any experience except now, but I still believe in a past and a future.

David: Okay, look at this directly. You speak of the Now as a concept, but when you say you feel in limbo, in between something and something else, you define these two somethings as the way you used to define relationship in the past. The hypothetical experience of real relationship you pretend to want, you still believe is in the future. If you feel in limbo, if you feel in between, if you feel confused, it must simply be that you are not clear now.

Friend: Yes. Oh I accept that, that I'm not clear now.

David: You accept it. But are you willing to question what you believe and your perceptions of yourself and the world? Belief clouds mind and perceptions of self and the world. Can you see that?

Friend: I accept that that is the case. I accept that that *must* be the case; otherwise I wouldn't feel in limbo. I don't know where to go with that feeling though. I don't know how to go deeper so I can be clear about this? I guess I'm not clear on what it is I'm not clear about.

David: Then let us retrace our steps a bit. Relationship problems, as defined in this world, are always specific. What are some specific relationship problems that come to mind for you? What are the things that are bothering you about relationships in your stream of consciousness? You must start with concrete, specific examples and work it back much deeper into the mind to discover what you still believe is real and true.

It shouldn't be a strain or effort, as if you were on a witch hunt looking for the conflicts in your mind. You can just relax and watch the thoughts go by, gently become aware of something that seems slightly distressing, annoying, or irritating about any relationship you may think of. Relax and try not to willfully search your mind. Just sink inward and be still a moment, and let the thoughts go by. Notice them. [Pause]

Friend: What comes to mind is the trivial stuff that we were laughing about at dinner, the stuff that use to block my experience of the Joy of the moment.

David: Be more specific.

Friend: Having my mind be occupied with what is really of no consequence, that which is all about form, that which is petty and doesn't support my remembering of the Joy of the moment. (I'm afraid of the Silence of this moment, afraid of the nothingness I believe it will bring, fearful to not have any of those trivial thoughts about the stuff of the world.) When I am in the flow of the moment, happy and content, I feel on Purpose, and it seems I am completely unaware of those trivial thoughts. I don't feel on Purpose when I'm having trivial thoughts.

David: From what you are speaking about it seems like you feel emotionally split. I hear that at times you experience yourself as having trivial thoughts that annoy you and at other times you feel that you are on Purpose with the Spirit, feeling happy and content. Yet you can't be two selves that are completely irreconcilable in every way, one being true and one being false. It is not possible to be one self at times and another self at other times. You must come to the point where you can identify the content of the false as false and see that the trivial thoughts and the emotional upset of any kind or degree are not and never have been the Real You. The illusion of upsetting emotion comes from the attempt to hold on to and make real that which has no reality whatsoever. All the trivial thoughts you speak of are thoughts of past or future and specific forms or images or scenes or events. Trivial thoughts are all the same in that they are all the past. They are believed to be the source of happiness by the deceived mind. Trivial thoughts are clung to and justified and defended by a deceived mind that believes the solution to a feeling of inner emptiness can be found among them. Yet the deceived mind is itself trivial stuff, for it is not real and it is not Who You are, the I Am Presence. The happiness of the Real You and the Real God Which created You is simply the experience of this moment. For there really Is only Now.

Friend: Then I can release those trivial thoughts.

David: Believing that anything exists apart from this moment, such as the belief in a self, a person, that has to stop thinking all this trivial stuff by force and effort if necessary, is simply a false belief that has no reality. God created you as Love and therefore You cannot be two selves, a person on a time line and an eternal Spirit. Spirit (Love) has no opposite. This very moment is Life ItSelf. There is nothing else. You can only truly experience What Is right now! Your Real Relationship is in God this very moment, and this Relationship is the only Real Relationship, for Divine Mind (Love) has no opposite.

Friend: So the frustration and the confusion about worldly relationships is really an attempt to be two selves. And you are saying that such an attempt is impossible in Reality. So I can only accept my Self as God created Me, as Spirit or Divine Mind, because there is nothing else besides my Self and God in an eternal, Loving Real Relationship. I have My Life in and of the Mind of God.

David: Yes! The Truth is Divinely Simple. It is the Silence, the Stillness of Life in Divine Mind. It is Spirit. It is Everlasting Happiness and Freedom and Joy! Letting go of the ego (deceived mind) is releasing all erroneous thoughts, including the belief in a self that could ever think such thoughts. Only the Idea of Christ, a Pure Thought in the Mind of God, is true. And You are That. That is All there Is.

Friend: Do I know how to let go of the ego?

David: Yes, you must.

Friend: Because Love is my natural State of Being, is that why you say yes I must? I must know how to forgive the ego and remember Love?

David: Conflict would be eternal if you couldn't remember the Love that You are. And the Holy Spirit is the how.

Friend: So you are saying that if I claim that I don't know how to release the ego, or I claim I don't know how to do it quite yet, that claim is just the ego making an excuse, afraid of the Love?

David: Yes. And excuses are illusions. It was the ego that believed in the need to make them. Effort itself is an illusion. It takes no effort to Be What You are right Now.

Friend: I still feel at times that I am just not trying hard enough and consistently enough to reach Enlightenment.

David: The I of which you speak is not You as God created You. Awakening is the experience of your Reality Now. Awakening is the release of the concept that there are two selves, a letting go of the belief that observed and observer are separate, that subject and object are separate. All strain comes from comparison, and all comparison presumes a split that is not real. How can the comparison of two illusions, both unreal, be meaningful? The comparison of nothing to nothing is meaningless. Illusions are one, not many. There is no split in the perceptual world, just a single erroneous belief in separation in mind. Seeing the impossibility of this belief is healing or coming to Wholeness.

Friend: I want to get this anchored in awareness. I feel like it is such an expansive awareness and yet it feels very tentative and elusive, like I'm just barely touching it. So it is a letting go of the idea that the thinker of time/space/matter thoughts has any reality whatsoever. Are you saying that that thinker is not real?

David: God is real. Christ, a Thought of God, is real. Eternity, eternal Thought, is real. The time/space/matter cosmos is not real because it has no source and no thinker and therefore follows nothing. Spirit creates Spirit, eternity creates the eternal, infinity creates the infinite, perfection creates the perfect. An erroneous belief is not Spirit, not infinite, not eternal, and not perfect. Christ is a Thought in the Mind of God, and God is a real Thinker. The thinker of the apparent temporal cosmos is not a real thinker, so the cosmos has no reality at all. There is no need to harbor or protect meaningless thoughts or to attempt to maintain a meaningless thinker. The thinker and the thoughts are one illusion, and that illusion has gone. You are as God created You right Now!

Friend: I am not so sure, at least not yet.

David: A "not yet" thought is simply an attempt to deny the Reality of That Which You are forever. Reality is beyond the need for acceptance. What Is remains forever What Is. To accept Reality only means to be aware of It. Any doubt or uncertainty is characteristic of the thinker and the thoughts that make up the ego/cosmos illusion.

Friend: So all the time-space thoughts are unreal and the mind that seemed to think the unreal thoughts is unreal – that's what it amounts to. The ego has no source and therefore does not exist?

David: Precisely!

Friend: And so that illusion can't be Who I am.

David: Indeed! You are as God created You.

Friend: It's that awareness I was trying to get at just a couple of days ago, when I was asking you to talk about real thoughts. That's what this is about isn't it? It's that distinction between real thoughts and unreal thoughts?

David: [Smiling] To Be or not to Be. To think with God or to attempt the impossible and make believe illusions are real. To feel Loving forever or to hallucinate the experience of upset and suffering.

Friend: Only the real "I" can think real thoughts, and everything else was from a make-believe I. And I can tell which I is the real I by how I feel right Now. Is that what you're saying?

David: Yes. We began this conversation by exploring the topic of relationship, but we have come to the point of healing the mind by releasing the single belief in separation, which was the underpinning of the entire time/space/matter cosmos. We discovered together that a fundamental assumption in defining all interpersonal relationships was the concept of personhood, of separate selves with separate bodies, minds, and thoughts. In sleep and deception it has appeared as if the split was within the perceptual cosmos, on the screen so to speak; i.e., subject/object, observer/observed, perceiver/perceived, person/other person, individual/cosmos; though in Light it is seen that the split was but an error in mind. Seeing the unreality of the error has demonstrated the unreality of the cosmos the error seemed to produce.

Reality is Whole as Divine Mind is Whole and as Spirit is Whole. Oneness is of and in God and cannot be broken apart. You are Vast as God created You. You cannot possibly be a fragment of mankind, a fragment of humanness among many other such fragments, in a cosmos which seems to be filled with hostility and conflict. All the former effort and striving were directed at protecting and defending this make-believe self-concept of multiple selves and a cosmos that has no reality at all. Happily that illusion of effort is past, for Who You are Now is a Fact of God. You are not multiple selves, just One. And your Real Self, the One Spirit, is indivisible. Such is the simple Truth.

Awakening is Inner Harmony and You simply cannot oppose anything. There is no one and no thing else for You to oppose, You Being Pure Oneness. One Self is Reality. All comparisons and judgments and concepts and opinions vanish when it is seen that they were all but one illusory self of meaningless thoughts. All opinions, every fragment, and every person that seemed to have an existence outside the Mind of God were one illusion. This was the past, yet the past is gone. The Truth is forever of God, in eternity, and Changelessly Now!

Friend: So beyond belief is Reality. Beyond concepts is a real experience.

David: Yes! Oneness can only be experienced Now, not described or explained. Oneness is beyond all beliefs, all concepts, all opinions, all specifics. Oneness or Truth or Enlightenment is an experience always available Now. By seeing everything that is false, in its entirety, the false is negated and only Truth remains. For Truth simply Is. And there is nothing but Truth.

Friend: Then Truth is not a personal experience?

David: Truth is Universal, Absolute Experience. "Persona" is a concept which means mask. When the mask is laid aside, the eternal Spirit is no longer hidden in awareness. In Reality Spirit is never hidden. Wholeness completely transcends the illusory concept of parts. Truth is openly revealed and revealing revelation.

Friend: Well that is a breakthrough! Mind watching, or noticing all those past and future thoughts, is not a personal thing. That's where the struggle seemed to come in my perception. I mean if it's a personal job it's a chore, and it's a big job that seems to take a lot of effort. If I release the personal me, I am "the watcher," "the awareness." There is nothing to defend and nothing to be assaulted in this gentle looking and awareness.

David: You see the personality construct was linear. This very moment has swallowed up the time line, all sense of personality, all concepts of interpersonal relationship, and the not yet concept. Heaven is surely a State of Mind that is Now. This is the Grand Simplicity of Love.

Friend: I may ask you to remind me of this a lot in the next few days. It feels very important to let this one in. I can feel the resistance hovering over it, kind of moving in and out of the clarity around it. I notice that this pattern has recently been the case. When I feel like there's been a real kernel here that can pop everything open, I feel an excitement and vitality and clarity. Then I feel this dense fog roll in very quickly.

David: Who is that I that is afraid? There's no striving in the Now. Just look.

Friend: I notice that I feel like I have to put so much mind energy forth to get some grasp of this experience, and to hang onto it. I feel like it takes so much focus, intention, and a great effort. It feels like something I have to work at. And you're saying it's not any of that?

David: Who is the I that has to work at something? The experience of Now is not linear. Work at implies continuation, process. Enlightenment is instantaneous.

Friend: So why do I feel that it takes a concentrated effort and intention on my part to stay with this, even in the conversation? Is it because I'm still looking through the ego filter?

David: Resistance.

Friend: So feeling like it takes effort is resistance?

David: Resistance is an illusory symptom of false belief. Do you want to attempt to think apart from God and believe that it is possible to do so?
Friend: No. But I feel like that's where I'll be if I don't keep applying this effort. I still believe vigilance is called for. I feel the struggle of being vigilant.

David: Go past the concept of vigilance. It is just a concept. Let it go. Persons are vigilant. You have seen yourself as a person who carried the vigilance torch, and it seemed to be a helpful concept for a while. Now, let it go.

Vigilance falls away in the recognition that there is nothing to be vigilant against; there is in fact no ego. Surrender to What Is, for Love is inevitable. End the search now. Accept your Self as God created You, Changelessly One forever.

Thinking *you know* continues to be an attachment that you have to let go of. Time plays heavily here. You believe you've figured out the past and present already, and you want to know the future so you can figure it out too. In that there is no Knowing whatsoever. You deceive yourself royally. Let the Holy Spirit show you how far reaching your "I know" belief is and what an obstacle it is to your awareness of Love and Truth. It is a needless protection from uncertainty and against surrender. You use it for a false sense of control because you are fearful. You fear the unknown. And that fear is actually reinforced every time that you think: I know. The I know belief is a mask over the dreaded I don't know. Quit denying I don't know with I know. Instead look at I don't know. Who is the I that does not know? Certainly, not the Self God created Perfect and One. The I who wants to know believes there is something in this world to know. It therefore feels it will be swallowed up if it doesn't hold onto that knowing.

So it comes back to self being lost in Self, I being lost in Being. Indeed, that's the way it goes, that's the way the little self disappears. The resulting Joy is indescribable. Judgment is how you demonstrate that you believe you do know, and in every instant it merely keeps hidden your unsubstantiated fear of the unknown that remains blocked from your awareness. You fear what you do not know only because it is unrecognized, it does not fit one of the mental boxes you use to hold the world together. Simply see that what you are attempting to hold together is only a hallucination.

Friend: Thanks for this opportunity to open to the Truth of Real Relationship.

David: You are most welcome. It is a delight! Thank You God for creating All as One. Amen.

Purpose is the Only Choice

- A conversation with David

When we look at choices in the world, our feelings of being overwhelmed can be expressed in a variety of forms. This dialogue, which takes place with David and several friends, begins with an expression of restlessness, which is a subtle form of upset or simply not being at peace. This provides a starting point for tracing the specific upset back to its source, the deceived mind, where perception is corrected by the choice of a new Purpose.

Part 1 - Choice of Specifics

Friend: I've been having a feeling of restlessness. Last night I woke up and the thought that kept coming to me was, "I'm just restless." It's still there and just came up again as I was in meditation. I had this feeling of extreme restlessness before coming to Cincinnati, too. Just now I've been thinking I want to be somewhere else and doing something else. I have felt my mind drawn to thinking of when I would go home. I have been letting my mind be drawn into thinking of the future.

David: Those thoughts don't go with a real contentedness in the moment.

Friend: The thing that was coming to me in meditation was that I have dropped many, though not all, activities from my calendar. I am still doing things that are not in line with my purpose, but it's not time for me to let them go yet. I know the time for that is going to come. I know a time of greater peace is going to come.

David: There are lots of unquestioned assumptions in what you are thinking and speaking about. What we want to do today is go deeply into the mind until it is apparent that peace of mind is available to us this very instant. We want to bring an end to the fallacy of: "I know it's going to come." This thought, "I know it's going to come," is very arrogant. Do you think God would put peace, happiness, and Enlightenment in the future? It can only be one's own mind that sets up blocks to Enlightenment. We want to come together in His Name, with a strong intention to be clear and take a close look at the false beliefs presently held dear that obstruct the awareness of God and Self. It may seem that we go step by step in our investigation, although recognition is instantaneous.

We can only have instantaneous Enlightenment. Future happiness used to be something that sounded good to me. It was better than no hope of happiness, I reasoned. Yet I discovered that this "reasoning" is circular and leads nowhere. What we want to do is come at this with such an earnest intention that we let the Spirit come among us and raise beliefs to the light, carefully tracing them back to their singular false cause.

My friend has said that today and at other times she has felt restless. Is there anyone here who hasn't felt restless at some time? We want to take an idea like restlessness and look at its underpinnings, so that we may reach an understanding that dissolves the experience of restlessness.

Friend: I really begin to wonder how much willingness I have for Spirit to clarify this in my mind. I keep wanting to take the ideas that are shared and put them in form. At one point in the meditation I asked to have my mind healed, to learn that healing has to do with my changing my thinking. This is what I want to do - to notice my erroneous thinking and then make a change. I want to remember that I have the power of choice. Right now, I just notice the pull to stay with the illusions as opposed to letting go and experiencing the peace that's available. This can take the form of restlessness and wanting to go outside myself and distract myself from the experience of God in my mind.

David: You bring up the very idea that I was going to bring into our discussion and that is choice. Does everyone here believe in choice?

Friend: Sure. I must.

David: Okay, choices. When I say the plural, what comes to mind?

Friend 1: My sense is that there is only one choice. When I look at choices, plural, then I am letting myself be pulled out into the illusion, all the illusions which are varied and many.

Friend 2: If there is only one choice, there is no choice. (Laughter)

David: We really want to follow this in closely. We want to look at our lives and what we believe. We want to trace it in slowly and examine this. Let's stay with the idea of choice and choices. What are some examples?

Friend 1: That I could choose to go home or to stay.

Friend 2: When I look at choices, I look at choices between illusions and the Truth.

Friend 1: We say that, but is that how we really see it? I know what David is alluding to when he asks "do you believe in choices?" If I look at my behavior and what I do, it leads me to believe I must still believe in choices.

David: Let's not go into the hypothetical or theoretical too quickly. If you say "I believe in choices," what are the things you choose between? What are some examples of these choices?

Friend 2: Deciding what words to use here, what ideas to put into a letter.

Friend 1: Waking up in the morning and deciding what I am going to wear is a choice.

David: These are the choices that are of the world. We have to admit it is like a menu. Every day seems to be a menu of choices. Can you see that choices, as we are defining them in this way, go together with the restlessness? Choices that are varied and complex are related to the feeling of restlessness. Can you see that?

Friend 1: Absolutely, because there is a multitude of these choices. There seems to be no end.

David: Could there ever be rest and the choices we are talking about in this way?

Friend 1: No. We would be at complete peace were it not for those choices.

David: Very well, let's pose this: If there is a choice that could end all choices, or an acceptance of something that brings an end to choice, when could that be?

Friend 1: Now. It would have to be Now.

David: Only now. So there is a discrepancy here. We are saying these words and yet it seems like choices of the world are either off in the future, or they are described as if they have already occurred. Therefore a present choice to end all choices must be in some way very different from the choices of the world, from personal choices.

Friend 1: We say, "I could have done this. I might do that. If I hadn't done this, maybe such and such wouldn't have happened." Is that what you mean?

David: Yes. When you describe the past, even in terms of recent events like the phone calls you made this morning, aren't the choices described as if they were real choices? It is as if one had to make real choices, such as who to call, how long to talk, what to talk about, etc. So we are discussing choices in the world, personal choices that seem to be in linear time. And what about future choices? Has anyone not experienced the strain of pondering a variety of future choices? Can you see that, if this is the case, you must believe that there are real future choices to make? These personal choices we are discussing, what are these choices between? Aren't these choices always perceived to be between options or alternatives within a dualistic world? Aren't these choices seen to be between two or more specific things? That's inherent in this concept of choice, isn't it? That's part of this definition of choice. Now, what is the commonality of the choices in the world, the personal choices that we are describing?

Friend 1: Illusions, behavior, choices of forms.

David: The key is that they are always choices between forms and specifics.

> The purpose of all seeing is to show you what you wish to see… Thus were specifics made. And now it is specifics we must use in practicing. W-161.2-3

There is always a restlessness associated with this, for this is an attempt to invest choice where there is no choice. Can you see the insanity of such an attempt? There must be something else other than this insanity; there must be a different kind of choice, if one is to reach Enlightenment, to bring an end to this restlessness and rest in peace. The key is this: If I am restless, I must still believe that there are choices between forms, behaviors, objects. I have to begin to see that this belief has brought me no rest.

What does restlessness mean then? Do I continue to justify and rationalize and say, "Well, I'm going to have lots of future choices to make?" Or shall we come closer to understanding the dynamics of what's going on with choices and belief? Is there choice in Heaven? In Nirvana? In eternal Bliss? What is your instant reaction?

Friend 2: No. Choice didn't happen until we separated.

David: There must still be an unquestioned false belief, then, if one agrees that Heaven or Nirvana exists forever as eternal Oneness. Choice rests on the belief in a dualistic, linear, time-space world of opposites, including past/future, does it not?

Friend 2: Yes.

David: So really, it comes down to this: the whole idea of choice between specifics must rest on the concept of linear time, as contrasted with simultaneous time: Now!

Friend 2: I just knew you were going to say that! (Laughter)

Part 2 - Choice of Purpose

David: There must be something to this if one agrees that Heaven is eternal Oneness and has nothing to do with choice, since there is nothing to choose between in Oneness. Now, what I am saying is that to approach an acceptance of something that's already happened such as the Correction to the belief in separation, one has to see choice where it is. In other words, one must first invest choice where it has meaning as a learning device, for example, at the mind level, before there can be remembrance of choiceless Oneness. Out of all the things you think you have to do, everything is as simple as one choice. All you have to do is make one decision. One decision!

Can you faintly grasp that peace and rest and joy and happiness must be related to the only decision that one need ever make? Really it's not even a decision; it's just an acceptance. What we want to look at is everything that seems to stand in the way of this acceptance. It's that simple.

> You need to be reminded that you think a thousand choices
> are confronting you, when there is really only one to make.
> And even this but seems to be a choice. W-138.4.

We want to be so thorough in tracing specific personal choices back to the false belief that underlies them all, that there is opening for the grand moment that seems to change everything and yet is changeless: this Instant. The teaching I share is that Enlightenment is available this very moment. And anything in one's mind that stands in the way of that recognition of Enlightenment right now must first be questioned, and then seen for what it is – illusion. Please don't get into comparing who is Enlightened and who is not. Enlightenment is not personal. Just consider these ideas and the holiness of the intention to be clear. Just say and mean: "I want peace! I want it more than anything else. I'm going to drop all my masks. I see that in order to drop them, I'm going to have to look at them. I want to see the masks for what they are. I want to discern the false from the true, to be right-minded. What a precious opportunity this is!" Can you think of anything more important than looking at one's own mind and examining the obstacles to this recognition? Is there anything that even comes close to that? This is a very precious opportunity!

From our discussion we have identified the belief that personal choices are choices between forms and images/specifics. So if one sees that there is no choice in form, wouldn't it follow that there would be just a watching or an observing, a state of bliss, a state of complete detachment. What bliss to stop trying to see choice where it isn't.

So we want to trace it back. Where would that releasing choice be if it's not between forms and images in the past or future?

Friend 1: I notice that I still want to say that there is choice between form and Spirit.

David: Do you understand this choice you speak of, this choice between form and Spirit? To understand this choice, one has to be clear about the distinction between form and content. That is the distinction we are investigating together. You believe choices are personal and between specifics; we have established that as our starting point. Form is the projection of specific thought-forms, images. Form is the projection of misthought. Is the Spirit specific?

Friend 1: I suspect you are saying that the Spirit is general or universal because the Spirit is a reflection of Reality and Reality is eternal and formless.

David: If we think of the word universal, doesn't it have a different connotation than specific? Spirit is universal. For our discussion when we move our attention to the mind, which is the realm of content, or purpose, we move to a meaningful context. The split mind is a context in which the idea of choice is meaningful as a metaphor or a steppingstone, a preparation for the last decision or final acceptance that brings an end to all decision. This final decision is a decision/acceptance of the content, or purpose, of the Spirit. One can believe there is a content or purpose in the world of form, but that doesn't make it so. What's the purpose of a car? What's the purpose of a couch? Do you see how these things seem to have separate little purposes? This is the learning of the world. The deceived mind has assigned names, meanings, or purposes to objects, behaviors, events, conditions, persons, and the relationships between them. How does the ecosystem work? How does the human body work? You see, all these bits and fragments and images have not only been given names, as separating devices, but the deceived mind thinks it knows how they all work together. There are no fragmented images and false associations between images in healed or true perception. There are none in Heaven or Reality either.

Let's examine for a moment the question: "How does the body work?" There are some self-concept beliefs that relate to the profession of nursing that may be helpful to examine now. [Note: Three of the friends in this discussion were trained as nurses.] The training you received when you were going through nursing school, what was it? Wasn't it to teach you how the parts of the body work, how the systems of the body work, how the systems of the body interact with one another? Was there any labeling of parts you had to learn in your education? Of course, and this is just a little shred of the learning of the world. There are seemingly many other disciplines. Worldly education has been all about giving purpose and meaning to specifics, and attempting to define and understand how the specifics relate to one another. Can one be open to the idea that there are no specific purposes and no relationship between specifics?

What if there is actually no purpose or meaning for anything in and of itself? What if everything perceived with the five senses is simply the past? It's like having a computer memory bank of past associations. For example, let's look at a memory of dropping a cup on the floor and breaking it. How else would one know that a particular cup would break in a specific situation unless it was based on the past? All the meaning that is given to everything, including how things relate to one another and what everything specific is for, is all based on the past. It's all made up. God doesn't know of a cup. Be not deceived by the "reality" of any changing form. M-27.7 He doesn't know the meaning of the cup or its texture, or the meaning of the word drop. And what would the cup drop onto, the floor? What is the meaning of the floor?

We are talking about a necessary and fundamental unlearning of everything that has been learned. When we talk about letting go of the past, we are talking about unlearning everything that has been learned. When we talk about letting go of the past, we are talking about unlearning the fundamental stuff of time/space, not just letting go of childhood memories or unpleasant memories. It is letting go of the world perceived with the senses. So the key thing, when we bring it all back to choice, is that the deceived mind thinks it sees meaning and purpose in the world. The teaching I am sharing is that purpose or content is of the mind.

How many of us have searched for truth and said, "If there is such a thing as truth, it should be simple?" Why would the truth be so complicated, so complex? It is meaningful, intuitively, to think of truth as simple. Well, doesn't it seem simple that instead of all the trillions of purposes and associations that make up this seeming world, there are only two purposes in a split mind, and of those only one reflects Reality? If one could know that there was just one decision to make between these two purposes, wouldn't that make everything very simple? If I think I have trillions of options and choices out there in the world of form, that seems to bring with it feelings of restlessness! That seems to bring fear. That seems to involve confusion. Is there anyone who has not experienced these things?

Friend 1: Or talked about them recently? (Laughter)

David: The notion that there are multiple choices and purposes based on the many images of the time-space cosmos is fearful, confusing, and overwhelming. So what we want to do is get very clear that there are just two purposes. That's not how it seems to the deceived mind. It doesn't make any sense from the worldly perspective. So there must be an entirely different context of choice than choice between images.

Now, postulate for a minute that there are only two alternatives, two purposes in the split mind – call one of these purposes forgiveness and the other separation. From this perspective, would the idea that every choice you make brings everything to you or nothing seem meaningful?

Friend 1: Yes.

David: So, we've got something interesting here. If I can just get really clear on the discernment between these two purposes in the split mind, then the simple choice for Enlightenment, for salvation, will be obvious. Isn't that good news!? Is there any higher priority than to come to that discernment?

We could call separation by many different names, such as fear, guilt, or death. The names do not matter. We could call forgiveness by many different names also, such as peace, love, and joy. Again, the names do not matter. If one can believe that there really are only these two purposes in one's mind, then one need only get in touch with the deception of what seems to come between my awareness of these two basic alternatives. If all the roadways I have pursued in this world have just been choices between illusions, and I still believe that there is a real choice to make in the world, I need to begin to see the scam of the game of the world. As long as I believe that there are still choices to make in the world between images, feeling restless is inevitable. The source of the restlessness is this: the mind cannot see the two alternatives clearly and accept the one that is real.

Another thing I want to mention is the framework of the mind. Metaphorically, let us say these two alternatives are in the basement of a large building. From the belief in separation sprang a system of subsequent beliefs, the many floors of the building. Most people would consider time a fairly abstract concept. Space seems fairly abstract as well, yet each of these concepts is specific in that it involves increments and degrees of measurement. Time is an idea of separation. Space is an idea of separation. Actually, they are just two forms of the same idea. All beliefs the deceived mind holds about itself involve the belief in levels: body level, emotional level, thinking level, cosmic level, microscopic level, etc. In Reality there are no levels. All is One in Spirit.

Thoughts such as "When am I going to go home?" need to be examined. For every past thought in the mind there are building blocks, so to speak, that are underneath that past thought. Unreal thoughts come from an unreal system of beliefs.

Part 3 - The Belief in Personhood

Friend 1: I believe I have a home in this world. [Laughter]

David: Who is this "I" that has to go home? Is it a person? Consider for just a moment that you believe your mind is full of real thoughts. What if you had a hint that this belief is not true? Then you would understand the need to take a look at every concept and thought, as basic as these that we are examining, and see that the beliefs about identity, and the world that these thoughts rest on, are untrue.

"Am I the way I am perceiving myself?" That is the question to ask. If one sees oneself as a person wanting to go home in a geographical sense, or home to a family in an emotional sense, is that the eternal Spirit? Or is that a mental construction, an image? How helpful, how powerful it is to examine these. If we get into a discussion about personhood, then we have to take a look at the thoughts and beliefs that comprise the person. What goes into the making of a person?

Friend 2: The color of their eyes and hair, whether they are black or white, their nationality, what they wear, what kind of car they drive, their vocation, parents, family heritage.

Friend 1: Aspirations and personal history make up a person.

David: Yes, every person seems to have an individual history. What if I mentioned the ideas of mind, soul, and emotions? Are they part of your definition of personhood?

Friend 1: Religion and spiritual outlook are both parts of personhood.

David: When we take it into a religious or a metaphysical realm, some people would say that everyone has a soul. And regarding the concept of reincarnation, for example, it is sometimes said that the soul incarnates and reincarnates, it comes and goes into and out of form repeatedly. Since God created the soul, it is eternal, changeless and limitless as God is. Well, if it were the case that the soul reincarnates into form, then something that is eternal, changeless and limitless would be temporarily contained in the form of a body. Yet that isn't meaningful. How could the infinite be contained in the finite?

Similarly, the whole idea of personhood has to be questioned very carefully. Every time someone seems defensive or upset and the upset is traced into the mind, it always comes down to the concept of personhood. Even if one is offended at pollution being put into the air, it still comes back to the belief that one is in this environment and that pollution is an affront to oneself, a person.

Every single upset can be traced to a basic subject-object split in which the person, the "me", is subject, and the rest of the cosmos is object. The way this world/cosmos seems to be constructed is as follows: there is the subject (or person) and there is the object that is always the surrounding and separated other, be it time, space, object, person(s), society, world, or cosmos. Personhood or personal identity is based on this duality, this basic split.

Friend 2: This is where I get hooked, because as you talk and I can see my beliefs and my attachment to personhood, then I think there is something to do. I would like you to address that because otherwise I don't feel I can go any further.

David: Every time you feel that frustration of thinking that there is something to do, it doesn't feel good, does it? There is an impetus for change, but the change seems to be too difficult or overwhelming to accomplish.

Friend 2: Then I go into this guilt and I feel whipped and I think, "I'm supposed to feel happy," but I don't.

David: Let's take a look at that idea that there's something to do. Now, doing is an action of what?

Friend 1: It would have to involve a body. Doesn't it always?

Friend 2: I don't get so caught up in the action as I do belief. I think I'm wrong because I have this belief and I have to change the belief. For example, I like nature. To change the belief I have that nature is real is where I feel stuck. I want to go on and see the fuller picture and feel joined with Spirit and, because I like nature, there is this dichotomy within me. I like nature. [Laughter] I . . .

David: I... do you hear it!? [More laughter] Let's look at the "I". Let's look at the coercive feeling of even having to make a mind shift or giving up a belief. Thinking that I have to give up a belief is a belief! It may seem like there is coercion. But is there really any coercion involved? I read a statement once that said "our egos are very invested in beliefs." Egos aren't invested in beliefs. Egos don't have beliefs. The ego is the belief in separation. And all beliefs based on separation are the ego. The deceived mind thinks that those beliefs are itself, having identified with them. What one mistakenly thinks one is and has to give up, doesn't exist. In other words, the True Self does not have to give up the ego. The True Self has no ego. There only seems to be coercion because of a belief that there really is something that one is right now that one has got to get rid of. But what if one is not that something!? In this realization, the feelings of coercion or of having to do something dissolve!

It gets back to purpose again. You need to get very clear in your mind about the two purposes. If you think you are imbedded in an illusory world of form and believe your life is a real person living in this world of nature, then the Spirit is going to be perceived as very threatening. You will perceive the Spirit as asking you to give something up that is real, that is good, that is beautiful, and you will not want to listen to the Spirit.

Friend 2: This morning when I was on the phone with my therapist and telling her about my inward journey she said, "There is one caution I have for you. I hope that you are not with people who are going to help you lose yourself, lose who you are." When she said that, I thought of a recent visualization in which I died. I told her of the visualization; I told her that self is being lost. Who is the self that I'm losing? That self must be something other than my True Self.

Friend 1: Yes, how could the True Self possibly be lost?

David: I hear people say, "Oh, the ego has to die!" Do you see there is something off about that idea? I say to them: "Ah, you are presuming it has lived!" The idea to fight the ego, to kill the ego, or just to have the ego die is missing the mark. Just calmly look at the ego and see its falsity. Light dispels darkness by its mere Presence – this is the whole message. "My purpose, then, is still to overcome the world. I do not attack it, but my light must dispel it because of what it is. Light does not attack darkness, but it does shine it away."

T-8.IV.2 So to me the phrase, "Die to self," is just a metaphor for the deceived mind that believes that life is of the world of bodies. There really is no life in the world of images. Images deny Life. Life is eternal and formless and changeless.

Part 4 - Seeing What I am Not

Friend 2: Let's go back to the idea for a minute that the ego is just a belief. Where personhood is concerned, in my mind I still have the True Self hooked up with it.

David: The other night when we were together, we had a gentleman tell about how he was feeling sad and he shared very candidly about a number of his judgmental thoughts. Most of them he identified as self-judgments of himself as a person. Yet even if the judgments had been so-called other-directed, it's all the same. All judgments are tied into the concept of personhood and the basic subject-object split. Unreal beliefs produce unreal appearances. If one can just begin to question the beliefs, then one can give up the entire belief system and the time-space cosmos it seemed to produce. Only then can one remember one's True Identity as eternal Spirit. Yet even to say "give up" implies that one had it, that the unreal belief system was real in the first place, that it is more than just an illusion. It seems as if what is unreal has a reality, as if the separation from God has really happened. That is the deception.

So, to me, it is essential to really question what one believes. Beyond that is coming to the realization that all the beliefs, all the branches of the tree, and the one belief that they sprang from, the tree trunk, or ego in this analogy, are all one. It is a reference point of clarity from which one sees the false as false. I don't have to do anything. I just see the false beliefs and thoughts, and the cosmos they seemed to produce, as false. It's a watching, seeing that all images are past, rather than selecting and sequencing the images into an ordering of objects and events. It is a state of stillness, of peace, and of joy!

Friend 2: Would you state the characteristics of Reality, or Truth, again?

David: It's eternal, changeless, formless, Ever-extending. It has no form components, no time, no space, no specifics.

Friend 2: I notice that I'm still not clear in my mind. When I look at nature, I see that it's changing and it certainly is form. So those are signs that nature is unreal. And I still think it's real. So I must be wrong.

David: Who is the "I" that thinks nature is real?

Friend 2: So that "I" is what has to go; that's what has to be questioned.

David: It just has to be looked at and seen in Light. You mentioned the other day, "I don't know who I am." The first question that was ever asked was asked by the ego: "Who am I?" The True Self never asked that question. It knows with certainty what it is, Spirit – One with All.

Friend 1: Not knowing who I am, yet thinking I do, is where the guilt comes in. When I've done something I think is wrong, it seems like I feel guilty because of what I've done. Guilt has nothing to do with what was done; it comes from misidentifying with the "I" that can do; isn't that it?

Friend 2: Even if I've done something and thought I felt worldly pleasure, it's all the same thing.

David: Yes, it is misidentification of the mind either way. Both pleasure and pain are misperceptions. Remember our two alternatives again: separation and forgiveness. The deceived mind believes that it is the ego. That belief is a decision that must be reversed before God and one's True Self can be remembered. That belief is projected onto the screen of the entire cosmos as guilt attributed to a doing or a not-doing, giving rise to thoughts such as: "I shouldn't have left my kids." "I didn't pay the money back." "I'm guilty because of something I did in the past." Yet can you see that personhood is the assumption on which all these thoughts rest?

Can you see how the ego wants the mind to believe that the guilt is because of something that has happened on the screen? The guilt is never because of anything on the screen. The guilt results from choosing the wrong mind, from believing one is something one is not; a person in a world of duality. It is nothing but an insane attempt to buy into a belief that has no reality and no existence.

So if one can work a perceived upset down to the core decision, the belief in separation from God, and clearly discern the ego's purpose unconcealed, one can laugh at the idea of ego. That is how peace of mind is reached. One sees what one is not, and what one is then gently returns to awareness. There is a scene that comes to mind from the movie *Being There*. The movie has some great symbols of innocence and defenselessness. When Chauncey, the gardener, leaves his sheltered place of residence and goes out into the world, he encounters the inner city. He's walking along and a street gang comes up to him, calling him names. One gang member pulls out a knife and holds it right up to his face. Although this situation could be perceived as threatening, Chauncey remains calm and defenseless. He simply pulls out a TV remote control he carries in his pocket, aims and clicks, as if thinking, "I don't like this channel, perhaps there's another alternative." The Spirit's purpose of forgiveness – that's the real alternative to choose, regardless of the situation. The Spirit is the choice, or the channel, to tune into for clear perception and peace of mind.

Friend 2: So while we are here, there's only one choice and that's between forgiveness and separation.

David: And that's only while one believes one is here. If one sees that one is the dreamer of the dream of separation, one is not denying the dreaming, but merely switching from being a dream figure to being the dreamer. For example, to think: "I'm a man, I live at such and such an address, and I do such and such for a living," indicates that the mind believes it's on the screen, in the dream. That's personhood. That's not being right-minded. Identified as a person, one will inevitably feel defensive about other persons, places, situations, events, or institutions such as the government, neighbors, co-workers, etc., for personhood is not true. But if one sees oneself as the dreamer of the dream, one can accept a different purpose for the dream. It's quite a detached place to just see the false as false. One watches and observes the thoughts of the world. One no longer reacts to them. In worldly perception it still seems like the body speaks. It still seems like the body is active, at times walking or talking. But one's attention is so far removed from the thoughts of the world that one feels disidentified from form and identified with the Spirit's purpose of forgiveness. In the flow of this purpose there is no awareness of separate persons, actions, situations or events.

Friend 1: One of the things I became aware of in the seminars I took was that I had a strong identification with my thoughts. I thought my thoughts were me. Of course, thoughts came up and I felt like I was being pulled in every direction. So I had the opportunity to see that I am not my thoughts. But a thought that you introduced is that I also think I am the thinker. So this is another step back from that. So I have just been sitting with that and noticing how attached I am to thinking that I am the thinker. This is part of the personification.

David: Yes, and it is good to stop and take a look at that. That error is the basic deception. If one thinks one is the thinker of judgmental thoughts, or the believer of false beliefs, then guilt and fear must follow. Often on the spiritual journey people will advocate, "Stop thinking. The problem is thinking instead of just feeling happy." But Life is Thought, so it's not the thinking itself that is harmful. But it is an important steppingstone to grasp that there are two kinds of thinking. Before one comes to see that fear (ego) does not exist and never has occurred, one has to use the steppingstone belief of two thought systems that comprise a split mind. And in one of the thought systems there are real thoughts, although they are currently covered over by the attack thoughts of the other system. This can be helpful. Instead of thinking, "I've got to stop thinking. I've done it again. I'll never get out of this trap of thinking," and feeling guilty, one need only ask for the discernment of the Spirit in sorting out the two thought systems. "There is need for help beyond yourself as you are circumscribed by false beliefs of your Identity." C-5.1 The whole point of the sorting out is to come to a realization that the two thought systems are mutually exclusive; the existence of one denies the other.

Part 5 - Purpose is the Only Choice

Friend 1: Are you saying that we are going to think and we'll want to have our thoughts correctly aligned since guilt comes from thoughts that are not aligned with the Spirit?

David: Yes. The deceived mind is full of unreal thoughts, which is not really thinking at all. Real thoughts of the Spirit remain available and can be heard if that is one's desire. Judgment denies Reality and therefore offers nothing. The release point is seeing the impossibility of judgment! If one can clearly discern between these two thought systems, then one doesn't fall for the ego's trick of personalizing everything and making problems specific, as in choosing which side to take. When judgment is seen as impossible, and the mind no longer identifies with the images and characters on the screen, there must be peace!

Friend 2: You make the distinction between attack thoughts and real thoughts. I'm thinking that loving, grateful thoughts are real thoughts, so being grateful for nature would be a real thought.

David: Let's look at this one. Let's take a look at the characteristics of a real thought. Everything has to have a source. If we examine cause and effect, what is the Source of these real thoughts? That's the way one can test thoughts out, so to speak. Ego attack thoughts are certainly not coming from God, but real thoughts, reflections of Reality, must come from God. Well, if one thinks that loving thoughts have to do with material nature, such as, beautiful forms, does one think those thoughts come from an abstract, eternal, changeless Source or not? The eternal comes from the eternal. Form is nothing but projected images. Can you see that after awhile one looks at every thought in one's mind, and runs it by the same criteria, the same test?

Friend 2: How do I get past judging? There seems to be a judgment between the real thoughts and the ego thoughts. How do I discern those thoughts without judging and making them wrong?

David: The only way that it's possible to look at the ego and not feel wrong is to be looking with the Spirit. In other words, there are two purposes - forgiveness and separation. If one is looking at the thoughts calmly with the Spirit, the purpose is forgiveness. Spirit knows the mind as it truly is; Spirit knows its wholeness. When there is complete acceptance of true forgiveness, it is seen that there never was anything to choose between. It is seen that even the metaphor of split mind was just a rung on the ladder, the top rung. What happens when you get to the top of the ladder? Even if you use a ladder in this world to get to the roof, when you get onto the top rung of the ladder, you step off. Once you reach the top rung, once you get to the acceptance of complete forgiveness, the ladder disappears.

Complete forgiveness is the acceptance of the Correction to the error called ego! The separation seemed to occur and the Correction was given as the immediate Answer. The Correction answered the instant of separation, the instant of time/space that seemed to separate into billions of stars, multiple images and separate persons. Seeing the deceived mind's inability to judge anything is the key to accepting the Correction and thus bringing an end to the error.

Here's a story for you: When the mind believed it separated from God, it was terrified that it had actually pulled off the impossible. The mind, in that instant of terror, seemed to project a world and identify with specifics on the screen of the world. The deceived mind zeroed in on the body to be its home. Spirit was forgotten. This body was selected to be the "me", and everything else in the cosmos, including all those other bodies that the deceived mind perceived, was selected to be the objective world in which the "me" would live. This subject-object split, and all ordering of the images of the world, was the deceived mind's attempt to bring some kind of order into chaos and minimize its terror. Ordering of images is judgment, a device for maintaining this illusory world and thus protecting the ego from the Light of Truth. Relinquishing judgment is letting go of the ego and its distorted world. All false beliefs and thoughts are self-judgments, but Self is beyond judgment.

Friend 2: So restlessness is simply believing that I am who I am not.

David: If we bring it full circle, restlessness is believing that there is a choice to be made where there is no choice. If you follow that in, it comes to a place of just examining the thinker and the thoughts in the mind. Choice between images is no choice at all. Forgiveness is just a state of seeing the false as false as one watches all the doing thoughts, all the body thoughts, all the personhood thoughts: "Oh, I need to do this. I need to take care of that. I'm ashamed of this. I'm afraid that will happen."

Friend 2: What am I doing then? I'm actively making phone calls to drop things from my calendar of activities. That's doing, not watching.

David: If one is asleep, if one is not to the point at which one has questioned all aspects of personhood, time and space, etc., one still has a false belief system. But the Spirit is able to infuse through that belief system, so to speak, and reach the mind where it believes it is. Let's say that you are beginning to question your beliefs about everything. What's on the screen of perception is just a motion picture of those beliefs. It seems like there is still a person who continues to do things in linear time. Remember, that is the dream. That's the interpretation or perception of the self as a person in the world. So one can say, "I seem to be getting more peaceful" or "I seem to be getting more upset." Do you see that that is an interpretation? Who is the "I" that seems to be getting more peaceful? Who is the "I" that seems to be getting more upset? It is still a person. As one steps back into one's right mind, so to speak, deferring to the judgment of the Spirit, one comes from a point of clarity or complete forgiveness and makes no interpretations by or of oneself. The individual perception dissolves into forgiveness, Spirit's one interpretation or judgment.

As long as one believes that one is in this world, there seem to be judgments and choices that are necessary. The Spirit is judgmental in the deceived mind, as it seems to undergo the process of sorting out the two thought systems. Here's an example of how that seems to play out: You tune into the Spirit and are quiet. You want so much to join with the Spirit and have a strong willingness. Thoughts that still involve form come to mind, thoughts to call so and so, to meet with someone, to leave this job, to take that job, etc. Obviously, those thoughts are still form thoughts. But Spirit understands that the deceived mind still believes it is a person in a world. The false belief system projects dark beliefs on the screen of the world as images. Spirit is working with the mind to let go of the false beliefs and thoughts that are producing the images. As the mind starts to loosen and to question these once protected beliefs, it feels disoriented, for example, "I'm not so sure, anymore, that I am a wife or a mother. I'm not so sure what I am." Symbolically, things still seem to be happening on the screen, but these are just the interpretations of the deceived mind about itself. That makes the issue of judgment clear. The Spirit isn't working in the world, but is working with "the mind that thinks it is in the world," so it can realize that it made up the world. One can meaningfully ask the Spirit to teach one to *perceive* the world differently. It is not meaningful to say, "Spirit, come into the world and change the circumstances; find me a parking space; help me win the lottery."

Thinking that Spirit works in the world can be a helpful steppingstone for a mind that believes it is a helpless person and seems to need a symbol that proves there is a loving, helpful God. Yet, Spirit does not come into the world. Truth does not come into illusions. The Spirit is working with the mind to let go of the false beliefs. One can choose to interpret oneself as a person and attribute situations and events to Spirit, such as, "Spirit helped me to lose twenty pounds." That would still be a personal interpretation, as if the Spirit was actually concerned with separate persons, objects, and situations instead of the mind that believes in these specifics. In summary, Spirit does not perceive the world the way it is perceived with the body's eyes. Vision is not personal.

Friend 2: I want to be a bit practical. Isn't it okay to be practical?

David: To me, what is *most* practical is looking at thoughts, concepts, and beliefs. I think an association is often made between practicality and specifics, or doing form things. But you said at the beginning of our discussion that there's something uncomfortable for you about the thought, "I have to do something." In questioning this, I'm asking you to just look at the beliefs. We start with something specific and then trace it back to the belief system in the mind. That is very practical.

Let's simply look, for example, at the idea: The girl ran across the street to get the ball. It may seem that what happens in the world of form is a fact, and that the only choice one has is how to interpret what happens. One must understand that actually seeing something that happens is an interpretation already because perception itself is interpretation. What happens is never a fact. It is a hallucination, a dream. It is an illusion of reality. God, or Reality, is the only true fact there is. So you can see how it is important to examine the belief system that produces the interpretation, "The girl ran across the street to get the ball." That interpretation assumes personhood, wouldn't you say? That interpretation assumes the concepts of "girl", "ran", "across", "street", "get", and "ball". These concepts, strung together and associated, make up the interpretation. Surely the subtleties of our inquiry today can lead one to appreciate questioning the purpose of everything one perceives.

Friend 2: We have talked before about inner-child work, psychotherapy, or looking into the past. Is it practical to look at all that? I want to question what I am looking at when I'm looking at my dysfunctional past. The dysfunction occurred when I believed I separated from God. Isn't that the dysfunction that occurred?

David: Yes, and the dysfunction can only be uncovered and

corrected right now! History would not seem to exist if one ceased making the same mistaken choice of separation right now. There would be no conception of a future if one accepted the Correction right now! Personhood has no meaning without history and the future. Do you see that?

Friend 2: You're saying the dysfunctional past is irrelevant in historical terms.

Friend 1: David pointed out earlier that every choice you make brings you everything or nothing. If you choose separation, if you choose to keep reliving that, then you think you are a separate person with a past and a future.

David: There is a point here that requires clarification. The big insight that we are talking about is this: upset is never because of what happened to a person in a personal dysfunctional past. How one is feeling now has nothing to do with an event that happened in history to a body or with what could happen in the future. How one is feeling is the result of a present decision of mind, a choice of perception. That, and only that, brings peace or upset. Remember, the split mind has only two contents or purposes. The perception or interpretation proceeds from the purpose the mind chooses. If you are feeling upset, it is only because you are presently choosing the ego, choosing separation. There is another way to say this: you must still believe the past is present, instead of seeing that the past is gone. This is deception, for the past is gone! Upset is always a sign that illusions reign in place of truth. So we are back full circle again. If one seems to be upset, it's not because of what somebody said, or what somebody did, or because of the weather, or what might happen. The upset, regardless of the form or intensity, is always because one is presently choosing the ego, and therefore still values the ego. The wish to be separate remains intact and needs to be questioned.

Once more, in order to make a clear decision for peace, one needs to get really clear about separation and forgiveness, the two different purposes of the split mind. Otherwise, one is going to stay plugged into the ego.

I would like to use the analogy of the ego as a kitchen blender that is running and making a loud noise. It has a cord that plugs into an energy source, and the way to stop the loud noise is to pull the plug. The blender doesn't run without the electricity.

In this analogy, the mind is the energy source that is giving the ego the electricity. The ego will not run, it can't even seem to exist, unless one gives it the power of one's mind. So the key is to follow the cord down to the plug (purpose), and unplug it. But if one is holding onto a belief system of linear time, of bodies, nature, and all the things of this world, then as one starts to go down, the ego shouts, "*Stop!* You don't want to do this. You'll be left with nothing! No identity!" And if the ego still seems to have value, if it still seems to give you something that you think you want and need, the mind will halt the search for the plug.

Ironically, in its attempt to handle the loud noise of the blender, the deceived mind will retain defense mechanisms and distractions on the surface, the projected world. Following the cord down in this analogy is the same as tracing upsets from specifics to the false belief that produced them or becoming clear on the distinction between form and content. Once this is clear, one is able to discern what comes from God and what doesn't, what is true and what is false, and thus realize that *only the truth is true and there is nothing to decide*. Until that realization is reached, purpose is the only choice.

Let's close with this quotation from the Course:

> The Father keeps what He created safe. You cannot touch it with the false ideas you made, because it was created not by you. Let not your foolish fancies frighten you. What is immortal cannot be attacked; what is but temporal has no effect. Only the purpose that you see in it has meaning, and if that is true, its safety rests secure. If not, it has no purpose, and is means for nothing. Whatever is perceived as means for truth shares in its holiness, and rests in light

as safely as itself. Nor will that light go out when it is gone. Its holy purpose gave it immortality, setting another light in Heaven, where your creations recognize a gift from you, a sign that you have not forgotten them. T-24.VII.5

The test of everything on earth is simply this; "What is it *for?*" The answer makes it what it is for you. It has no meaning of itself, yet you can give reality to it, according to the purpose that you serve. Here you are but means, along with it. God is a Means as well as End. In Heaven, means and end are one, and one with Him. This is the state of true creation, found not within time, but in eternity. To no one here is this describable. Nor is there any way to learn what this condition means. Not till you go past learning to the Given; not till you make again a holy home for your creations is it understood. T-24.VII.6

Reversing Effect and Cause – Getting to the Bottom of the Belief in Linear Time

- A conversation with David

Part 1 – Cause and Effect Are Simultaneous

David: Let's start our discussion on Cause and Effect with the following quote:

You may still complain about fear, but you nevertheless persist in making yourself fearful. I have already indicated that you cannot ask me to release you from fear. I know it does not exist, but you do not. If I intervened between your thoughts and their results, I would be tampering with a basic law of cause and effect; the most fundamental law there is. I would hardly help you if I depreciated the power of your own thinking. This would be in direct opposition to the purpose of this course. It is much more helpful to remind you that you do not guard your thoughts carefully enough. You may feel that at this point it would take a miracle to enable you to do this, which is perfectly true. You are not used to miracle-minded thinking, but you can be trained to think that way. All miracle workers need that kind of training.

I cannot let you leave your mind unguarded, or you will not be able to help me. Miracle working entails a full realization of the power of thought in order to avoid miscreation. Otherwise a miracle will be necessary to set the mind itself straight, a circular process that would not foster the time collapse for which the miracle was intended. The miracle worker must have genuine respect for true cause and effect as a necessary condition for the miracle to occur.

Both miracles and fear come from thoughts. If you are not free to choose one, you would also not be free to choose the other. By choosing the miracle you have rejected fear, if only temporarily. You have been fearful of everyone and everything. You are afraid of God, of me and of yourself. You have misperceived or miscreated Us, and believe in what you have made. You would not have done this if you were not afraid of your own thoughts. The fearful must miscreate, because they misperceive creation. When you miscreate you are in pain. The cause and effect principle now becomes a real expediter, though only temporarily. Actually, Cause is a term properly belonging to God, and His Effect is His Son. This entails a set of Cause and Effect relationships totally different from those you introduce into miscreation. The fundamental conflict in this world, then, is between creation and miscreation. All fear is implicit in the second, and all love in the first. The conflict is therefore one between love and fear. T-2.VII.1-3

So without jumping the gun too much we can say that all miscreation is the wrong mind, in which cause and effect are split off and turned around. It seems as if something in the world or the cosmos is the cause of the state of fear and upset. And all creation or the true cause and effect relationships would be reflected in the right mind, in which the mind is seen to be causative and not at the mercy of anything.

> It has already been said that you believe you cannot control fear because you yourself made it, and your belief in it seems to render it out of your control. Yet any attempt to resolve the error through attempting the mastery of fear is useless. In fact, it asserts the power of fear by the very assumption that it need be mastered. T-2.VII.4

So, we could say that all magic in this world, every attempt to protect the body, shelter the body, insure the body, improve the body and everything else in the world, is a way to change externals to reduce fear. Then the fear is not recognized where it is, nor what its true cause is. The cause is believed to be out on the screen. So if the fear is that I will be flooded out or blown away by a hurricane – all the protective barricades that I set up, whether they are physical or relate to insurance or medical concerns – are all attempts to master fear.

Friend 1: By protecting against what is mistakenly believed to be the cause of it.

David: And of course it doesn't work because the cause of the fear is not out in the world; it has just been set up to appear to be there. Every attempt to deal with it is magic. And the reason that magic is so believable is because it seems to work. If I make a lot of money, if I have a lot of insurance, if I become civilized and tame nature and use technology to seem to surround myself with the best available means of keeping the body healthy, protected, safe and secure, then ego error (what is actually going on in the mind) is doubly shielded from awareness because the magic of projection seems to work.

That is why it feels like some people who go to twelve-step programs or people who hit a deep rock bottom may be more open and ready for a change of mind, a spiritual transformation, because they have tried certain things and nothing seems to work. They come to the point where they feel like their lives are unmanageable and they need something else beyond them to make a change.

Projection is a subtle and seductive defense. In the world it seems that there are underprivileged people and underprivileged countries, and abundance is strongly associated with material wealth, technology and advances in medicine. It is not seen that it is all a cover for attempting to resolve fear through magic and keep it from awareness. The world is not where the fear is at all. So it's quite sneaky.

True resolution rests entirely in mastery through love. To choose the miracle is mastery through love, since forgiveness is a reflection of love. Earlier we discussed desires in the mind and repression and indulgence. To try to block the thoughts from awareness doesn't do anything because they just resurface. Repression doesn't get rid of them. And indulgence, or using magic and pursuing the ways of the world to the nth degree in an attempt to solve the problem or escape from the fear, the loneliness, the isolation doesn't work either. Neither one of these defenses works. But true resolution, the miracle, does work. And that's what we are trying to get clear on. That there is a present decision, which is a miracle, that can be chosen at any instant. And that it will work because it ends the isolation and the experience of fear, anger and conflict.

> In the interim, however, the sense of conflict is inevitable, since you have placed yourself in a position where you believe in the power of what does not exist. Nothing and everything cannot coexist. To believe in one is to deny the other. Fear is really nothing and love is everything. Whenever light enters darkness, the darkness is abolished. What you believe is true for you. In this sense the separation has occurred, and to deny it is merely to use denial inappropriately. However, to concentrate on error is only a further error. The initial corrective procedure is to recognize temporarily that there is a problem, but only

as an indication that immediate correction is needed. This establishes a state of mind in which the Atonement can be accepted without delay. It should be emphasized, however, that ultimately no compromise is possible between everything and nothing. T-2.VII.4-5

To deny that there is a problem is not helpful. But to have a sense that there is a problem in awareness, i.e. I am feeling upset, depressed, uncomfortable, angry or whatever, is needed temporarily to see that there is a problem, but then it should be instantaneously given over to the Holy Spirit, because there isn't any value in holding onto the problem or upset.

Friend 1: And to deny it keeps it twice removed from any kind of solution.

David: From that last statement, "It should be emphasized, however, that ultimately no compromise is possible between everything and nothing," you can see that all that preceded it was just a stepping stone because, as you see cause and effect in their true relationship, then that initial corrective procedure of recognizing the problem vanishes. Instead of saying, "I've got a problem, now where's my torch?" you can just hold Purpose, your torch, out in front. As it says in the Setting the Goal section, the goal belongs at the beginning T-17.VI. Then in the Rules for Decision section, he says that it is easier to have a happy day if you remember what question to ask and you hold your purpose in front, than it is to try to regain the sense of peace by grasping it back after it has seemed to slip away T-30.I. It is much more difficult to regain than it is to just hold firm to your goal and keep the goal out in front. But early in the text it is appropriate to speak of recognizing the error where it is - in the mind.

Time is essentially a device by which all compromise in this respect can be given up. It only seems to be abolished by degrees, because time itself involves intervals that do not exist. Miscreation made this necessary as a corrective device. T-2.VII.5

He's giving us a hint there, because it seems to be a process in time. But Jesus ultimately says that there can be no compromise between everything and nothing, so that's how he is foreshadowing that it is going to be one complete instant of forgiveness and that the whole idea of process is a metaphor.

> The statement "For God so loved the world that He gave His only begotten Son, that whosoever believeth in Him should not perish but have everlasting life" needs only one slight correction to be meaningful in this context; "He gave it to His only begotten Son." T-2.VII.5

That phrasing, "He gave it to His only begotten Son," does not make sense from a physical standpoint because God doesn't know of form. But we can say that God gave the real world to his only begotten Son. In other words, the Holy Spirit Answered the dream of separation by making the real world. Not created in Spirit, but made the real world as a correction for the distorted perceptual world that was made by the ego as an attack upon God.

> It should especially be noted that God has only one Son. T-2.VII.6

When Jesus talks about parts and Sonship it has to be a metaphor, because the unified Spirit is the Son of God, or Christ. And yet to a mind that believes firmly in separation, it is a good stepping stone to talk about all parts of the whole, as if there are parts in a whole. And we talk about this in terms of mind. In the Course it's described generally as if every brother has a mind of his own. And in many sections it's written in that metaphor, "Can [the teacher of God] change the patient's mind for him?" M-5.III.1. We will be working towards, there is only one Son of God; there is only one Mind. And, in a metaphorical sense, there is only one ego. And ultimately, in reality, there is *no* ego.

> If all His creations are His Sons, every one must be an integral part of the whole Sonship. The Sonship in its Oneness transcends the sum of its parts. However this is

obscured as long as any of its parts is missing. That is why the conflict cannot ultimately be resolved until all the parts of the Sonship have returned. Only then can the meaning of wholeness in the true sense be understood. Any part of the Sonship can believe in error or incompleteness if he so chooses. However, if he does so, he is believing in the existence of nothingness. The correction of this error is the Atonement. T-2.VII.6

Friend 1: I read that part on Oneness transcends the sum of its parts and I think of the experience of synergy, joining with another person, and holding the intention at that metaphorical level of their being another person. There does seem to be a synergy when two come together that is greater than two times one.

David: This is pretty early on in the text and one could conclude from reading: "However this is obscured as long as any of its parts is missing," T-2.VII.6. that this is going to be a long correction process. The quote that is coming to mind is, "Just as the separation occurred over millions of years, the Last Judgment will extend over a similarly long period, and perhaps an even longer one." T-2.VIII

You could take those two statements and say that this correction process is going to take millions of years. But that is within a time context. If you look at other parts of the text, it says is that time doesn't exist, that it just takes one instant, that once my mind is healed all minds are healed. These are more top-rung-of-the-ladder kinds of statements. The early statements seem to imply that it is going to be a long process and get back to the perception that if I accept my part in the Atonement then I have done my part, but the many parts have to do their part. And when I accept my part completely and return to creation with my father, that this world of time and space will continue on for millions of years until every part has accepted the atonement; and you're backing away from the ultimate metaphysical reality that none of time-space can ever exist at all.

How can all minds be healed in all places and in all times? That is what it says in the workbook. If I accept the Atonement then that is how the world is saved. The salvation of the world depends on me. The salvation of the cosmos depends on me. You can see this viewpoint implies that there is cosmos outside my mind, and, when I accept the correction, that takes care of the cosmos. That is a huge leap from the linear sense that, as a fragment, as I accept the Atonement, then all of my brothers have to accept the Atonement as well, and it will take millions of years before the mind is healed. But the two viewpoints can't go together. One is obviously deeper than the other. I think this is an area where there is a lot of confusion.

Friend 1: I was very confused initially by the fact that there are different levels represented in the Course. Just as I thought I was getting a hold of one idea, then I would come across another idea that seemed to contradict what I thought I was starting to understand, not realizing that there were just different levels represented.

David: Once a rung is transcended it seems to be just what it was, a metaphor or stepping stone you have hopped off. And this makes sense because the mind believes that perception is fragmented and it has all these beliefs and levels. The Course ultimately says, "You will learn this course entirely or not at all." When you reach the top of the ladder, the ladder disappears. This is a journey without distance to a goal that has never changed. And now, right now, is the only time you can ever accept the Atonement, because right now is all that there is. Time is simultaneous. It is not sequential, not linear. When you transcend those levels, then the whole idea of process just collapses in on itself. It can't be both an instant and a process. It is just a matter of coming to be very clear on that.

We are being called, in a metaphorical sense, to be teachers of God, to speak to our brothers about experiences that are beyond this world, that what is to come has already happened. That is a pretty far-reaching idea, but when we speak about this, we will be speaking as the Spirit uses us, it will also come out like the Course with different rungs. So if you later went back and viewed all of your writings and tapes of conversations with all the people, you would find a mosaic of steps on the ladder much like the Course itself. If you read the teachings of Jesus you see some statements are obviously spoken to the level of the hearer and at other times the author is speaking of a deeper metaphysical understanding. "The Kingdom of Heaven is at hand" is a good example of that instantaneous thing we are talking about, whereas describing the "messengers of the Kingdom" or "the light of the world" or "you will go forth and carry my message to all parts of the earth" do not come close to the metaphysical purity of "the Kingdom of Heaven is at hand." Now is the time of Correction, not in the future. There really is no future, and that is quite a leap.

> I have already briefly spoken about readiness, but some additional points might be helpful here. Readiness is only the prerequisite for accomplishment. The two should not be confused. As soon as a state of readiness occurs, there is usually some degree of desire to accomplish, but it is by no means necessarily undivided. The state does not imply more than a potential for a change of mind. Confidence cannot develop fully until mastery has been accomplished. We have already attempted to correct the fundamental error that fear can be mastered, and have emphasized that the only real mastery is through love. Readiness is only the beginning of confidence. You may think this implies that an enormous amount of time is necessary between readiness and mastery, but let me remind you that time and space are under my control. T-2.VII.7

That's reminiscent of you may believe that your accomplishment of the Holy Spirit's goal lies far in the future and that can be a depressing thought. But later in the text he reminds us that this is not the case, that time is under the Holy Spirit's use. It is a different way of thinking about time and space. The other day someone said, "Maybe I have this backwards because I feel like I had a list of reasons why I wanted to move to Chicago, the pros and cons. And I have been trying to set this thing up and that thing up. And then, if I have enough money and the right conditions, then I am ready to go."

Friend 1: Into the spiritual pursuit?

David: Yes, more deeply into the spiritual pursuit. And this was when we discussed the idea that all it takes is readiness on our part and willingness to have miracles performed through us, and Jesus will arrange time and space for us. Literally time is in the hands of the miracle worker. The miracle worker isn't stuck in time trying to hack his way out the best he can.

But literally all it takes is readiness and then time and space are set up. Even with these sessions we have, it is just our willingness and our readiness that sets up time and space for the teaching and learning for us to extend the miracles and extend the clarity. It's not that we have to go through a whole process of setting up all these things. That is the worldly way of doing things, making a production out of it. All I have to have is the willingness.

Friend 1: That's when it's really effortless I think. It's when that intention is strong and it just unfolds from that.

David: It's been called synchronicity. In the world's eyes it looks like things just click and flow effortlessly in sync. For the mind that is ready, able and willing to perform a miracle, everything is lined up for it. The next section, The Decision for Guiltlessness, is in Chapter 14.

> The miracle teaches you that you have chosen guiltlessness, freedom and joy. It is not a cause, but an effect. It is the natural result of choosing right, attesting to your happiness that comes from choosing to be free of guilt. Everyone you offer healing to returns it. Everyone you attack keeps it and cherishes it by holding it against you. Whether he does this or does it not will make no difference; you will think he does. It is impossible to offer what you do not want without this penalty. The cost of giving is receiving.

Either it is a penalty from which you suffer, or the happy purchase of a treasure to hold dear. T-14.III.5

Friend 1: So the cause is right-mindedness. And the effect is the miracle. Is that what this is saying?

David: Yes, the miracle is a reminder of Cause. "In gentle laughter does the Holy Spirit perceive the cause, and looks not to effects." T-27.VIII.8 He sees the falsity of the effects of the world because He sees that they all come from a false cause, and He reminds the mind of the Cause that is present. So when it says, "The miracle... is not a cause, but an effect," T-14.III.5. it is an effect of choosing the right mind.

Another way to say it is that the world brings witness to what the mind wants. And if the mind chooses the right mind, the miracle brings witness to that choice. It brings a witness of guiltlessness, freedom and joy.

> Those who remember always that they know nothing, and who have become willing to learn everything, will learn it. But whenever they trust themselves, they will not learn. They have destroyed their motivation for learning by thinking they already know. Think not you understand anything until you pass the test of perfect peace, for peace and understanding go together and never can be found alone. Each brings the other with it, for it is the law of God they be not separate. They are cause and effect, each to the other, so where one is absent the other cannot be. T-14.XI.12

Friend 1: So in this respect, it is clear that unless I am consistently in a state of peace, I don't know anything.

David: It calls to mind a few different passages in the Course. The one in the text says, "You are still convinced that your understanding is a powerful contribution to the truth." T-18.IV.8 It is speaking to the ego mind, or the deceived mind. And in other places it refers to what the Bible called "the peace that passeth understanding." T-2.II.2 It is talking about accepting the Atonement, about being in your right-mind. That is what it means to understand. That would also mean to be the "dreamer of the dream," to have completely reversed cause and effect in all respects, to have no confusion, to be absolved of conflict. That's equated with understanding and peace. Cause and effect are almost used interchangeably. They are cause and effect, each to the other. Where one is absent, the other cannot be. That reminds me of other parts in the text where Jesus talks about "The cause a cause is *made* by its effects," T-28.II.1. In other words the Father is a Father because of the Son. Not in the sense that the Son created the Father, but in the sense that creation gives Fathership. It is just another way of saying that cause and effect are together, that cause and effect are not split off, and through relationship they go together.

Friend 1: They're simultaneous.

David: Yes. There's no time gap in between them. In the world linear time is a gap between cause and effect, as if something has come in between the Cause and Effect, the Father and the Son. The whole point of the Course is to show that this is impossible. Ideas leave not their source, cause and effect are simultaneous. Another way of saying this is that the mind gets exactly what it wants. And when it wants only peace it cannot perceive anything but a peaceful world. But, as long as it is not sure about what it wants, then there seems to be a gap between cause and effect. Yesterday the question was raised about the hypothetical situation. Someone said "I just don't see how you can go along without conflict. What if I asked you to have lunch on the same day that you have already said that you are going to speak at Unity?" And I described to him that listening to the Holy Spirit and following that Voice eliminates all conflicts. It is no longer a menu of options. You are following inner guidance and you are at a place where you feel like the dreamer of the dream, because you are not trying to change or control the script. You are flowing along observing something that has already happened. That is where the effortlessness comes in. You're not looking back and saying "This could have been different," or "We need to do this differently." And you are also not looking forward, planning, scheming, straining and trying to get it to go the way that you want it to.

Friend 1: What seems like a key factor is that there really is only one thing that I want. When my personal wants are not a factor, and all I want is just to listen and follow the Holy Spirit, then it takes the conflict right out of it.

David: The deceived mind really believes that it has options and that when it is thinking, "I wish I was somewhere else but here," that there is a "somewhere else." But there isn't. Cause and effect are simultaneous. There isn't a hypothetical somewhere else. The script is written and the outcome is always what it must be. All things do work together for good. The shadows are moving in a pattern of Divine Order, and it is just a matter of seeing it as the dreamer of the dream or observing what has already happened. That is where the ease and the peace come in. Strain is believing that you are in the dream, that you are a person thinking, "I could be somewhere else" or "this should be different than it is." Whatever hypothetical is going on in the mind when a conflict is arising there is a sense of coercion: "I'd be doing that if I really had my druthers, instead of this," and the deceived mind is still trying to split off cause and effect. It is denying that cause and effect are simultaneous, that this is just a projection of thought.

Friend 2: I am unhappy because I don't like where I am and think that being somewhere else would change how I feel; that's the reversal of cause and effect.

David: Yes, and that's the ego's answer to the belief in separation. It's always holding out something in form, a thought of something in the future or the thought of some imagined place, to remove this person and put this person in another environment.

Ultimately if we bring it back to the self-concept and the subject / object split you see what's beneath "I think I would be better off if I were in a different place" is the belief that I am a person. It makes no sense to think that I can go to another place or situation without the belief that I am this little, teeny fragment, a little person. The ultimate realization is that if the entire cosmos or the entire world is just a projection from the mind, that cosmos is the effect of this mistaken cause – the belief that I am separate.

It seems that events are sequential and that some events happened last week or decades ago or, like Cleopatra, centuries ago. But the Course is teaching us that those things seem to have been projected from the mind in terms of time. Those are seen as happening long ago. An event closer to where it seems to be projected from is thought of as space. This thumb and Cleopatra don't seem to have a lot of relationship, and yet, they are both ideas. One has been projected from my mind in terms of time, living centuries ago, and this thumb seems to be very literally close at hand! This thumb is so many inches away, very close to the projector. Whereas events that seem to have happened many years ago have been projected beyond the mind to time.

But ideas leave not their source. Cleopatra is in the wrong mind just as much as this thumb. Time starts to collapse when you start to see that there is no linear, or sequential, time. To make up linear time and believe that I am a fragment moving in and through that linear time is just an ego attempt to hold cause and effect apart from one another.

A miracle collapses time. What is a miracle but a look on the dream world or the script from above the battlefield, seeing the falsity of the whole thing? That is what a miracle is, a leap above the battlefield where you recognize the false as false. It doesn't do anything. It just reminds the mind that what it sees is false and that collapses the need for time.

Part 2 – Time is an Illusion

David: Our next segment is from Chapter 16, The Reward of Teaching.

> You may have taught freedom, but you have not learned how to be free. I said earlier, "By their fruits ye shall know them, and they shall know themselves." For it is certain that you judge yourself according to your teaching. The ego's teaching produces immediate results, because its decisions are immediately accepted as your choice. And this acceptance means that you are willing to judge yourself accordingly. Cause and effect are very clear in the ego's thought system, because all your learning has been directed toward establishing the relationship between them. And would you not have faith in what you have so diligently taught yourself to believe? Yet remember how much care you have exerted in choosing its witnesses, and in avoiding those which spoke for the cause of truth and its effects. T-16.III.2

This whole world is learned and based on upside down and backward thinking where cause and effect have been reversed. Even if you ask, "Where are you from?" "Well, I was born in 1958" and so on, it is obvious cause and effect have been reversed to place my origin in the time/space universe. Look at questions like "Were you raised in a dysfunctional family?" or "What were the social conditions at the time you were born?" The social and cultural conditions seem to be a factor in who you are; the cause of who you are seems to be determined by the time/space cosmos.

That has been taught. This world has been carefully built up based on that backward thinking, with enormous care in choosing its witnesses. Whether you are talking about a dysfunctional family, being mistreated in school, or having certain horrifying events that seemed to happen, when someone recounts their personal life history it's still based on reversed cause and effect. It is believed that these events have caused a lasting effect on the mind. It is not seen that the mind has believed that it is guilty and it called forth witnesses to reinforce the guilt. Instead, through the ego's lens, it is seen as if these events and conditions in the world are somehow causative.

Friend 1: It helped me to remember that I told the world what to teach me.

David: And it keeps it in past tense too. If someone says, "Yuck! Why would I do such a thing?" it is still a "why" question instead of "What is it for, what is the Purpose? I can make a different choice right now." The unholy purpose – that the world was made as an attack upon God, as a place to hide from love and to reinforce guilt – was a past decision. But right now I can choose to be free of that unholy purpose. That's what it means to hold on to a new purpose; that right now is offered to me as correction for that. So it would be the correction of, "I taught the world to teach me" which keeps it in the past tense.

Friend 1: Oh, yes, I remember the last time we talked about this, I said it's the belief that comes first, and you reminded me that that was just a stepping stone idea because the belief and the effect, or the cause and the effect are simultaneous.

David: Yes, they're one, the ego tree trunk and the branches. The thought that seemed to give rise to the world, the wish to be separate from God, and all the effects of that wish, the cosmos... are one. It's all history so to speak. Jesus says at the very end of the Course, "Where is the ego? Where the darkness was." C-2.7.

Friend 1: And it's only the seeming linearity of time that obscures the fact that they are simultaneous.

David: Time is the belief that cause and effect are separate. That's the gap, the gap that doesn't exist. That's the point of the whole Course. You've put many toys in your gap and now you believe that you can play with these toys and that you brought these toys to life. It's the Pinocchio thing. You have projected out a bunch of images and this thing that seemed to be a static wood puppet seems to have a life of its own. And it scares you when these toys squeak and do certain things. Maybe you think you have to lock up or avoid some of these events or these toys. And the Course says, these are "children's toys." You must see that you made these toys up, and by giving another purpose to the toys or to the whole script you can see that they aren't real, that they don't have any life. There is no life in the toys. This runs against all the thinking of the world, the ideas of making the world a better place, saving the starving children, all the dramas on TV, etc. There is this horrible thing called death that seems to be waiting with a hook to get every living thing at a certain time, and life is precious, to be saved. Yet there is no life on the screen. That is fundamental. As you start to see that, the implications are far reaching; then it makes more sense to sink down beneath the images in your mind and to let them go, let go into the awareness that there is a real world of real thoughts beneath all these wrong-minded attack thoughts and dark shadow images.

> Does not the fact that you have not learned what you have taught show you that you do not perceive the Sonship as one? And does it not also show you that you do not regard *yourself* as one? For it is impossible to teach successfully wholly without conviction, and it is equally impossible that conviction be outside of you. You could never have taught freedom unless you did believe in it. And it must be that what you taught came from yourself. Yet this Self you clearly do not know, and do not recognize It even though It functions. What functions must be there. And it is only if you deny what It has done that you could possibly deny Its presence. T-16.III.3.

To try to teach that the world has existence in and of itself as an objective reality is to try to teach an impossible lesson. The mind is without conviction when it is trying to teach the impossible lesson, because some part in the mind knows it can't be taught. These ideas can't be shared because they don't come from God. They are delusional ideas. The attempt to share ego ideas is denying the Self, denying Reality. That is where guarding the mind comes in, where watching the thoughts carefully and withdrawing the mind's allegiance from these backwards thoughts is so important. If I want to get clear, why would I attempt to teach something that can't be taught? When you start to get down to cause and effect, you get to watching your mind more closely.

I was talking the other day about little phrases that fill up the gaps of silence like, "Isn't this lovely?" You start to tune your mind in so much to be a channel for the Holy Spirit that there is not that uneasiness of silence that needs to be filled in with those comments or wonder questions, "I wonder why it's snowing so hard?" They seem to be conversation to fill up the silence and the fear of that silence. Just be able to watch the thoughts and not give allegiance to them, to bask in the silence, to sink into it.

"This is a course in how to know yourself. You have taught what you are, but have not let what you are teach you." T-16.III.4 In a sense the Holy Spirit is a reminder of our Self, what we truly are.

> You have been very careful to avoid the obvious, and not to see the real cause and effect relationship that is perfectly apparent. Yet within you is everything you taught. What can it be that has not learned it? It must be this part that is really outside yourself, not by your own projection, but in truth. And it is this part that you have taken in that is not you. T-16.III.4

So we're back to that wrong-mind again. The ego – all of consciousness – is the split mind, the wrong mind, and as long as the guilt and fear are believed to be within, it's not seen that they are truly outside of you. You have to sink down below them into the mind and go beneath them to see that they are really outside instead of within. But as long as the mind believes that there is guilt and sadness inside, then it prefers to stay focused on the screen and believe that the cause of the guilt and pain is out there on the screen; the world remains a good distractive device, a way of avoiding looking within.

It's just separating the wheat from the chaff, separating the attack thoughts from the real thoughts, discerning between the wrong mind and the right mind. What can it be that has not learned it? It can only be the wrong mind that hasn't learned what we really are, that doesn't realize the cause/effect relationship that is perfectly apparent.

Friend 1: Well, my thing is feeling like I'll forget it.

David: Yes. Ultimately it's about learning the Course entirely or not at all. There are lessons in the workbook that say you are not two selves, but one. What part of the statement, "I am a spiritual being having a human experience" has to be forgiven? The latter part! This human experience stuff. "I'm only human" is justification for error and mistakes. You aren't two selves. You think that you're part good, part bad. You can't be two selves. It comes down to a big either/or. You are Perfect; infinite, absolute, changeless... or, what is the option? In the end what else can it be? You can't be anything but that. It brings it down to one decision.

> And it is this part that you have taken in that is not you. What you accept into your mind does not really change it. Illusions are but beliefs in what is not there. And the seeming conflict between truth and illusion can only be resolved by separating yourself from the illusion and not from truth. T-16.III.4

The final realization is simply that the truth is true. It sounds funny when you read it in there, that the truth is true. But to see that, you have to see what is false. The self-concept is not just little personal beliefs. It is the belief that made the world and the cosmos. All backward thinking is false. So the self-concept is not just a persona, but a part of what the mind has wrapped around itself. The deceived mind has wrapped a body around it, and a couch and a room and an area with snowflakes and a lake and some clouds and the rest of the world and a solar system. It has spun a cobweb of time, space and form all around it. And so the underpinning of all that – cause and effect, the belief that it really is possible to separate from the Creator – is what seemed to produce all that. Simply going into the mind and seeing that the cause is false is also to see that it can't have real effects. What you are left with is seeing that you dreamed this whole thing up. And secondly, that you can give a new purpose to this whole cosmos that you dreamed up. And finally, in the ultimate sense, that there is no need for this cosmos anymore. The only purpose of this world is that you pass it by without remaining to see some glimmer of hope in something you believe it offers. It is not like there is some value that is left in the cosmos, that you can have a paradise on earth or whatever. That is where the Course takes us literally beyond all the channeled writings that say that there is a world of perfection where everyone lives in peace and harmony. The closest the Course would come to utopia would be the real world, which is simply seeing that the entire world is an illusory projection, not finding any inherent value or meaning in any aspect of it.

The next section is from the Responsibility for Sight:

> We have already said that wishful thinking is how the ego deals with what it wants, to make it so. There is no better demonstration of the power of wanting, and therefore of faith, to make its goals seem real and possible. Faith in the unreal leads to adjustments of reality to make it fit the goal of madness. The goal of sin induces the perception of a fearful world to justify its purpose. What you desire, you will see. And if its reality is false, you will uphold it by not realizing all the adjustments you have introduced to make it so. T-21.II.9

If I ask myself, "Why do I have to do this?" I would say, "I need to do this because of that" and trace it back into beliefs that I have different levels of needs: basic survival needs, emotional needs, physiological needs and so on. The mind is splintered into different levels and different needs. And beneath that is the belief in lack and scarcity and sacrifice. Beneath that is the belief in separation, the belief that separation is possible. From the belief that I could separate from my Creator the belief in lack arose and I was suddenly lacking something, that I wasn't whole and complete. It is helpful to look at all the adjustments, the different attempts at magic and the attempts to build a self-concept, to become a mature, respected, healthy, responsible adult. That first belief in separation has involved all kinds of adjustments in my mind.

It is like when a dam starts to break. You start to plug one hole and then have to run over and plug another. This world was made as a hiding place but it requires so many adjustments. All of the defenses that the mind uses are based on the underlying belief that there is something to be defended, and that the defenses are necessary or useful. Mind tricks and magic of all kinds are used to conceal this despair that is believed to be real. Ultimately the only way to lay down the defenses and attempts at magic is to look into the mind, to look right into the cause and see that the big bad wolf, the wizard of Oz, the one that seems to be controlling and powerful, is nothing but this little mouse that is of no consequence at all. You just quit believing in it. That is quite a release.

"When vision is denied, confusion of cause and effect becomes inevitable." T-21.II.10 When the light in the mind is denied then backward thinking becomes inevitable because it is seen as a necessary part of the hiding place idea.

> The purpose now becomes to keep obscure the cause of the effect, and make effect appear to be a cause. This seeming independence of effect enables it to be regarded as standing by itself, and capable of serving as a cause of the events and feelings its maker thinks it causes. T-21.II.10

This is a world apart from Heaven, where ideas seem to have left their source and where God is powerless over what has been made. It is the birth of objective reality apart from the mind of the thinker. The dream figure seems to be at the mercy of the dream world. The dream figure also is seen as causative. So it can do things; it can be a cause of events on other things. Someone who seems to murder or whatever is seen as a causative agent that can act in and of itself. It is not seen as just part of a play in the mind, that I am the executive producer/director , and that I have set it up this way. It is seen as if the characters have wills of their own, making them causative as well. For example: "You cause me great misery. You hurt my feelings. You made me laugh." It is not seen that the mind has chosen all the emotions and all the states of mind.

> Earlier, we spoke of your desire to create your own creator, and be father and not son to him. This is the same desire. The Son is the Effect, whose Cause he would deny. And so he seems to be the cause, producing real effects. Nothing can have effects without a cause, and to confuse the two is merely to fail to understand them both. It is as needful that you recognize you made the world you see, as that you recognize that you did not create yourself. *They are the same mistake.* T-21.II.10-11

That is the "authority problem." That is where we come to the point of saying, "I was wrong about everything, wrong about the belief that I pulled apart from my creator, could make up a world apart from God, and could make myself." That's the belief behind the self improvement movement, that I am an image of my own making and can improve and shape my own destiny.

Friend 2: Explain a little bit about the "authority problem."

David: The authority problem is the denial of Spirit. To believe that you can make up a world or make up a self in the direction of your own making is to deny that you are what you are; for what you are is an Effect of God, Spirit, as God created you.

Friend 1: And that can't be changed.

David: And that can't be changed. Reality is only yours to accept, not to select from. To make yourself there first must be the belief that reality is yours to choose from; I can choose to stay with this family or I can choose to leave. I can choose to live where I want to live. I can choose to go where I want to go. I can choose to retain my cultural or ethnic identity. I can choose to speak the language I want to speak I can choose to go back to college or not. I can choose to work out and improve my body or I can choose to let it go. All the attempts to make a better person are perceived from the basic assumption that I can make myself, and that reality is mine to select from. It's the value for pluralism. Even respect for diversity doesn't go down to wanting to see the sameness that is, or accepting the universal Reality that is. It is still an attempt to cling to variety and diversity, to cling to the belief that you can make yourself.

Friend 1: That phrase that you used, believing that reality is mine to choose from. Would that be equated with "I invent reality"?

David: Yes. "I can order my own thoughts" is another way of saying it. "I can pick and choose from reality." And Jesus clearly says in the Course that if you believe that you can order your thoughts you will have this disordered thought system, and then you will feel responsible for the chaos and disorder, and you will feel guilty. Guilt automatically comes from a mind that believes it can order its own thoughts. It's inescapable. And the Course says, "God Himself orders your thought because your thought was created by Him." T-5.V.7 This is where Divine Order comes in.

Let's move ahead.

> Forget not that the choice of sin or truth, helplessness or power, is the choice of whether to attack or heal. For healing comes of power, and attack of helplessness. Whom you attack you *cannot* want to heal. And whom you would have healed must be the one you chose to be protected from attack. And what is this decision but the choice whether to see him through the body's eyes, or let him be revealed to you through vision? How this decision leads to its effects is not your problem. But what you want to see must be your choice. This is a course in cause and not effect. T-21.VII.7

This is a course in thinking and not in forms, behaviors and appearances. The sentence, "How this decision leads to its effects is not your problem," means you do not have to figure out how vision works, but just to have the desire and willingness for vision – that is the whole thing.

In Chapter 24 we see another way of saying what we were just talking about:

> In dreams effect and cause are interchanged, for here the maker of the dream believes that what he made is happening to him. He does not realize he picked a thread from here, a scrap from there, and wove a picture out of nothing. For the parts do not belong together, and the whole contributes nothing to the parts to give them meaning. T-24.V.2

The deceived mind believes that it can pick from and assemble reality the way it wants it, and that's what it sees. And not only does it label the parts and set them apart from one another, but it starts to define how it wants the parts to relate to one another. That is a lot of the learning of the world, not only what the parts are but how they relate to one another.

Friend 1: And there is no relationship between illusions. That has been coming to me a lot lately. And the mind's attempt to see relationship where there is none is simply the mind's attempt to order the chaos and make the illusion seem that it's not an illusion.

David: Yes, it's very important to understand this. In the Kingdom of Heaven, the one eternal law is "what you extend you are." And in this world, the law becomes twisted to "what you project you will believe." So the false concepts have to be revealed in the mind and let go of because attack thoughts, false ideas, must be projected. In other words, they can't be held together. You can't hold onto the Holy Spirit's thought system and attack thoughts because holding onto two opposing thought systems makes an intolerable conflict. So attack thoughts must be projected. And what the mind projects it believes. That is what we read earlier, that in this sense the separation has occurred because you have accepted it in your mind. You believe it and to deny it would be an inappropriate use of denial. When the deceived mind holds a delusional thought that is not of God, it must be projected because every thought must be either extended or projected. Thoughts of God are extended and thoughts of the wrong mind are projected. So it is imperative that the mind raise to awareness and let go of the concepts that are not of the Father... every concept that is not of the Father, every belief.

Friend 2: When I started to read this information, I began to see all the reversal of the cause and effect and it was almost this bombardment. I felt bombarded by the backwards thinking, and I suppose what it comes down to is me just calling forth these witnesses to say, "Yes, it is impossible for you to believe this." But at the same time I remember the kids walking through the door and talking reversing cause and effect! And my husband comes in and then he starts doing it. And I thought; If I'm going to totally reverse my thinking and not buy into it anymore, then how do I fit into this picture? I'll just go sit over in the corner and keep my mouth shut! Cause there won't be anything for me to say! [Laughing]

Friend 1: The picture will change though...

Friend 2: I'm sure it will.

Friend 1: As the mind changes, the picture it uses for witnesses has to be changing.

Friend 2: There's the reversal of the cause and effect too. I am not even sure what it is I am doing but I see that there is reversal of cause and effect in it... that I think that me changing my mind, that that is going to cause a problem.

Friend 1: Because the witnesses to your mind aren't seen as witnesses to your mind, they are seen as apart from your mind and separate from you as individual minds that will go on caught up in this backwards thinking and you'll think "How can I go on being around all this backward thinking?"

Friend 2: Or even as a parent, the kids come to me and say, "How did this happen?" or "What about this?" and I think, "Wow, what do I say? Give them the expected answer or ..."

Friend 1: Give the answer a teacher would give them, or give them an answer that a teacher of God would give them.

Friend 2: Right. And it's just separating it out. Instead of just seeing myself as a chance for the Holy Spirit, it's like I have to know the answer ahead of time and be prepared so that when they ask me the question it's not like "Oh my gosh, I've got to think about this. Can you hang on for ten or fifteen minutes and I'll get back to you because I've got to really work this all out in my mind before I give you an answer."

David: I think behind the "How can I fit into the picture?" is the dreamer of the dream vs. dream figure. The basic thing beneath it is, "I belong in this picture," whether it's this picture or just in general; this picture of the world or this picture of a home.

Friend 1: I am in it, I am in the picture! And I belong here. [Laughing]

David: And your mind seems to be shifting and seems strange now. Early on for me, the more I plunged into the ideas of the Course, the more I felt that friction. Going to family gatherings, there was all this talk about all this stuff... and I just felt "Oh my gosh! if I keep going with this... I feel strange, I feel I am out in left field right now. And it could only get worse." That's the way I perceived it because it seemed to be going dramatically away in the opposite direction. And I think I projected my fear out into the future and I pictured myself alone. I pictured myself in the monastic mode of just going off into a hut or something somewhere.

Friend 1: Ostracized by anybody that might have been around before.

Friend 2: Who'd want to be around you?

David: And the surprise or turnabout has been that of just feeling Called internally to go places, to do things, to speak, and to meet people. It is like when I described going to Roscoe and having all these meetings in the community kitchen. It was like I was drawing forth witnesses that wanted to hear what I was saying, but before what I perceived as my biological family didn't care; they weren't in a place to receive.

Friend 1: And they even said, "I think you need to find someone else to talk to about these things," right?

David: Yes, once, early on. And it was just following that Guidance and going to spiritual center, and sitting and talking and immediately clicking in at a place where there was a you-can-see-it-too experience. Drawing forth a witness to my shift of mind was bringing back, reflecting back to me those ideas I was feeling. Actually there were those who could hear what I was talking about and could understand. That counterbalanced the idea that I would be alone. And then just going with that direction more and more whether it has been with the travels or with the conversations we're having. The pain was trying to fit this new kind of experience into the old picture.

This was a journey or a Guidance that I really had to follow; I really wanted to follow. All along, even through the college years of trying to put something together and make a career out of something, I felt this Call to I didn't know what. But along with it was "I have to go. I have to go with this Guidance even though I don't have a clear picture. I can't know what it will look like." I think of some of the stories of the different saints and so called wise people; I think of Meher Baba who went into silence, complete silence. And there was such a light in his eyes and such an attraction, such a strong draw that people would come to sit in his presence. And finally they got him a spelling board. He would point letter by letter and his teachings came through that. But in conventional thinking it's like, Come on, what is this? Everyone talks. What you do think God gave people mouths for?

Earlier we discussed the thoughts of Jesus on readiness and mastery. Readiness does not imply mastery but it means that the potential for a real change in mind is there. Readiness is not something that you can cultivate outside yourself because there isn't any readiness outside yourself. It is really readiness in your own mind. To really go within and focus on watching your mind and to really want to have that mind shift, the shift from readiness into mastery, to really generalize... is a highly internal matter. You know how the Course says the curriculum is highly individualized. When you really look at it in those terms you see that you can't rush your brother along. You can only go with where you are, and it takes the strain out of wondering.

There is a part of the mind that says, "I like relaxing and watching a football game. I enjoy fine dining or hobnobbing with people. I like some of that. I am not ready to generalize. I am not ready to take this thing and generalize it across the board, but I have a sense that you are on to something and I am watching. And beyond that I know that we are connected in a way that I know what you do for you, you do for me and for everyone." When I extended this with a lot of friends, I really opened and tried to make myself available and there was a real attraction, and with some there was a pulling back, like "This is threatening to my everyday life and threatening to the way I conceive of my life. There are certain parts of the way I conceive of my life that I like. I'd like to be at the place of commitment where you all are, but I am not there and I need to go splash in the pond a little more." And that's okay. That's fine. But the whole point is that it is peripheral to "I want to go from readiness to mastery. I want to get the lesson."

I read something using a bird metaphor that said the formation of a flock is not necessary to staying on the homing beacon. There may be a flock; there may not be a flock. There may be some in the flock that will say this leader is crazy and leave the flock, and some of those may even seem to get to the destination more quickly in another flock. None of that is your concern. Your concern is to stay focused on the beacon; don't lose sight of the beacon. Reading that helped me, because there is a tendency to watch the flock. Whether it's a biological family or a Course community or certain people, the same thing happens. The mind may think it will be different now because you're a Course student or something like that. But that's not the case either. It still comes down to having to stay on the beacon and pull your attention away from who is flying in formation and who is not in formation, who is with the flock and who is leaving the flock, all of the drama of spiritual awakening, to speak in the ego sense, that is all just a distraction as well.

I think our teaching/learning sessions are very helpful and we've all said that we'd like this to continue, to be in communication. If we feel strong guidance to call or to write to someone, to go with that guidance, to really trust and just keep open. We want to keep getting clearer and clearer through these teaching/learning situations however it unfolds.

So, we're continuing on with cause and effect and moving to Chapter 28, section I, The Present Memory.

> The miracle does nothing. All it does is to undo. And thus it cancels out the interference to what has been done. It does not add, but merely takes away. And what it takes away is long since gone, but being kept in memory appears to have immediate effects. This world was over long ago. The thoughts that made it are no longer in the mind that thought of them and loved them for a little while. The miracle but shows the past is gone, and what has truly gone has no effects. Remembering a cause can but produce illusions of its presence, not effects. T-28.I.1

That's a biggie. That explains a lot of what we have been talking about. In the next paragraph it says, "Remembering is as selective as perception, being its past tense." That's an interesting idea, that remembering is the past tense of perception.

It continues:

> It is perception of the past as if it were occurring now, and still were there to see. Memory, like perception, is a skill made up by you to take the place of what God gave in your creation. And like all the things you made, it can be used to serve another purpose, and to be the means for something else. It can be used to heal and not to hurt, if you so wish it be. Nothing employed for healing represents an effort to do anything at all. It is a recognition that you have no needs which mean that something must be done. It is an unselective memory that is not used to interfere with truth. All things the Holy Spirit can employ for healing have been given Him, without the content and the purposes for which they have been made. They are but skills without an application. They await their use. They have no dedication and no aim. T-28.I.2-3

That is clearly stating what we have been saying about removing all the purposes that we have given to everything... tables, chairs, bodies, houses, cars, green paper strips, metal discs.

Friend 1: Unselective memory is an interesting phrase.

David: All selective memory is using the past and picking out what you want things to mean to you. Unselective gives the impression that it's universal, that the Holy Spirit's purpose is a universal application and that all the things in this world have no dedication and no aim. They really have no relation to each other. All specifics are related through the Holy Spirit's purpose, but they have no relation to one another. A car and a body seem to have a pretty strong relationship. Cars are very necessary it seems, in the world's eyes, to get those bodies around. And yet all objects in the world and all skills have no inherent, intrinsic meaning or use in and of themselves because that whole idea in and of themselves is erroneous. There is no specific in and of itself. The whole world that's been constructed starts to teeter if that is accepted.

Friend 1: What was the metaphor you used of beads strung on a golden cord?

David: That the golden cord is the Holy Spirit's purpose and the beads are the specifics that, of themselves, would just be scattered and have no meaning or use without the cord running through them. And taking the metaphor a little further you could see the beads in a necklace. Because the cord has no beginning and no end, therefore neither do the necklace beads. The circle is the whole, like the Holy Spirit's purpose, with no beginning and no ending.

> The Holy Spirit can indeed make use of memory, for God Himself is there. Yet this is not a memory of past events, but only of a present state. You are so long accustomed to believe that memory holds only what is past, that it is hard for you to realize it is a skill that can remember now. The limitations on remembering the world imposes on it are as vast as those you let the world impose on you. There is no link of memory to the past. If you would have it there, then there it is. But only your desire made the link, and only you have held it to a part of time where guilt appears to linger still. T-28.I.4

The part of time where guilt appears to linger still is the unholy instant. Every time the unholy instant is called and believed to be the present, then the present is denied. The holy instant is denied when the past is brought into the present. So every time you order thoughts or judge, you are attempting to deny that these are just images and that the ego thoughts and the projected images are already over and done. They are part of that unholy instant. So the wrong mind exists entirely in the unholy instant because the wrong mind is past tense. And the right mind, which would be analogous to forgiveness, is in the present. So if we talk about wrong-mind, right-mind, or guilt versus forgiveness, we talk about past versus present. Forgiveness is in the right mind or in the present moment.

Something that has been coming to me the last couple days is a metaphor that the miracle is like a point. The wrong mind is like a line and the miracle is like a point, only a point, and always a point. In fact if you turn a line, like a strand of dry spaghetti, perpendicular to your eye, it's a point that collapses the line. So instead of thinking "I am the Holy Son of God, I am One, I am Allness," you could think "I am a point, not a line." Whenever I am tempted to think of what I have done in the past or what is coming up I can just think of "I am a point, not a line." It's simple, a geometric metaphor.

Friend 1: I like the image of recognizing when I am thinking of myself as a line and then it shrinks down and it is just a point.

David: Some of you may question how that fits with "I am everything and everywhere," because a point can be seen as very tiny. The miracle is a perception, but it is as if the entire cosmos of time and space is that point. You can observe that point from the miracle and you see that all of time and space is simultaneous. It is not linear and it is all contained in that unholy instant. You can think of the unholy instant as kind of a point that you can observe from the miracle. And in that sense, it includes everywhere that you could possibly be, all included in that point. It takes away the sense of distance and location and place.

> The Holy Spirit's use of memory is quite apart from time. He does not seek to use it as a means to keep the past, but rather as a way to let it go. Memory holds the message it receives, and does what it is given it to do. It does not write the message, nor appoint what it is for. T-28.I.5

Memory is just like time and the body and relationships and everything else. It's this neutral thing that will serve the purpose like everything else in the mind. It's a skill that was made up by the deceived mind. It has no inherent purpose in and of itself. We are back to "What is my purpose? What is it for?"

> Like to the body, it is purposeless within itself. And if it seems to serve to cherish ancient hate, and gives you pictures of injustices and hurts that you were saving, this is what you asked its message be and that it is. Committed

to its vaults, the history of all the body's past is hidden there. All of the strange associations made to keep the past alive, the present dead, are stored within it, waiting your command that they be brought to you, and lived again. And thus do their effects appear to be increased by time, which took away their cause. T-28.I.5

We've got some good stuff in there. This is a good paragraph for the computer memory analogy where all of history, all of the body's past is hidden there in this vault of an enormous hard drive. And literally when it says "all the body's past" we are talking about the past-past and the future-past, meaning future, all of the perception.

"And thus do their effects appear to be increased by time, which took away their cause."

So the ego is a splintering thought and is all of the fragmentation, and we could even say procreation because there seem to be more and more bodies. It is a population explosion basically, "and thus do their effects appear to be increased by time." It seems as time goes on that there are more and more bodies, and it says "which took away their cause." It's still that reversal of cause and effect as if time and procreation appear to be the cause of more and more bodies when really the cause of the entire world including the bodies and all of the fragments and everything, is the ego, the belief in separation in the mind. So time seems to have done a very nice thing for the deceived mind. It seems to have taken on causation. Time seems to have causation, when time is really just a belief that has spun from the belief in separation. So the cause is in the mind, not in time.

A lot of times people ask: "Is the world getting better or worse?" Some people will say it's getting worse with pollution and getting more complex and so on. But that's still not getting at the issue, that the cause of the world is in the mind and that time is not really multiplying the problems. There still is only one problem, that's the belief in separation; even though the many hides the zero of everything. It doesn't matter how many times you multiply an illusion by zero you still have zero, because the cause is not in the world or in time. And still there are the scientists looking into the cosmos for the beginning of it, the Big Bang, for they still believe that there is a cause out there on the screen. What we are here learning in the Course is that the cause is in the mind. So now the next paragraph really starts to put time in its place, so to speak.

> Yet time is but another phase of what does nothing. It works hand in hand with all the other attributes with which you seek to keep concealed the truth about yourself. Time neither takes away nor can restore. T-28.I.6

This is a very important idea. When you read a statement like "...just as the separation occurred over millions of years, the last judgment will occur over a similarly long period and perhaps an even longer one'" and you still aren't clear about the right mind and the wrong mind, you could conclude wrongly that the healing is subject to time, to millions of years. It says so right here! But what we are seeing here, much later in the text, is a clear statement that time neither takes away nor can restore. It's not the millions of years that are going to restore the Sonship back to its original place. Time is just as neutral as anything else, just another phase of what does nothing. It's the purpose given to time that is the crucial thing. If the mind can just accept the Holy Spirit's purpose completely and wholly in one instant, that's what it means to accept the Atonement. That doesn't take any time. That is where the whole idea of process collapses, in that one decision to accept the Correction that's always been in the mind.

Friend 2: So, why would He make a statement like that; that it's taken millions of years and that it's going to take millions more? How do you see that as helpful?

David: Well I see it first of all in the context of its coming on page 34. If I was new to the Course and started reading some of what we are reading now on page 590, I may just chuck the book. Without careful study, application, insights and experiences that make way for the mind to accept an idea like this, the mind is not ready. Remember it's always an interpretation. The deeper the insights go and the more you become aware of the deeper ideas expressed in the Course, an early statement like that is just seen for what it is – a stepping stone. I see it as one of those lower rungs or one of those stepping stones along the way. There are a lot of things that can be interpreted as discouraging. For example, there is a statement in the Teacher's Manual about stages of the development of trust, and some would say, "Well, the manual is at the very end, so it should be pretty far along."

And on page 11 of the Teacher's Manual it says, "And now he must attain a state that may remain impossible to reach for a long, long time." People read that and this other one about it taking millions of years and conclude that this is going to be a long, drawn-out process. But there are other parts in the Course that clearly point out that it can be an instant. It cannot be accepted in any other time but now!

Friend 1: What appears as discouraging certainly depends on where you are coming from. I'm thinking of the woman who was discouraged reading the idea that it takes only an instant because she felt, if it took only an instant, why hadn't she already experienced that instant?

David: It's based on the interpretation. The ego can go either way and seem to make it discouraging for the mind: that it's going to take a long time or just an instant and I can't do it. But when you start to get clarity on the dreamer of the dream and on the urgency that we have been talking about, the need to make an interpretation on that dissolves.

Friend 1: Just let it go. Use it as long as it's helpful and then let it go.

David: It is gone. It's not even an active thing like, "Okay, thank you. You've served me well, I kiss you goodbye." At a certain point in the insight, in the Aha...! the past is gone, is dissolved.

> Yet time is but another phase of what does nothing. It works hand in hand with all the other attributes with which you seek to keep concealed the truth about yourself. T-28.I.6

"All the other attributes," you could throw the whole kit and caboodle in with that: time, space, abilities, skills, personhood, size, degrees, levels, all those are "the other attributes with which you seek to keep concealed the truth about yourself." The truth about our Self is completely abstract. There are no levels in the truth about our Self, no intervals, no degrees.

> Time neither takes away nor can restore. And yet you make strange use of it, as if the past had caused the present, which is but a consequence in which no change can be made possible because its cause has gone. T-28.I.6

This is a big sentence because it takes the whole underpinnings of the world away. It's the strange use you give time, the idea that the past caused the present, that needs to be let go of. And that last part of the sentence, "which is but a consequence in which no change can be made possible because its cause has gone" is how the ego skips over the present. If the past caused the present, then the present is just an effect. There is no way to change it. You are sunk; you are determined. The ego says, just skip over the present because...

Friend 1: There's nothing you can do about it.

David: There's absolutely nothing you can do, the ego says, because the past caused the present.

Friend 1: I never saw it that way before.

David: So you can see why linear time has to collapse; the mind has to let go of the belief in it because, other than that, we are back to determinism. For example, in psychological terms, you are a product of your environment or you are a product of your past conditioning.

Yet change must have a cause that will endure, or else it will not last. No change can be made in the present if its cause is past. Only the past is held in memory as you make use of it, and so it is a way to hold the past against the now. T-28.I.6

So if we go back to our computer analogy, the deceived mind's use of memory is to call up certain programs. The deceived mind always goes back to the giant vault of the past and continues to ask for memories out of that. Instead it needs to call forth the memory of the Present, the Holy Instant or of God.

Remember nothing that you taught yourself, for you were badly taught. And who would keep a senseless lesson in his mind, when he can learn and can preserve a better one? When ancient memories of hate appear, remember that their cause is gone. And so you cannot understand what they are for. T-28.I.7

This fits in with lessons such as "Nothing I see means anything" and "I do not know what anything is for." Those lessons are important because the mind has to accept those ideas in relation to what the body's eyes seem to be seeing and hearing. That's where disorientation can come in. Life has been constructed as sequential daily life, and Jesus is saying that as "ancient memories of hate appear," in whatever form, remember that their cause is gone so you cannot understand what they are for. That means don't try to figure it out. Don't try to rationalize it or break it apart. You cannot understand what they are for. Stop trying. And it fits in with you still think you know. *You cannot understand what they are for.* So now we are moving to the idea of substituting a new purpose, a new cause.

Let not the cause that you would give them now be what it was that made them what they were, or seemed to be. Be glad that it is gone, for this is what you would be pardoned from. And see, instead, the new effects of cause accepted now, with consequences here. They will surprise you with their loveliness. The ancient new ideas they bring will be the happy consequences of a Cause so ancient that it far exceeds the span of memory which your perception sees. T-28.I.7

Ideas that are not of God cannot be shared in reality. It is the attempt to share these concepts and ideas that seems to make the world have objective reality. The mind not only makes up a dream in which the dream figures seem to come along and reinforce the reality of the world, the mind gives a specific name to each dream figure and the dream figure answers to the name. That is pretty convincing, that there is a separate reality apart from my mind, not seeing that my mind is doing the asking and the answering, so to speak, and it's all a delusion. I see so-and-so and they say hi. They answer to that name. So that is why all the senses and everything that comes through the senses just witness to the reality of the world. It seems to be that there are two people or two minds agreeing upon some fictitious concept and it seems to have a reality because of that.

Part 3 – The World is Causeless

Our next quote jumps to Chapter 26:

> Cause and effect are one, not separate. God wills you learn what always has been true: That He created you as part of Him, and this must still be true because ideas leave not their source. Such is creation's law; that each idea the mind conceives but adds to its abundance, never takes away. This is as true of what is idly wished as what is truly willed, because the mind can wish to be deceived, but cannot make it be what it is not. And to believe ideas can leave their source is to invite illusions to be true, without success. For never will success be possible in trying to deceive the Son of God. T-26.VII.13

Ideas leave not their source means that the world has not left the mind of the thinker. We are speaking of the wrong mind. But before the mind can make a clear discernment between the right mind and the wrong mind, between forgiveness and illusions, it has to see the false as false; only then can the false disappear. So to skip the steps of really looking at the ordering of thoughts or the subtle means of judgments or of making error real and try to hop over that to "I am the holy Son of God," is like trying to go from somewhere in the middle of the alphabet to z. It is important to have tremendous clarity of what is false, to see the false as false.

Friend 1: So, what transpires to make the transfer from seeing the false as false to seeing that it is nothing, that it doesn't exist at all?

David: Those are the same, those things you just said. What I was referring to is the idea in the Course that says you'll reach the real world and you'll barely have time to enjoy it. To say that God takes the final step is still a metaphor, but the step that He takes is creation. The first and only step that God takes is creation of His Son. And so the final step in terms of the Course is really the first step.

Friend 1: It's a return to awareness of what's always been the case.

David: Yes. It's really not a step at all in the sense of a sequence at the very end.

> The miracle is possible when cause and consequence are brought together, not kept separate. The healing of effect without the cause can merely shift effects to other forms. And this is not release. T-26.VII.14

This is another way of talking about magic. All attempts at magic try to shift effects to other forms or to heal effects without a cause – to heal something in the world, some consequence, situation, some event that seems not right, by shifting around the forms. Or, as Krishnamurti phrases it, "to juggle the contents of consciousness." This is what the shifting of forms is. You've got all these concepts and if you keep trying to juggle the concepts, hoping that you will arrive at the perfect combination, then you are deluded, because you'll never have a transformation of mind as long as you just shift and juggle the concepts. There has to be an entirely different way of looking at consciousness from an entirely different point of view – from the miracle or above the battlefield – before the shift is a meaningful shift.

> God's Son could never be content with less than full salvation and escape from guilt. For otherwise he still demands that he must make some sacrifice, and thus denies that everything is his, unlimited by loss of any kind. T-26.VII.14

Here comes that word "sacrifice." Jesus shares that sacrifice has no meaning in Heaven, but while you believe you are in the world he defines sacrifice as the giving up what you want. And as long as the mind sees some glimmer, even some small value in anything in the world, then it will perceive giving up the world as sacrifice. Even a tiny thing that still is held onto reinforces the concept of sacrifice. If there is even a little bit of ordering, if there is something in the corral that the mind doesn't want to willingly expose to the light, then it denies that everything is His.

> A tiny sacrifice is just the same in its effects as is the whole idea of sacrifice. If loss in any form is possible, then is God's Son made incomplete and not himself. Nor will he know himself, nor recognize his will. He has forsworn his Father and himself, and made Them both his enemies in hate. T-26.VII.14

This is a different way of coming at the theme of "You will learn this Course entirely or not at all." That kind of idea can be perceived as threatening through the ego lens. But I think it's a relief to embrace that idea, even though initially you want to avoid it. Avoidance is part of thinking it is impossible to transcend the ego entirely. Non-compromise dispels that kind of notion. The beginning of the paragraph contains the central idea we've been talking about. "The miracle is possible when cause and consequence are brought together, not kept separate." That precisely eliminates the past and the future because the past and the future are attempts to keep cause and consequence apart. Separation is where linear time came in.

Friend 1: In the margin I've got a reminder to myself of why I want to see cause and effect clearly. Simply that if I can maintain peace of mind in every seeming situation in the world, that is how my mind comes to see that the world has no effects and what has no effects must have no cause. And that is the undoing of the ego. Sometimes I get caught up in trying to understand the concepts and I forget why this makes any difference, how it really relates to anything.

David: I think too that this idea: "The miracle is possible when cause and consequence are brought together and not kept separate," relates to that section in the text called The Immediacy of Salvation where Jesus says, "Why should the good appear in evil's form?" T-26.VIII.7 Why are you thinking that God would place salvation in the future? When the mind believes that salvation is in the future, it is separating cause and consequence. It is saying that there was a past, a real past. There is a future yet to come, it is a real future. It is denying that there is cause for freedom now. It is still the wanting to hold onto the gap of time and to project correction into the future. When the mind does that it can't help but feel that it will suffer fear from now until the time when the correction is accepted. It is simply projecting fear to time and it is saying that old thing about time healing all wounds. Well, right now is a new purpose for time that heals all wounds. It's not time itself. Linear time has never healed anything. Linear time is part of the problem, not the solution.

Friend 1: That's one of those old sayings that's backwards isn't it?

David: It could be reinterpreted though. Instead of saying that time heals all wounds, you could say that the correct use of time, the Holy Spirit's purpose for time, heals all wounds because his purpose is to make time unnecessary. The ego's purpose for time is its purpose for everything – death – it maintains the belief that separation from God is real, has occurred, and will be punished. So it is interesting to come at cause and consequence from the sense of time to see that everything points to: "Now is the point of release." T-13.IV.5.

The next section is The "Hero" of the Dream, in Chapter 27.

> The body's serial adventures, from the time of birth to dying are the theme of every dream the world has ever had. The "hero" of this dream will never change, nor will its purpose. Though the dream itself takes many forms, and seems to show a great variety of places and events wherein its "hero" finds itself, the dream has but one purpose, taught in many ways. This single lesson does it try to teach again, and still again, and yet once more; that it is cause and not effect. And you are its effect, and cannot be its cause. T-27.VIII.3

David: "This single lesson does it try to teach," is the ego. The ego is a lesson in the mind and the Holy Spirit is a lesson in the mind and the mind that is trying to learn two lessons is very confused. The lessons don't go together. They are an either/or proposition. What the ego is teaching is that the world is the cause and not effect and that you are its effect and cannot be its cause. In the world's eyes the mind is clearly identified with the body or the hero of the dream. Bodies are born from other bodies. From the ego's perspective you are clearly the effect of this world.

If you want to take it back to theories of evolution, there having to be the right conditions for that spark of life to arise from the dust and the single cell organism evolving to higher and higher forms of life. What's still behind those theories is that you had your beginning in form. Even the attempts to bring God into it by making man and woman out of clay reinforce the notion of the body being an effect of the world. To say that God had *anything* to do with making form, is trying to bring God into form. The whole dream analogy is about the dream seeming to be the cause and you being its effect.

Thus are you not the dreamer, but the dream. And so you wander idly in and out of places and events that it contrives. That this is all the body does is true, for it is but a figure in a dream. But who reacts to figures in a dream unless he sees them as if they were real? T-27.VIII.4

It is a vast turnaround from thinking that I'm just this tiny person in a vast world and there are all these other people, personality traits and languages to realizing they are all part of the one dream that is the projection from my own mind.

The instant that he sees them as they are they have no more effects on him, because he understands he gave them their effects by causing them and making them seem real. T-27.VIII.4

There is that "gave" again. Not give but gave. The past tense is always important in these sentences because it constantly puts the ego and the whole world that it seemed to bring about into the past tense.

How willing are you to escape effects of all the dreams the world has ever had? Is it your wish to let no dream appear to be the cause of what it is you do? T-27.VIII.5

There we are with fear of consequences. If you let go of all fear of consequences, then you can truly be in the miracle and whatever you seem to do or say is literally automatic, coming from right-mindedness.

Then let us merely look upon the dream's beginning, for the part you see is but the second part, whose cause lies in the first." T-27.VIII.5

This is setting the stage for when he gets into Self-Concept versus Self T-31.V and he talks about the part that you gave away. Now we are getting into the two tiers of the self-concept. The first part is the belief that I have separated from God. The second part is the dreaming of the world, made as a cover you would never look below. The dreaming of the world is the part that has been given away, projected and forgotten. The mind forgets it's a mind and then believes it's on the screen.

"No one asleep and dreaming in the world remembers his attack upon himself." T-27.VIII.5 This is the belief in separation.

> No one believes there really was a time when he knew nothing of a body, and could never have conceived this world as real. He would have seen at once that these ideas are one illusion, too ridiculous for anything but to be laughed away. How serious they now appear to be! And no one can remember when they would have met with laughter and with disbelief. We can remember this, if we but look directly at their cause. And we will see the grounds for laughter, not a cause for fear. T-27.VIII.5

The ego always pays extreme attention to the screen and do not go within and look at your mind. Or if we use the Wizard of Oz analogy, when they finally get to Oz, to the room where they see this giant thing on the screen, a huge face with a loud voice, Toto pulls the curtain in the projection room, and the wizard says "Pay no attention to the man behind the curtain!" [laughing] Pay no attention to the thought in the mind, to the true cause, stay focused on the horrifying picture that you see on the screen so you will tremble before it. That movie has many good metaphors in it. No wonder people love it even if they don't know why; because it's a metaphor for their release. There's no place like Home. You've always had the power to go Home.

> Let us return the dream he gave away unto the dreamer, who perceives the dream as separate from himself and done to him. Into eternity, where all is one, there crept a tiny, mad idea, at which the Son of God remembered not to laugh. In his forgetting did the thought become a serious idea, and possible of both accomplishment and real effects. T-27.VIII.6

"In his forgetting" is where the accomplishment and real effects seem to occur.

> Together, we can laugh them both away, and understand that time cannot intrude upon eternity. It is a joke to think that time can come to circumvent eternity, which means there is no time. T-27.VIII.6 A timelessness in which is time made real; a part of God that can attack itself; a separate brother as an enemy; a mind within a body all are forms of circularity whose ending starts at its beginning, ending at its cause. The world you see depicts exactly what you thought you did. T-27.VIII.7

The mind believes that it is guilty, that it separated from God, and the world demonstrates to it that separation is real, that guilt is real.

> Except that now you think that what you did is being done to you. The guilt for what you thought is being placed outside yourself, and on a guilty world that dreams your dreams and thinks your thoughts instead of you. T-27. VIII.7

This is getting down to day to day living versus abstract purpose and seeing that we can't hold onto both at once, that it really is an either/or kind of thing. The fear is in the belief that to give up my conception of day to day life is going to be some kind of a loss. The status quo is familiar, comfortable, not always the best, but still it's not so bad.

Friend 1: At least I have a handle on it.

David: A seeming handle in the way that things are constructed and the way things work.

Friend 2: Even if I said I wanted to give it up, it seems impossible. I can imagine coming to a place where I say I am ready to give it up, but what I can't imagine is how that would be, how that would look.

Friend 1: There is no point of reference.

David: It needs to be a free floating. For example, I am asked, "Where do you live?" I say, "I live in my mind." It is a real detachment. There is no box for that. It doesn't fit in any of the boxes. The follow up question is usually, "Where do you receive your mail?' or something like that – "let's nail this down to some kind of a box." It is very different to be in a place of not conceiving of yourself as living in a particular place.

Friend 1: To even come to thinking of yourself as mind would have to mean that there is a transfer of the whole cause and effect idea. It seems like that's how the mind would come to recognize itself as what it is, by recognizing that the cause and effect is the opposite of what it once thought it was.

David: Yes. When thoughts come to mind like "This is interesting now but what about next week? How will things be then?" they are just more future thoughts in linear time.

I think of the lesson, "I place my future in the hands of God." When you do that, you give over your mind. When you are giving over the future, you are giving over the past as well.

It says in Lesson 135, it's not planning on your own but "listening to wisdom that is not its own." W-135.11. "If there are plans to make, you will be told of them." W-135.23. Even when those Guided things seem to take shape it is swept into the same category as the script is written. It is not like our gatherings are apart from anything else that seems to happen in the world of form. There is no breaking it up into free time and work time. Our metaphor of ebb and flow is still a metaphor because the whole point is to have sameness. It just takes one decision, one instant right now to do that. It is not like it must be projected out; it is just a present decision, a present intention.

Friend 1: That's the only thing that can make it all the same.

David: Let's bring it back to practicalities. If you have thoughts like "I'm off somewhere else" or "How will this work with my family and my kids?" take a look at those thoughts as they come up. You start with your concerns – this is my concern, this is my thought – not with the abstract dreamer of the dream.

> The secret of salvation is but this: That you are doing this unto yourself. No matter what the form of the attack, this still is true. Whoever takes the role of enemy and of attacker, still is this the truth. Whatever seems to be the cause of any pain and suffering you feel, this is still true. For you could not react at all to figures in a dream you knew that you were dreaming. Let them be as hateful and as vicious as they may, they could have no effect on you unless you failed to recognize it is your dream. T-27.VIII.10

David: That's all you need. That's it. That's the summary.

> This single lesson learned will set you free from suffering, whatever form it takes. The Holy Spirit will repeat this one inclusive lesson of deliverance until it has been learned, regardless of the form of suffering that brings you pain. Whatever hurt you bring to Him He will make answer with this very simple truth. For this one answer takes away the cause of every form of sorrow and of pain. The form affects His answer not at all, for He would teach you but the single cause of all of them, no matter what their form. And you will understand that miracles reflect the simple statement, "I have done this thing, and it is this I would undo." T-27.VIII.11

> Bring, then, all forms of suffering to Him Who knows that every one is like the rest. He sees no differences where none exists, and He will teach you how each one is caused. None has a different cause from all the rest, and all of them are easily undone by but a single lesson truly learned. T-27.VIII.12

He's speaking of the Atonement.

> Salvation is a secret you have kept but from yourself. The universe proclaims it so. Yet to its witnesses you pay no heed at all. For they attest the thing you do not want to know. They seem to keep it secret from you. Yet you need but learn you chose but not to listen, not to see." T-27. VIII.12

So if we consider, "Yet to its witnesses you pay no heed at all." I sometimes say that every brother you meet is a witness, but I am not speaking in terms of form because it has nothing to do with bodies. In fact, as long as you see bodies, you can't see the lesson because you can't see the face of Christ and see bodies. You could extend this to situations as well. In the Workbook Jesus says "You could, in fact, gain vision from just that table." W-28.5 He means that forgiveness involves withdrawing all the meaning or interpretation from the past completely and letting the Word of God be written upon it; or to let the purpose of the Holy Spirit be exchanged for the ego's purpose. That is the witness that proclaims that you are the dreamer of the dream and that you are but doing this to yourself.

> How differently will you perceive the world when this is recognized! When you forgive the world your guilt, you will be free of it. Its innocence does not demand your guilt, nor does your guiltlessness rest on its sins. This is the obvious; a secret kept from no one but yourself. And it is this that has maintained you separate from the world, and kept your brother separate from you. T-27.VIII.13

David: There's the subject/object split.

> Now need you but to learn that both of you are innocent or guilty. The one thing that is impossible is that you be unlike each other; that they both be true. This is the only secret yet to learn. And it will be no secret you are healed. T-27.VIII.13

It is obvious in that sense, why any grievance, even a little tiny grievance, is an attack upon God's plan for salvation. Because a grievance is saying that there is still someone, some thing that is different than it should be, that it's wrong, that it's guilty and apart from yourself. This healing statement is just saying that this is impossible.

Friend 1: There is no "apart from myself."

David: Right. There is no "apart from myself," and the mind that believes that there are others believes that one could be guilty and one could be innocent, that you are guilty and I am innocent or that I am guilty and you are innocent. It doesn't matter which way you go. The secret yet to learn is that they must be the *same*. I remember this past winter when we were teaching a class and one fellow was talking about being sick and I said, "You can't be sick apart from me. Either we are both sick or we are both healed."

Friend 1: That part about the secret of salvation and You are doing this unto yourself... is really what we were talking about before in terms of the child abuse issue. But how can you say that the mind brings witness to itself when you are talking about a two-week-old baby.

David: It would be making an exception saying guilt is seen as justified because there has been a real abuse that has taken place, totally apart from the will of that child. Thinking that the mind is somehow related to the body is all part of level confusion. Bill Thetford went through the same kind of thing when he had difficulties going to conferences or rehab conventions where there were broken bodies, handicaps, and disabilities all over the place, and it was a reinforcer or a reminder in the belief of the frailty of the belief in life in the body.

Friend 1: And that's why he was having so much trouble with it?

David: Yes, and what Jesus says is that you have some level confusion going on. Level confusion is making an exception. You are confusing the brain with the mind. The mind is invulnerable. Even the level of "I can be hurt only by my thoughts" is just a description of the wrong mind. But the release is that I don't have to choose the wrong mind. I am not the wrong mind. My mind holds only what I think with God. That is a description of the right mind. That is what we are to embrace. That's the Correction.

Friend 1: Only my loving thoughts are true.

> The ancient new ideas they bring will be the happy consequences of a cause so ancient that it far exceeds the span of memory which your perception sees." T-28.I.7

David: Beneath the span of memory which the deceived mind's perception sees is the memory of the Present, the memory of God. So the present isn't in between the past and the future, the present is before time was. That is beyond what the wrong mind can see. The wrong mind cannot perceive the present. Now is back farther, beyond time. And when he says ancient new ideas, he is talking about the real thoughts in the mind that are buried beneath the attack thoughts. And a lot of times someone will say, "Give me an example of a real thought" and a good one you can throw out is "I am as God created me." There is not a hint of perception to that idea. That's an ancient new thought buried in the mind that brings salvation with it because it is not perceptual. Is that the only one? No. "I am spirit." If you look in the Workbook you can find them. "My mind holds only what I think with God," has no hint of perception. There are the other ones that say, "I am determined to see" or "What I see is a form of vengeance," that are clearly pointing to the way the mind seems to see now. Those are clearing away concepts, making ready for the real thoughts which are totally abstract.

Now we see him shift from lower case "c" to capital "C." "This is the Cause the Holy Spirit has remembered for you, when you would forget." T-28.I.8 So now God is coming into the discussion:

> It is not past because He let It not be unremembered.

It has never changed, because there never was a time in which He did not keep It safely in your mind. Its consequences will indeed seem new, because you thought that you remembered not their Cause. Yet was It never absent from your mind, for it was not your Father's Will that He be unremembered by His Son. T-28.I.8

That Cause is literally the memory of God. "It was not your Father's Will that He be unremembered by His Son...what you remembered never was..." So here He's speaking to the ego self. This can be confusing at times for people when they are reading the Course because they'll say, "Well, when he says you are the Holy Son of God himself, he seems to be speaking of a different you than when he says what you remembered never was."

It came from causelessness which you confused with cause. It can deserve but laughter, when you learn you have remembered consequences that were causeless and could never be effects. T-28.I.9

[Laughing] There we have it! The laughter...

The miracle reminds you of a Cause forever present, perfectly untouched by time and interference. Never changed from what It is. And you are Its Effect, as changeless and as perfect as Itself. T-28.I.9

So we're back to the idea that real Cause and the only Cause is God. Now he's shifting to "and you are His Effect"; he is not speaking to the ego now. He is speaking to the Son of God.

Friend 1: The true You.

Its memory does not lie in the past, nor waits the future. It is not revealed in miracles. They but remind you that It has not gone. When you forgive It for your sins, It will no longer be denied. T-28.I.9

"It is not revealed in miracles"… that's the difference between revelation and miracles. Miracles are time collapses that are the means that prepare the mind for revelation. But miracles are not revealing or revelatory in the sense that they are still perceptual. And revelation is not a perceptual experience. The mind, when it is in a revelatory experience, absolutely has no memory of fear.

As we come together with our intention we are able to transfer the training to all the seeming separate aspects of the deceived mind's life including pap smears, food, sex and so on. In reality there is no separation between all those things because there's that golden cord or the necklace that ties them all together. But to the mind that believes that they are separate aspects that have a true experience and existence in and of themselves, then the mind needs miracles just to remind it that the false is false.

> You who have sought to lay a judgment on your own Creator cannot understand it is not He Who laid a judgment on His Son. You would deny Him His effects, yet have they never been denied. There was no time in which His Son could be condemned for what was causeless and against His Will. T-28.I.10

People will raise this question: "How could I have done this?" or "Why do I keep doing this?," and that is just the ego speaking. That is the ego that has the question. It is the ego that is frustrated and seeming to beat itself up. All those statements are just coming from the wrong mind. They are statements of a mind that is deceived that is still trying to deny the fact of Christ. "You would deny Him His effects, yet have they never been denied." If you really follow where this is going, you see that this world is a hallucination. And to really see it as a hallucination you must simultaneously, spontaneously spring into Reality. To just see the world in that way, as a hallucination, and not think of it as a good metaphor, but just to see it for what it was, certainly with that kind of an experience, the attempting to do anything on one's own vanishes, because it seems to be impossible. It is seen that I cannot act on my own, for that was not me.

"What your remembering would witness to is but the fear of God."
T-28.I.10 He is speaking more to the deceived mind here.

> He has not done the thing you fear. No more have you.
> And so your innocence has not been lost. You need no
> healing to be healed. T-28.I.10

That seems to fly against some of the other things, that you're
function is healing and so on, but now we are getting down to the
nitty gritty.

Friend 1: But nothing ever occurred that calls for healing, is the
essence of this.

David: Right, it's the very basis for the metaphysics. What you
thought you did has not occurred. You need no healing to be
healed.

Friend 2: The impossible never happened. [Pause] Something else
came to my mind as you were talking, I had this memory of a
time when I was in college and I had taken some drug and I had
hallucinated and it was so scary to me. I hated it and I thought, that's
the fear because things were not as I expected them. Walls moved
and distances were altered. Something looked real close, then when
I walked towards it, it would be far away. So my perception that I
knew or thought I knew was all distorted.

It was very scary to me. And I can remember having this feeling
of being out of control and I just wanting to go somewhere and
hide until it went away. I thought, "I can't be with people. I can't do
anything. I can't function." All those feelings came back to me just
now and Wow! All those feelings are still there in this hallucination.
It only makes sense that you would feel that way when your
perception is distorted, when nothing is as it appears, when nothing
is as it is supposed to be. I don't even know who I am or how I
relate to any of this; just the tremendous fear that is there.

David: Kind of like an extreme version of the seemingly minor upsets when things don't go the way you think they should. And really what we have to see is, that is the way that the world is constructed.

Friend 2: Yes, and I thought "I'm living with that fear everyday!" But I am just so used to it, that I am not even aware of it anymore. I have just put it aside or covered it up so well that I don't even know it is there.

David: The mind chose the hallucination of the world to cover over what it is really afraid of. And as we have gotten into it you have had some kind of a fear come up. You start to project fear into the future or feel drawn to other things. Or you have gotten into the defense of "Hey I don't have it so bad" and that's where the mind will try to cling to this covering-over that it has done, saying that I've got it good, I shouldn't complain or I should be able to have it both ways. I should be able to hang onto this and that, when there is a real fear of going into the Light, of just letting go of everything else *but* that Purpose. That's what the real fear is. The fear of the hallucination is just the cover for the big one: the fear of Love.

Friend 2: So that gives me some sense of what kind of fear we're talking about. It's tremendous. It's terror, but I guess I'd never really felt that or imagined what that really is about and, wow, when I get a glimpse of it...

David: And loss of control. You said you also felt a tremendous loss of control.

Friend 2: Yes, I remember that feeling very strongly. I remember thinking that I never want to do this again because I do not like this feeling. I knew people who thought it was really cool to hallucinate, but not me. This is not for me.

David: This is one side of it. Your self-concept has been focused toward order and control. The flip side of it would be, my life is too in control. We saw that in something we were watching to lose control and let go. In that sense the interpretation of hallucinogens is: I'm letting go of my inhibitions and control. So, really it's just two sides of the defense. And the control issue is the authority problem, believing that I am who I think I am in this world; that I have constructed a world and a self, and I am me. I am unique... I have my likes and dislikes. I have my opinions and conclusions and that's the way I want it to stay. I want a peaceful me, a peaceful person. I want to retain something.

Friend 1: Peace on these terms.

David: Right, on my own terms. And it's impossible. That's the joy I see in what we've been doing because it is starting to come to see the absolute absurdity and impossibility of control. Trying to bring the truth to the illusion, or trying to mix Spirit and time and space and matter, as if they can be reconciled or mixed, like oil and water, stirring and stirring – they do not go together. If it seems extreme, it is extreme. All attempts to reconcile the two are futile.

> In quietness, see in the miracle a lesson in allowing Cause to have Its Own effects, and doing nothing that would interfere." T-28.I.10

This is another support for that idea, "I need do nothing." It is explained right there in that sentence. That's the metaphysics behind I need do nothing.

> ... he does not believe that he is Love's Effect, and must be cause because of what he is. The Cause of healing is the only Cause of everything. It has but one Effect. And in that recognition, causelessness is given no effects and none is seen. A mind within a body and a world of other bodies, each with separate minds, are your "creations," you the "other" mind, creating with effects unlike yourself. And as their "father," you must be like them. T-28.II.3

The whole illusion of other minds and other bodies that seems to be causative and the whole world of reversed cause and effect seems to be set in motion just from the belief that you can create yourself, that you are a person with a separate mind. There are so many different rationalizations, so many attempts to deny that I am the Son of God and I am created by my Father, "I'm only human" is a common one. That seems to be soothing. But when you really look at the content beneath it, it is an attack thought. There is nothing soothing about being who you are not.

Friend 1: There is also nothing realistic about being who you are not.

David: That's another thing that comes in a lot: let's be realistic let's be practical. But to be practical in those terms, you're back to: "Am I this instant denying the truth or will I choose to accept it?" The ego schemes get unveiled.

> Nothing at all has happened but that you have put yourself to sleep, and dreamed a dream in which you were an alien to yourself, and but a part of someone else's dream. T-28.II.4

So if I think I try to do the Course the best I can but I can only go so far at work. I can only go so far in my family or whatever the rationalization, underneath it is "I am dreaming a dream and I am alien to myself, but I am part of someone else's dream." The people-pleasing that comes in about what someone else will think is basically just a restatement of this sentence: that I am part of someone else's dream. The ego is saying that I can't just wake up. There are other people to be dealt with. The fear of letting someone down is tied in with believing that I am part of someone else's dream. Once you get clear that you are the dreamer of the dream you don't have to constantly compromise to the dream figures because you are not in their dream. Remind yourself: "This is my dream."

> The miracle does not awaken you, but merely shows you who the dreamer is. It teaches you there is a choice of dreams while you are still asleep, depending on the purpose of your dreaming. Do you wish for dreams of healing, or for dreams of death? A dream is like a memory in that it

pictures what you wanted shown to you. T-28.II.4

An empty storehouse, with an open door, holds all your shreds of memories and dreams. Yet if you are the dreamer, you perceive this much at least: That you have caused the dream and can accept another dream as well. But for this change in content of the dream, it must be realized that it is you who dreamed the dreaming that you do not like. T-28.II.5

We are back to reversing cause and effect, bringing causation back to the mind. Once again, the tense is so important: "...it must be realized that it is you who dreamed the dream." This realization is definitely a step, it is not reaching the level of "My mind holds only what I think with God" but it is the step that comes before that idea. I have to accept my responsibility for it, but I don't have to feel guilty for it because it is past tense. And I am in the present. There is a present cause that I can give for the dream. When we say present cause we are not talking about the capital C Cause, Which dispels the dream entirely, but the Holy Spirit's purpose (cause) is a reflection of the present. There is no purpose in Heaven (Abstraction), so it's not a component of Heaven. But take the first things first.

It is but an effect that *you* have caused, and you would not be cause of this effect. In dreams of murder and attack are you the victim in a dying body slain. But in forgiving dreams is no one asked to be the victim and the sufferer. These are the happy dreams the miracle exchanges for your own. It does not ask you make another; only that you see you made the one you would exchange for this. T-28.II.5

That sentence, "in forgiving dreams is no one asked to be the victim and the sufferer" reminds me of the line, "Those who see themselves as whole make no demands." W-37.2. That is a phenomenal idea because in this world the mind can't even imagine what that would be like, because all of it's relationships involve reciprocity. "Make no demands." You could say that the Holy Spirit reminds, the Holy Spirit suggests... but never commands or demands. You can see what a wonderful release that would be and how you would have to give up all conceptions of the world as you think you know it. All business relationships, all relationships according to roles that are predetermined have to be abandoned because as long as you have predetermined roles, functions, duties and obligations you are still in an ego reciprocity set up. And Jesus gives us the model for that. Since forgiveness was his only function, he did not claim to be the king of the Jews or hold any kind of earthly position. He did not require anything. He made suggestions and he said things like, "Follow me," which is a pretty strong suggestion, but without a sense of commanding or demanding.

Friend 1: There wasn't any sense of do this or else.

David: Right. No threat involved.

Friend 2: And no implied expectations. I was thinking of the terms that might be used... suggest or invite, but as soon as I put an expectation on it, then that is the demand. Because I can suggest something to you, but if I have an expectation that you are going to follow my suggestion, that is where the demand lies.

David: If there's an implied expectation in your own mind, then that is still a demand. The guru trap can be a temptation in the spiritual path as well. If there is an ego temptation to have some type of control, even subtly, over what goes on, that is the way the ego wants to raise itself up by still having a personal identity, still wanting to give some direction to the students. It can be a very subtle thing. And once again the guru trap is just another form of ego distraction. It cannot exist apart from one's own mind, but it takes very careful learning and careful watching to stay beyond that because of the temptation. The ego still wants to maintain some type of control.

> This world is causeless, as is every dream that anyone has dreamed within the world. No plans are possible, and no design exists that could be found and understood. T-28.II.6

There is an implication in the second sentence. We are told that all of the pursuits and the plans deemed necessary in this world don't make any sense.

> What else could be expected from a thing that has no cause? Yet if it has no cause, it has no purpose. You may cause a dream, but never will you give it real effects. For that would change its cause, and it is this you cannot do. The dreamer of a dream is not awake, but does not know he sleeps. He sees illusions of himself as sick or well, depressed or happy, but without a stable cause with guaranteed effects. T-28.II.6

So that is coming back to "Without a cause there can be no effects," and "The cause a cause is *made* by its effects." T-28.II.1 It's saying that the world is causeless so you can't try to give reality to the effects. You can make illusions, but you can't make real effects. All of the sciences and the attempts to understand the world and how it works presume a world that has real parts in it and that has real interactions, real cause and effect relationships between those parts. And all of them deny the spiritual fact that Now is the only time there is. That is where true religious experience – inner peace, transcends science, all the disciplines, all the theories, all the schools of thought.

When I was going through all of my years of searching I asked myself what I was to be? This was something I pondered even in high school when I looked into the different menus of the world, the professions and vocations. From aptitude tests and career planning they were able to generate a large number. I looked up and down the computer printout, and there was nothing there for me. I felt out of place. I felt awkward and weird, like everyone else has something leap off the paper for them, but not me. I believed I had to do something to make a living, even though I saw nothing attractive to do. When I went on to study engineering my heart wasn't in it.

Friend 1: I remember that feeling. After I had recognized teaching wasn't it and I was working in social work, I remember taking a career direction test, and it indicated a number of different things. I looked at them all and thought, "Yuck. Maybe I can do them, but I don't want to."

David: I had a sense, too, that I could do any number of the things that I saw on the printout, but my heart wasn't in it and after ten years of college it was the same thing. I had pursued and gone into education very deeply. By then I had investigated a lot of disciplines and their schools of thought. I had actually dabbled in and tried several of them out. But by then there was a sense of something internal Calling me and Guiding me. I didn't know what it was or where it was going. It was like a mission. I had read some of Maslow's ideas about self-actualizing people, and he said they had a strong sense of mission, purpose or meaning for life. I related to that but didn't know what it was.

Friend 2: So how does this relate?

David: Well, when I read "This world is causeless, as is every dream that anyone has dreamed within the world. No plans are possible, and no design exists that could be found and understood," I begin to understand the difficulty of working with the Course and trying to fit it in – for example, taking metaphysics into corporate America or trying to shape Course principles into a business. I ran into a lot of that in the Association of Humanistic Psychology, where they were attempting to take ideas like that into various structures. Many of the conferences would have those aims and directions. What we are seeing as we get into the depth of the Course is that there is no reconciliation between Spirit and the time/space/matter continuum, which would include daily life as it is experienced and concepts including careers, disciplines and institutions. "No plans are possible, and no design exists that could be found and understood."

Friend 1: You can't bring truth to the illusion.

Part 4 – Letting Go of False Beliefs

David: This world is a hallucination. There seem to be healthy well adjusted people walking around on this planet and there seem to be others that are so psychotic and insane they are locked up. Anyone who appears to walk this world holding beliefs of separation in their mind is literally psychotic. There has been a break with reality in the sense that the mind is dreaming a world and hallucinating and thinking it sees meaning and life in this world. This world was made as a denial of life. The only life is the Light deep down within the mind. In Lesson 132 Jesus literally says, "There is no world."

"I loose the world from all I thought it was." W-132 These ideas are the underpinnings for that experience. The question comes up about the phrase from the Bible, to be in the world and not of it. We have to look at that idea of being in the world. I have also heard it said that I have a feeling that if I keep following this that I am not going to be functional in the world. Surely one will not function the way one functioned in the past. It is a complete transformation where one isn't a separate being perceived as functioning in the world. It will be a sense of totally letting go and giving no thought to behavior. It will be an out-picturing of holding to the intention that peace comes from being aligned with the Holy Spirit. Being in that Purpose or intention is everything. And the ego will immediately jump in and say, "How will that look?" It is irrelevant in the ultimate sense how it will look. How it will look to whom? If there is no world outside my mind and there is no person outside my mind – I have constructed them all – then that question dissolves. Another way of looking at it, aside from a material standpoint, is Jesus saying, "I am determined to see. I am determined to see things differently. Above all else I want to see things differently." That seeing that he is talking about, that vision that he is leading the mind to, is not seeing in the sense of the physical eyes. Reversing cause and effect is like turning an upside down world right-side up.

> The miracle establishes you dream a dream, and that its content is not true. This is a crucial step in dealing with

illusions. No one is afraid of them when he perceives he made them up. The fear was held in place because he did not see that he was author of the dream, and not a figure in the dream. T-28.II.7

That gets to our point: it can't be both. You can't be author of the dream as well as a figure in the dream. All fear is held in place by believing and perceiving one's self a figure in the dream. It is like saying, "I don't want to look at the fear inside. I don't want to look at the cause of the whole dream; I have already accepted that there is a real cause for the dream and that I am a figure in it." So the fear can't be released because the fear is held in place; it remains covered over in the mind and unconscious.

He gives himself the consequences that he dreams he gave his brother. And it is but this the dream has put together and has offered him, to show him that his wishes have been done. Thus does he fear his own attack, but sees it at another's hands. As victim, he is suffering from its effects... The miracle does nothing but to show him that he has done nothing. T-28.II.7

This is about accepting the metaphysical connections, like in the discussion of sexual abuse the other day. The woman was saying that you can't say that it didn't happen. If you follow this metaphysically that is precisely what you come to, that it didn't happen. The very thing that seemed absurd is what you end up with as being reality. The past is gone and never happened.

What he fears is cause without the consequences that would make it cause. And so it never was. T-28.II.7

Every cause must have an effect; every cause must have consequences. Since the dreaming of the world is not a real cause, it doesn't have real consequences. In the deceived mind the cause is believed to be real and the effects are believed to be real and causative in themselves. But that doesn't make them true; because the mind's belief in them doesn't make them true. It's like eternal Knowledge.

It can be kept from awareness but that doesn't keep It from being what It Is.

> The separation started with the dream the Father was deprived of His effects, and powerless to keep them since He was no longer their Creator. In the dream, the dreamer made himself. But what he made has turned against him, taking on the role of its creator, as the dreamer had. And as he hated his Creator, so the figures in the dream have hated him. His body is their slave, which they abuse because the motives he has given it have they adopted as their own. T-28.II.8

That is very applicable to what we were discussing about the child abuse. That is the exact word, abuse.

> ...which they abuse because the motives he has given it have they adopted as their own. And hate it for the vengeance it would offer them. It is their vengeance on the body which appears to prove the dreamer could not be the maker of the dream. Effect and cause are first split off, and then reversed, so that effect becomes a cause; the cause, effect. T-28.II.8

This is just another way of saying what we read in The Dreamer of the Dream section, that the hero of the dream seems to go in and out of all these places that are contrived by the dream and the mind seems to have no power over the events that seem to happen.

> This is the separation's final step, with which salvation, which proceeds to go the other way, begins. This final step is an effect of what has gone before, appearing as a cause. T-28.II.9

The Course says that time actually goes backwards instead of forwards. When visual images come, it is like having walked on a beach and seen the footprints in the sand and then taking a broom and stepping back, back, back, along the beach sweeping the broom over them. So you are retracing the steps until you come back to the final point and are off the beach, without any footprints or any trace of anything that has happened. This is important, because it is saying that this is the separation's final step, splitting off cause and effect and reversing them. Salvation then proceeds to go the other way.

So we begin with a specific event, "I am feeling upset right now, and turn it around and say that I am projecting this upset and I look at it so I can turn cause and effect around in my mind right now. That is a retracing, coming to the realization that there is no external cause in this particular event. This is a necessary step before I come to transfer of training and the final generalization that there is nothing outside of my mind that can cause anything.

> This final step is an effect of what has gone before, appearing as a cause. The miracle is the first step in giving back to cause the function of causation, not effect. T-28. II.9

And another way to word that would be that the miracle is the first step in giving back to the mind the function of causation, not effect.

> For this confusion has produced the dream, and while it lasts will wakening be feared. Nor will the call to wakening be heard, because it seems to be the call to fear. T-28.II.9

So as long as the mind believes in backward thinking and holds to it and clings to it, then the Holy Spirit is associated with terror because the Holy Spirit seems to be a threat to the self-concept, to the way that the world has been constructed.

> Like every lesson that the Holy Spirit requests you learn, the miracle is clear. It demonstrates what He would have you learn, and shows you its effects are what you want. In His forgiving dreams are the effects of yours undone, and hated enemies perceived as friends with merciful intent.

Their enmity is seen as causeless now, because they did not make it. And you can accept the role of maker of their hate, because you see that it has no effects. Now are you freed from this much of the dream; the world is neutral, and the bodies that still seem to move about as separate things need not be feared. And so they are not sick. T-28. II.10

If the dream figures don't have any sense of intent or purpose in and of themselves, then it's seen that as the dreamer of the dream I gave them all the meaning that I perceived in them. They never had a hateful or spiteful intent. That is just something that was once projected onto them. That is why the crucifixion is such an extreme teaching device, because in the world's eyes Jesus was betrayed, abandoned, torn, hated and eventually killed, yet he projected no hateful intent onto the dream figures. We could say, at the scene of the crucifixion that the world is neutral and bodies that seem to move about as separate things need not be feared. Part of the backward thinking that creeps in with the crucifixion is that there was suffering for Jesus. What we are seeing in the Course is that there was no suffering involved, nothing in the world that would reinforce the separation being real, because he saw that he was the dreamer of the dream.

Friend 1: So there was no more projection.

David: And if he sees the world as causeless then there is no guilt in the mind and therefore there is nothing on the screen that would reinforce guilt. Certainly pain and suffering are simply reinforcements of the belief that guilt is real.

The miracle returns the cause of fear to you who made it. But it also shows that, having no effects, it is not cause, because the function of causation is to have effects. And where effects are gone, there is no cause. Thus is the body healed by miracles because they show the mind made sickness, and employed the body to be victim, or effect, of what it made. T-28.II.11

So he is dropping down a metaphorical level to, "thus is the body healed by miracles." We've talked about that in the ultimate sense the body can't be sick and the body can't be well. The mind in the miracle sees it is not in a body, and therefore the body isn't being used as an effect or employed to be the victim. The body is seen as causeless and not a real effect. It is perceived to be outside the mind instead of containing the mind. We have seen in the case of sickness, where the deceived mind so much wants to be right about being a separate self that it uses the body as proof. That is the witness that it calls to the stand. And in the miracle it is seen that the mind was mistaken about what it thought it was, it no longer sees that it is in the body and no longer needs to see the body as a symbol of sin or as proof that separation is real. That is where the patient can rise up in the miracle and say, "I have no need of this." Because the decision is seen to be a decision of mind and returned to the mind. The body is no longer victim.

> Yet half the lesson will not teach the whole. The miracle
> is useless if you learn but that the body can be healed,
> for this is not the lesson it was sent to teach. The lesson
> is the mind was sick that thought the body could be sick;
> projecting out its guilt caused nothing, and had no effects.
> T-28.II.11

When we are in workshops someone will bring up the thing, "But I feel guilty because I was sick and it seemed like I couldn't do anything about it." Underneath that statement is the belief that the mind knows what sickness is and the premise that the body could be sick.

Friend 1: That that's possible.

David: Yes, that it's possible. It's really just a statement that I believe I know what can be sick. And once again, the lesson is that "the mind was sick that thought the body could be sick; projecting out its guilt caused nothing, and had no effects." It is back to the hallucination. That is the most you could say of it. Not speaking as if it's a fact: I was sick with the flu, or with cancer.

It is about staying with the single lesson consistently. In the Teacher's Manual Jesus says that it is rare that the lesson is consistently applied to all situations. He is pointing to how much vigilance it takes to stay with that lesson – that the mind is sick, and that it is impossible for bodies to be sick – to generalize that and transfer that to all situations and settings. It is trying to maintain vigilance about what can be sick. There is a temptation to talk about symptoms. It is easy to go from what we just talked about to talking about it at the symptom level. A key point today is the idea of trying to maintain a constant vigilance against that.

Temperature is another one. There has been a lot of talk when we are in the building about moving the temperature up and down and stoves and so on. Can you withdraw your mind from all the ego chatter and watch the blah blah blah in the workshop? Try to be very attentive to the mind all the time; keep a close watch. Is there anything in particular that anyone wants to go into today?

Friend 1: To go more into sickness would be helpful for me. I would like to be clearer. When I cough part of me feels like I shouldn't be coughing.

David: So there is a real focus on the symptom. Do you feel uneasy or guilty?

Friend 1: To me it seems like a failure to get clear in my mind, if I am coughing and blowing my nose.

David: That's good. So right now you are saying that you would like to get clear. That is important. You are making an interpretation that is a fearful interpretation and if you continue on and feel like you are not getting it, not teaching what you should be teaching, the fear doesn't get reduced at all. There's no shift. And one person seems to ask, meaning well, "How are you doing today?" Maybe the person wants to fix special kinds of foods, and it can seem to be a counter to everything we have talked about, because it seems to be lending support to something that can't be shared. That would be an example of not sharing ideas that don't come from my Father and yet to go right along and do it anyway. It has to be clear that this is an either/or thing. It can't be something that you talk about and give lip service to and then you turn around and slide into something else.

When we get into the theme of magic, the whole belief in the mixture of magic and miracle is that if the mind is too fearful of the miracle, it recommends a mixture of miracle and magic. This could seem to play out as taking medication or getting up and leaving. It could be anything external: doing something on the outside to try to bring about some kind of relief within.

Friend 2: Sometimes I leave. When I have had symptoms before I didn't put myself in situations where I knew people were going to be asking me about it. If I am coughing or blowing my nose I don't want people asking how I am feeling; I don't want to discuss it.

David: Well, we always say, "Bring it up." In other words, where two or more are gathered... that's a golden opportunity for the mind shift. To be able to bring it up, trace it back with the intention to get clear with the belief so that there can be a shift of mind. It is not like we are coming together with other topics to discuss and we won't discuss that. But to actually, if you feel willing and comfortable enough, bring it up and use it as something to go into and get clear on. The guilt is coming from the interpretation of the symptoms. What we are trying to get at in the mind is that the body cannot be sick, like we talked about the other day, a pencil or a shoe being sick. The wrong mind is the only thing that can be sick. We start to see that a learning device cannot be sick, and sickness is only a faulty interpretation of the learning device. Guilt has nothing to do with what is happening on the screen.

Friend 2: And the Course is telling us to overlook the mistakes that are made. I recognize that is something I really need to work at because I don't overlook mistakes and instead point them out to myself. And so a cough or any symptom is just another mistake. It's getting into that order of difficulty too, saying that if you cough, that is different than if you have breast cancer. It is just a mistake.

Friend 1: So the mistake is that I associate coughing with sickness.

Friend 2: The mistake is that you think the body can be sick.

David: When we take it to a broader realm of looking at your whole life under this thing of Purpose, how you use and see the body is what is important. Do I see the body as insignificant and completely apart from me and as a learning device or are there ways in which it still seems very important to me. That is why we go into that deeply. We can use the vehicle of talking about sickness and go into it as deeply as we can to get clearer on this. To see a chair as a chair is sick. To see a clock as a clock is sick. Because, in the ultimate sense, to see anything as if it has a separate existence in and apart from everything else is sick. It's a sick interpretation. You see how different that is from seeing a body as sick in the world's eyes. To the world a chair is a chair, a clock is a clock, and a sick person is a sick person because they have symptoms that let us know that they are sick versus healthy. Yet it's the mind that is breaking the world up into little boxes and categories. That is sick. That is what we have to start to see. That is where the sickness lies. Not so much reading meaning into particular symptoms and saying that some bodies are sicker than others, that cancer is more serious than a hangnail. You see all those different categories, but it goes much deeper than just coughs or things like that.

The mind believes it is guilty; and it is so determined to hang on to that concept, that, to it, sickness seems like a small price, because sickness is a witness that the body can tell the mind how to feel. It is a witness that smallness, that vulnerability must be true. It can come back to something as subtle as, I want something to be this way instead of that way, all that we have talked about, our ordering of thoughts, our preferences. The mind that believes it can order its own thoughts is a sick mind, but it doesn't want to see that, it doesn't want to see that it is *wrong*. So by making it seem as if something like sickness happens to the body completely without the mind's intention, then sickness is a witness proving its vulnerability and that guilt is justified.

No one can heal unless he understands what purpose sickness seems to serve. For then he understands as well its purpose has no meaning. Being causeless and without a meaningful intent of any kind, it cannot be at all. When this is seen, healing is automatic. W-136

So it all comes back to the mind. What is the cause of sickness? First let's look at it in terms of the wrong mind. The wrong mind is the sick interpretation of reality. It is the assertion that says I am what I wish to be rather than as God created me. And when the Course says sickness, "Being causeless and without a meaningful intent of any kind, it cannot be at all," sickness has to be traced back to where it came from. Did it come from God? That's the ultimate question that it comes back to every time. It is just that simple.

Friend 2: I have had times when healing was not automatic. In the Manual where it says, "If [the patient] even suspected it, they would be healed," M-5.III.1. and I think that I certainly suspect it! I feel like I have a clue of what's going on. Then I think I must be kidding myself. I must not understand it at all.

David: We have to keep trying to train our minds to hold to that intention and to let go of everything we think we know. If you put it into Course terms "Only God's plan for salvation will work." W-71 God's plan for salvation is change your mind about your mind in this instant. That's it. Then there is the ego's plan... if someone acted differently or if I was in a different place, if this circumstance was different than it is... I can be right about who I think I am and something on the screen has to change. The only thing that doesn't change in the ego's plan is changing my mind about my mind. That lays it out. There's God's plan and there's the ego's plan. And Jesus says, "Yet after we have considered just what the ego's plan is, perhaps you will realize that, however preposterous it may be, you do believe in it." W-71. You are trying to do the preposterous all the time. You are trying to change something external to bring about salvation and it will never work.

Friend 1: Talk about this idea of what is most useful. I want some clarity on when to hold that in front of me and when I am using that as an excuse or an escape or a judgment.

David: You put it in the context of the stages of Development of Trust M-4.I.A.3. First you go through a stage where you start to have a sense that everything is helpful, wherever the body seems to go, whatever you seem to be doing. Then is the phase of increasing the helpfulness. And it is still obviously an illusion because the mind still thinks it knows what is most helpful or what will increase the helpfulness. So it is really a stepping stone. But in the next stage, the teacher of God who wanted to let go of the false and accept the true realizes he had no sense of what the false and the true are. His mind is still so tied in to the idea of sacrifice and the belief in form that he still doesn't know. So that stage of what can increase the helpfulness is still an early stepping stone because it involves changing circumstances. It is a subtle ego error to make a haven to hide from the guilt. The Course talks about it in terms of special love relationships, but it could include, for example, a student on the spiritual path, trying to find the easiest most helpful path, sliding into that haven of "when I'm in a quiet setting and can talk comfortably, I want to stay there forever because that is most helpful."

In answer to your question, it's really important to just stay attentive. You can instantaneously use any situation that seems to be on the screen. You can look at your reaction and use that as a starting point to see where you are making an interpretation of the particular situation that is hurting you right now. We get back to right-mind and wrong-mind. There are two mindsets and whenever I am feeling coercion, confused, doubting or restless, I ask myself, "Can Christ be restless? Can Christ be doubting?" The uncomfortable feeling means that there is fundamental identity confusion and that I want to cling to the way I have constructed it rather than the way it is.

Friend 2: Until you know what your function is and you fulfill it, you will be restless.

David: Yes indeed. When we are relaxed and on purpose it just unfolds effortlessly. It doesn't even feel like it's a big job. It's not even thought of as a job. It is a different framework for everything. Thinking about the past or thinking about the future entails enormous strain because the ego wants us to hold these both in mind, when there is just the Holy Instant, Now.

> No one can heal unless he understands what purpose sickness seems to serve. For then he understands as well its purpose has no meaning. Being causeless and without a meaningful intent of any kind, it cannot be at all. When this is seen, healing is automatic. It dispels this meaningless illusion by the same approach that carries all of them to truth, and merely leaves them there to disappear. W-136

We are talking about sickness in bodily terms, but you could also say it about someone that seemed to be upset psychologically.

> Sickness is not an accident. Like all defenses, it is an insane device for self-deception. And like all the rest, its purpose is to hide reality, attack it, change it, render it inept, distort it, twist it, or reduce it to a little pile of unassembled parts. W-136

What this whole world is — whether you are talking at the cosmic level, the microscopic level or the personality level — is just a pile of unassembled parts. You look around a room at coats, rugs and a chair.... unassembled parts. It doesn't matter what you are talking about, but it seems as if they have existence in and of themselves. You see the microwave is set off by space from the teapot. That just shows how deep this sickness of mind is, because everything that is assumed to be everyday reality is just this pile of unassembled parts.

> The aim of all defenses is to keep the truth from being whole. The parts are seen as if each one were whole within itself. W-136

Friend 2: So looking at the world, not being attentive, and seeing all these parts every day is just further proof that it is a chaotic mess.

David: We are redefining what sickness is, from being a few so called symptoms in the body or dysfunctional communication in the family, to just looking out on a winter scene and seeing separate trees and separate snowflakes... As long as the mind is seeing separation everywhere and believes that those things, snowflakes and trees, have an existence in and of themselves, that is a sick perception. The deceived mind wants to hang on to sick perception and therefore sickness seems to serve a purpose. "This sickness is being done to me completely without any intention of my own." So the mind then pretends it doesn't have a choice in the way it sees it. That it doesn't have a choice in the matter.

Friend 2: So, using that example, the only thing I have to do with perception is the purpose that I give it.

David: Yes.

Friend 2: If I'm using the ego's perception then it's a bunch of unassembled parts. If I'm using the Holy Spirit's purpose then it's what?

David: The entire scene becomes unified in perception. It becomes almost like a backdrop that's unimportant because of the shining Purpose that is being held out in front. It is a happy dream.

Friend 2: The scene becomes peripheral. That's how we described it in the past. That makes sense.

Friend 1: So, it's kind of unseen when it's that peripheral.

David: It's unnoticed because perception is selective and when you are zooming in and focusing on your Purpose, then background is just unimportant or irrelevant.

Friend 2: So, with your example before, you were saying when you are focused on the sickness symptoms, that is picking out one of the pieces and holding it up as separate and saying, "let's look at this" and try to see how it fits into the whole, which it can't if I am holding it out as separate.

David: And it takes two minds to agree that there's a sickness. If one mind absolutely will not buy the bait of seeing sickness, then that is what healing is. You hold in mind how impossible sickness or separation is. Anything that is judged or valued, like a haircut you say is better than one you had before, is ordering of thoughts. That judging is what makes the error real. As long as there are better haircuts and worse haircuts, higher jobs and lower jobs, error seems real. You see how that makes the error real. It's not nothing if it's valued positively or negatively. And that is the underlying metaphysics of why you don't want to buy into a judgment, because it makes the error real. It makes the world real in the mind of the thinker.

This need not be. For all is One in Truth.

The Five Levels of Mind

Introduction

How can you attain peace of mind and have it as a consistent experience? It can never be found by changing circumstances in the world. It can only be found by going into the mind, where truth is found.

Let's begin with the introduction to *A Course in Miracles*. "Nothing real can be threatened; nothing unreal exists. Herein lies the peace of God." This is saying that anything that is not peaceful is an illusion. The process of forgiveness is recognizing illusions as unreal. The metaphor of a dream is helpful. In a dream you think the images you see are real, but on waking you realize they are false. Freud said "Dreams are wish fulfillment" and that's what they are.

The wish that made up this world was the wish to be separate from God. In Heaven all is the same so there is no need for learning, for forgiveness. But everyone who seems to come to this world is in need of forgiveness. What needs to be forgiven is the perception of a world of images.

Nothing we see with the eyes or hear with the ears is of any value. The body is not even necessary for perception. The mind perceives. The body as the perceiver is only a belief. If you identify with the body, you may fear losing your eyesight. But the body is just a communication device for the Holy Spirit to use for a while. Then you lay it aside. The ego made the body and the cosmos to keep the mind asleep, dreaming and guilty.

Jesus said "My Kingdom is not of this world. I am calling you out of the world. I am calling you to wake up from this dream of separation." This world is not natural. Love is natural. Freedom is natural. But a sense of limitation or fear is not natural.

The way to wake up is called forgiveness. But it is not the forgiveness of this world, in which someone is seen as doing a harmful act and then forgiven. The world of perception has come from the ego. It is a trick, a deception. It seems very convincing, very real. So convincing that six billion people seem to think it's real too. This is a world of differences. No two people see the same world. Each has their own perspective. The way out is to realize that the ego made it all up. As long as you believe in the ego you will experience conflict.

You must forgive everything of this world to be happy. The word "person" comes from the Greek word *persona*, which means mask. Can you be a happy mask? No, you can never be a happy mask. You have to drop the mask and be very transparent with everything you think and feel in order to be truly happy. Let me illustrate this with a story.

I started a workshop in Florida and a woman raised her fist and said, "Here we go again. You left-brained intellectual men…" I just watched. I didn't identify with or believe in any of those concepts: brain, intellectual, male. I was at peace. When she stopped talking, I just continued on. But in your daily life the ego may find things people say to be insulting. The ego mind takes offence. This is why it is important to release the ego, to drop the mask, so you can experience peace of mind.

The ego has two major defenses: denial and repression. If you believe you can separate from your Creator then you can believe in emotions like guilt. We are talking about the ontological guilt that arises from the idea that you could leave the Mind of God. The ego's response to guilt is to push it out of the mind, to pretend it is not there. This is what denial and repression are: a mechanism in the sleeping mind to pretend guilt isn't there.

In the very instant of separation, the Holy Spirit was given as the answer to the problem. All problems are already over because they have already been answered. But because of denial and repression, the sleeping mind has pushed the separation idea out of awareness. It has pushed the Holy Spirit out of awareness. The Holy Spirit and God have been reduced to mere concepts.

The reason this lack of awareness continues is because of projection. The ego tells the sleeping mind to push out anything it doesn't like with projection. Projection is a way of seeing outside of you something that you are still holding on to. So the world is a cover to keep you from seeing that your mind believes in separation.

This is why it gets so intense in relationships. On the first date you don't talk of your darkest moments or you may not get a second date. You each present a mask because there is fear of dropping the mask. As the relationship progresses, the masks do gradually get lower. The ego is what the mask is and it is in terror of being removed. So the ego brings up lots of past memories, "Remember when you were open and trusting; it was used against you!" The ego doesn't want you to know that if you dropped the mask completely you would experience only love. So when you get into a relationship, there is a lot of denial and repression; you keep dark memories buried. But, because it is difficult to hold these things inside, they are projected out onto your partner. When you get irritated with your partner, it is because of something in you that you have not raised up for healing.

For example, if you have a partner whom you find controlling, it is because you still believe in the unconscious mind that control is possible. This is projected out as if your partner wants to control you. This is the trick of the world: that other people seem to do to you what you have not allowed into awareness. Letting the Holy Spirit use your relationships is a fast way to healing. It undoes the denial and repression.

Once you begin to understand how your mind works, the mystery goes away. You realize you are doing this to yourself and that you can stop. So for our discussion I have drawn a map of the ego mind that was given to me by Jesus. This is a practical tool for you to use.

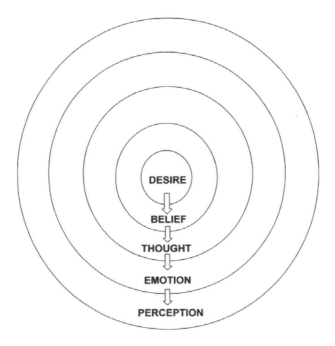

This preliminary illustration shows the chain of causation, originating at desire and resulting in perception.

These are the layers of the ego mind and the outermost layer, caused by all of the others, is perception. The world is *seemingly* perceived through your five senses, but is *actually* perceived through your consciousness. Perception includes all the images you see and all the images in your imagination, which are the same. The world of perception was made by the ego to blind you from the truth. The Holy Spirit shows you what you have forgotten: that you are asleep and dreaming. The Holy Spirit awakens you very gradually and softly so as not to frighten you. This is why the Holy Spirit *uses* the symbols of perception to reach your mind, to reach your consciousness. Consciousness is the realm of the ego that believes in images. This circle of consciousness is a mere speck before the experience of the vast eternity of Spirit.

THE LEVELS OF MIND DIAGRAM

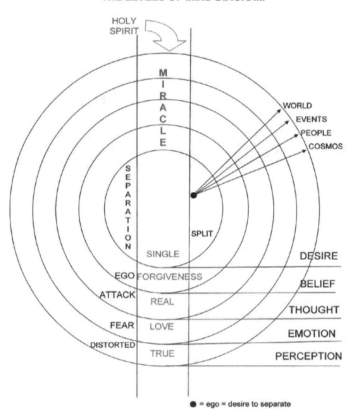

● = ego = desire to separate

Key Points on the Levels of Mind

Mind is beyond levels. Mind Is. Mind reaches to itself. T-18.VI.8 It does not go out. Complete abstraction is the natural condition of the mind. W-161.2 And abstraction is now unnatural. The ego mind does not look on everything as one. It sees instead only fragments of the whole. God dwells within, and your completion lies in Him. No idol takes His place. Look not to idols. Do not seek outside yourself. T-29.VII.6.

Desire - Desire is in the center, your altar, the prayer of your heart that is always answered. The world was created in an instant by your desire for something other than love, your desire to separate.

> You will remember everything the instant you desire it
> wholly, for if to desire wholly is to create, you will have willed
> away the separation, returning your mind simultaneously
> to your Creator and your creations. Knowing them you will
> have no wish to sleep, but only the desire to waken and be
> glad. Dreams will be impossible because you will want only
> truth, and being at last your will, it will be yours. T.10.I.4

You are created as pure divine love by God. But you had a crazy
thought, "Could there be more than everything?" This desire for
more than everything is the dot in the diagram. When prayer or
desire becomes split, purity is lost. From the split prayer all the rest
spreads out. The belief becomes the ego and the thought becomes
attack and the emotion becomes fear and the perception becomes
the entire cosmos. It all springs from the desire for more than
everything.

To go within for healing, to where the prayer is pure, you must start
with perception and move back through the layers to the center. It
is a journey into your consciousness to discover truth. Everyone
has all of the answers within them. This is the purpose of the Holy
Spirit, to take you back inward step by step. The Holy Spirit is the
voice leading you back to God.

Belief - In the instant of the tiny mad idea of separation came
the first belief: the ego, the belief that you could be something
other than what you truly are. What you believe you are is now the
question.

> Belief produces the acceptance of existence. T-1.VI.4
> You believe in what you make. T-1.VII.3 You still believe
> you are an image of your own making. Belief is an ego
> function, and as long as your origin is open to belief you
> are regarding it from an ego viewpoint. A decision is a
> conclusion based on everything that you believe. T.4.II.4

Thought - Your thoughts come from the ego and spring from your belief in it. They are always partial, concerning such things as relationships, judgment and money. These will never make you happy. You always want more and you are left chasing dreams.

> Thoughts can represent the lower or bodily level of experience, or the higher or spiritual level of experience. One makes the physical, and the other creates the spiritual. You are responsible for what you think, because it is only at this level that you can exercise choice. Thoughts are not big or little; powerful or weak. They are merely true or false. T.1.I.12 Your ability to direct your thinking as you choose is part of its power. T.7.VI.2.6

Emotion - Your thoughts produce your feelings: fear, depression, anxiety. The world you see is just a reflection of your emotions.

> You have but two emotions, love and fear; one you made and one was given you. Each is a way of seeing, and different worlds arise from their different sights. T-13.V.10 That you do listen to the voice of your ego is demonstrated by your attitudes, your feelings and your behavior. T.4.IV.1

Perception - What perception sees and hears appears to be real because it permits into awareness only what conforms to the wishes of the perceiver.

> Perception is a mirror, not a fact. And what I look on is my state of mind, reflected outward. W-304.1 Judge how well you have done this by your own feelings, for this is the one right use of judgment. T-4.IV.8

When you are asleep in the dream, you believe in the specifics that you perceive. So this is where the journey back must start. Once you are in touch with what you perceive you need to get in touch with your emotions. There are many dark emotions buried in the subconscious mind and you must go through them on the way inward.

The power is in the center. The cause is in the center and the effect is on the outside. Your desire influences your belief. And your beliefs control your thoughts. Your thoughts control your emotions and your emotions control your perceptions.

The ego never wants you to learn this. It wants you to think that cause is at the level of perception. The ego would have you think that the past causes the future. You need to understand what is underneath the level of perception. As soon as you learn how things work in the mind you have the tools to undo the ego completely.

Let's look at an example. One partner in a marriage has an affair. The other partner finds out and feels angry. But this person's anger really has nothing to do with the affair. Their anger is coming from a deeper place: their egoic desire to have more than everything and from their attack thoughts. The anger is part of their emotions of fear and guilt. All this is the result of what is happening deep down in the mind. This cosmos is just a projection of what is going on in consciousness.

This person who is angry at their partner's infidelity must first recognize that they have an emotion. They are not angry for the reason they think, their partner's behavior. "I can be hurt by nothing but my thoughts." W- 281 This is why you must go down into your mind and release the ego in order to perceive a peaceful world. We ask the Holy Spirit's help to let our desire be single, rather than split. The Holy Spirit teaches us that there is only one helpful belief – forgiveness. Jesus spent his life on earth teaching forgiveness.

The Holy Spirit is the Love that you really are. He uses the symbols of the world to lead you back inside your mind. The Course is just to help you hear your Internal Teacher. Then you no longer need it. To learn to follow the Holy Spirit, pay attention to your emotions. When you are upset you know you need a new thought. The Course gives you new thoughts to practice with to train your mind to think in a different way so you feel in a different way and perceive in a different way. It is that simple.

At first you may need to think about things. But as you become more intuitive you don't have to figure anything out. Because you are told from within what is most helpful. You have no need for opinions and learn to say "I don't know," because your real focus is to be happy and peaceful. Your intuition knows the words to speak; sometimes no words, just a smile. You learn to laugh a lot, not to take the world so seriously, to relax and come into the present. If you think you need help, someone shows up to help you.

You see that the world is coming from your own thinking. You no longer believe in luck. If you are happy it is because of your thoughts, because of your own mind training. That is the reward of forgiveness. Forgiving is a way of aligning all the levels.

At the center is your desire to know who you are. If you practice it will come, because your belief becomes forgiveness. You realize that the only purpose for this world is to practice forgiveness. Nothing else works. Release everything in your mind that is not of God, and your thoughts are happy thoughts. The witnesses to your happy thoughts will appear, and you will have no enemies. The emotion that comes from these thoughts is love.

It is only judgment that drains you of your energy. When you don't judge the dream it is very peaceful. Do not try to fix the dream or to obtain a future goal. Be happy in the happy dream now.
This model of the levels of mind can be used to see that your behavior comes from your thoughts and your feelings. You can take full responsibility and hold no one else responsible. When you trust Spirit you are filled up from the inside. With the use of this mind training you come to have very loving relationships.

Forgiveness

Looking at the surface circle, to the upper right of the diagram, we have an event. Imagine that someone says something to you and you feel angry. The event seems to cause your painful emotion of anger. The ego has tricked you into blaming a person and circumstances for your pain. This is a reversal of cause and effect. Your pain is not because of the event. It is because of your ego interpretation of the event. Spirit has a completely different interpretation of the event, even if it appeared to be an attack.

Look at the central column of the diagram, which represents the miracle. When Jesus was bleeding on the cross he said, "Forgive them, for they know not what they do." Those words only make sense from inside the miracle, because Jesus did not perceive that he was being attacked. He could see that it was just a dream and that he was spirit and not a body.

If you practice the forgiveness process I'm going to show you, you will become more identified with the spirit and less identified with the body. When an event seems to occur, rather than staying with the ego mind to blame the person or circumstance, go with the Holy Spirit inside your mind. The circumstances never cause the emotion. It is the mind that causes the circumstances. Everything starts in the center at the desire and moves out, seeming to produce the effects.

Say to yourself: "I have given everything I see all the meaning that it has for me." W-2 You acknowledge what you are perceiving. But you are not upset because of the projection that you perceive. The upset is coming from the thoughts underneath the projection. It is these thoughts that produce the projection, the circumstances. To use a movie projector analogy, when there is a glitch in the film, you would not go up to the screen and bang on the screen to fix it. You have to go back to the projector room. You have to do the same thing in your everyday life; go back to the mind.

It seems as though the person's behavior made you angry. So you could say to yourself, "I think I am upset because of what the person said to me." But then say to yourself, "I am never upset for the reason I think." W-5 Ask yourself what false thoughts and beliefs you may be holding.

Your ego thoughts are all part of a false identity. When you think you are upset by somebody else, it just means that you are holding on to an ego identity. The ego doesn't want you to know the real cause. It wants you to believe that you are a person and somebody else is doing something wrong. As you go into your mind, however, you begin to undo the ego thoughts and the ego identity.

As you do this you discover your true identity. This identity cannot be attacked because it is pure oneness. To have an attack there must be two parts, one to attack the other. As you forgive and go inward you are unifying your mind. If you want only peace, then you will see only peace in the world, because everything starts with desire. The black dot on the diagram represents a split desire. That is what makes the world seem fragmented in pieces. But when you're in the miracle you see that everything is unified. There was no attack.

Forgiveness takes a lot of practice. But it is worth it. It reverses the process of the world. You perceive the world differently, with stability. Nothing outside yourself, be it noise, pollution, people, or events, can disturb you. As you let go of ego attack thoughts, of justifying your anger, you become clear inside. You learn to follow the guidance of the Holy Spirit inside you. You become free of your expectations of the world. You give up a vulnerable, false identity and find your real identity in Christ. You become profoundly peaceful and happy.

The Five Levels of Mind
Selections from *A Course In Miracles*

1) Perception

What perception sees and hears appears to be real because it permits into awareness only what conforms to the wishes of the perceiver. This leads to a world of illusions, a world which needs constant defense precisely because it is not real. The world we see merely reflects our own internal frame of reference – the dominant ideas, wishes and emotions in our minds. "Projection makes perception."

T-21.in.1. We look inside first, decide the kind of world we want to see and then project that world outside, making it the truth as we see it. We make it true by our interpretations of what it is we are seeing. If we are using perception to justify our own mistakes – our anger, our impulses to attack, our lack of love in whatever form it may take – we will see a world of evil, destruction, malice, envy and despair. All this we must learn to forgive, not because we are being "good" and "charitable", but because what we are seeing is not true. We have distorted the world with our twisted defenses, and are therefore seeing what is not there. As we learn to recognize our perceptual errors, we also learn to look past them and "forgive" them. Perception is a function of the body, and therefore represents a limit on awareness. Perception sees through the body's eyes and hears through the body's ears. It evokes the limited responses which the body makes.

You who believe that God is fear made but one substitution. It has taken many forms, because it was the substitution of illusion for truth; of fragmentation for wholeness. It has become so splintered and subdivided and divided again, over and over, that it is now almost impossible to perceive it once was one, and still is what it was. That one error, which brought truth to illusion, infinity to time, and life to death, was all you ever made. Your whole world rests upon it. Everything you see reflects it, and every special relationship that you have ever made is part of it. You may be surprised to hear how very different is reality from what you see. You do not realize the magnitude of that one error. It was so vast and so completely incredible that from it a world of total unreality had to emerge. What else could come of it? Its fragmented aspects are fearful enough, as you begin to look at them. But nothing you have seen begins to show you the enormity of the original error, which seemed to cast you out of Heaven, to shatter knowledge into meaningless bits of disunited perceptions, and to force you to make further substitutions. T-18.I.4-5

The ego is the questioning aspect of the post-separation self, which was made rather than created. It is capable of asking questions but not of perceiving meaningful answers, because these would involve knowledge and cannot be perceived. T-3.IV.3

Perception is a choice and not a fact. But on this choice depends far more than you may realize as yet. For on the voice you choose to hear, and on the sights you choose to see, depends entirely your whole belief in what you are. Perception is a witness but to this, and never to reality. T-21.V.1.

2) Emotion

Fear... has many forms, for the content of individual illusions differs greatly. Yet they have one thing in common; they are all insane. They are made of sights that are not seen, and sounds that are not heard. They make up a private world that cannot be shared. For they are meaningful only to their maker, and so they have no meaning at all. In this world their maker moves alone, for only he perceives them.

It is through these strange and shadowy figures that the insane relate to their insane world. For they see only those who remind them of these images, and it is to them that they relate. Thus do they communicate with those who are not there, and it is they who answer them. And no one hears their answer save him who called upon them, and he alone believes they answered him. Projection makes perception, and you cannot see beyond it. Again and again have you attacked your brother, because you saw in him a shadow figure in your private world. And thus it is you must attack yourself first, for what you attack is not in others. Its only reality is in your own mind, and by attacking others you are literally attacking what is not there. T-13.V.1,3

What would you see? The choice is given you. But learn and do not let your mind forget this law of seeing: You will look upon that which you feel within. If hatred finds a place within your heart, you will perceive a fearful world, held cruelly in death's sharp-pointed, bony fingers. If you feel the Love of God within you, you will look out on a world of mercy and of love. W-189.5.

Love's messengers are gently sent, and return with messages of love and gentleness. The messengers of fear are harshly ordered to seek out guilt, and cherish every scrap of evil and of sin that they can find, losing none of them on pain of death, and laying them respectfully before their lord and master. Perception cannot obey two masters, each asking for messages of different things in different languages. What fear would feed upon, love overlooks. What fear demands, love cannot even see. The fierce attraction that guilt holds for fear is wholly absent from love's gentle perception. What love would look upon is meaningless to fear, and quite invisible.

Relationships in this world are the result of how the world is seen. And this depends on which emotion was called on to send its messengers to look upon it, and return with word of what they saw. Fear's messengers are trained through terror, and they tremble when their master calls on them to serve him.

Send not these savage messengers into the world, to feast upon it and to prey upon reality. For they will bring you word of bones and skin and flesh. They have been taught to seek for the corruptible, and to return with gorges filled with things decayed and rotted. To them such things are beautiful, because they seem to allay their savage pangs of hunger. For they are frantic with the pain of fear, and would avert the punishment of him who sends them forth by offering him what they hold dear. T-19.1V.A.11-13

The Holy Spirit has given you love's messengers to send instead of those you trained through fear. They are as eager to return to you what they hold dear as are the others. If you send them forth, they will see only the blameless and the beautiful, the gentle and the kind. They will be as careful to let no little act of charity, no tiny expression of forgiveness, no little breath of love escape their notice. And they will return with all the happy things they found, to share them lovingly with you. Be not afraid of them. They offer you salvation. Theirs are the messages of safety, for they see the world as kind.

If you send forth only the messengers the Holy Spirit gives you, wanting no messages but theirs, you will see fear no more. The world will be transformed before your sight, cleansed of all guilt and softly brushed with beauty. The world contains no fear that you laid not upon it. T-19.IV.A.14-15

I am never upset for the reason I think. ...The upset may seem to be fear, worry, depression, anxiety, anger, hatred, jealousy or any number of forms, all of which will be perceived as different. This is not true... W-5.1

I am upset because I see something that is not there. W-6. I see only the past. W-7 I am upset because I see a meaningless world. W-12 A meaningless world engenders fear because I think I am in competition with God. W-13 I can escape from the world I see by giving up attack thoughts. W-23

3) Thought

The truth is that you are responsible for what you think, because it is only at this level that you can exercise choice. What you do comes from what you think. You cannot separate yourself from the truth by giving autonomy to behavior. This is controlled by me automatically as soon as you place what you think under my guidance. Whenever you are afraid, it is a sure sign that you have allowed your mind to miscreate and have not allowed me to guide it.

It is pointless to believe that controlling the outcome of misthought can result in healing. When you are fearful, you have chosen wrongly. That is why you feel responsible for it. You must change your mind, not your behavior, and this is a matter of willingness. You do not need guidance except at the mind level. Correction belongs only at the level where change is possible. Change does not mean anything at the symptom level, where it cannot work.

The correction of fear is your responsibility. When you ask for release from fear, you are implying that it is not. You should ask, instead, for help in the conditions that have brought the fear about. These conditions always entail a willingness to be separate. At that level you can help it. You are much too tolerant of mind wandering, and are passively condoning your mind's miscreations. The particular result does not matter, but the fundamental error does. The correction is always the same. T-2.VI.2-4

Everything you see is the result of your thoughts. There is no exception to this fact. Thoughts are... merely true or false. ...Salvation requires that you also recognize that every thought you have brings either peace or war; either love or fear. W-16

It is a mistake to believe that a thought system based on lies is weak. T-3.VII.1.

The thoughts the mind of God's Son projects... are his beliefs. And it is these, and not the truth, that he has chosen to defend and love. They... can be given up by him. T-14.1.3.

If you are willing to renounce the role of guardian of your thought system and open it to me, I will correct it very gently and lead you back to God. T-4.1.4.

The Ordering of Thoughts

Delusional ideas are not real thoughts, although you can believe in them. But you are wrong. The function of thought comes from God and is in God. As part of His Thought, you cannot think apart from Him. Irrational thought is disordered thought. God Himself orders your thought because your thought was created by Him. Guilt feelings are always a sign that you do not know this. They also show that you believe you can think apart from God, and want to. Every disordered thought is attended by guilt at its inception, and maintained by guilt in its continuance. Guilt is inescapable by those who believe they order their own thoughts, and must therefore obey their dictates. This makes them feel responsible for their errors without recognizing that, by accepting this responsibility, they are reacting irresponsibly. If the sole responsibility of the miracle worker is to accept the Atonement for himself, and I assure you that it is, then the responsibility for what is atoned for cannot be yours. The dilemma cannot be resolved except by accepting the solution of undoing. You would be responsible for the effects of all your wrong thinking if it could not be undone. The purpose of the Atonement is to save the past in purified form only. If you accept the remedy for disordered thought, a remedy whose efficacy is beyond doubt, how can its symptoms remain?

The continuing decision to remain separated is the only possible reason for continuing guilt feelings. We have said this before, but did not emphasize the destructive results of the decision. Any decision of the mind will affect both behavior and experience. What you want you expect. This is not delusional. Your mind does make your future, and it will turn it back to full creation at any minute if it accepts the Atonement first. It will also return to full creation the instant it has done so. Having given up its disordered thought, the proper ordering of thought becomes quite apparent. T-5.V.6.-8

4) Belief

Belief produces the acceptance of existence. That is why you can believe what no one else thinks is true. T-1.VI.4

Although you can perceive false associations, you can never make them real except to yourself. You believe in what you make. If you offer miracles, you will be equally strong in your belief in them. T-1. VII.3

What you believe is true for you. T-2.VII.5

Eating of the fruit of the tree of knowledge is a symbolic expression for usurping the ability for self-creating. This is the only sense in which God and His creations are not co-creators. The belief that they are is implicit in the "self-concept," or the tendency of the self to make an image of itself. Images are perceived, not known. Knowledge cannot deceive, but perception can. You can perceive yourself as self-creating, but you cannot do more than believe it. You cannot make it true. And, as I said before, when you finally perceive correctly you can only be glad that you cannot. Until then, however, the belief that you can is the foundation stone in your thought system, and all your defenses are used to attack ideas that might bring it to Light. You still believe you are an image of your own making. Your mind is split with the Holy Spirit on this point, and there is no resolution while you believe the one thing that is literally inconceivable. That is why you cannot create and are filled with fear about what you make. The mind can make the belief in separation very real and very fearful, and this belief is the "devil." It is powerful, active, destructive and clearly in opposition to God, because it literally denies His Fatherhood. Look at your life and see what the devil has made. But realize that this making will surely dissolve in the Light of truth, because its foundation is a lie. T-3. VII.4-5.

The Holy Spirit will teach you to perceive beyond your belief, because truth is beyond belief and His perception is true. The ego can be completely forgotten at any time, because it is a totally incredible belief, and no one can keep a belief he has judged to be unbelievable. The more you learn about the ego, the more you realize that it cannot be believed. The incredible cannot be understood because it is unbelievable. The meaninglessness of perception based on the unbelievable is apparent, but it may not be recognized as being beyond belief, because it is made *by* belief. T-7. VIII.6.

You cannot evaluate an insane belief system from within it. Its range precludes this. You can only go beyond it, look back from a point where sanity exists and see the contrast. Only by this contrast can insanity be judged as insane. T-9.VII.6.

Every idea has a purpose, and its purpose is always the natural outcome of what it is. Everything that stems from the ego is the natural outcome of its central belief, and the way to undo its results is merely to recognize that their source is not natural, being out of accord with your true nature. I said before that to will contrary to

God is wishful thinking and not real willing. T-11.V.5

To learn this course requires willingness to question every value that you hold. Not one can be kept hidden and obscure but it will jeopardize your learning. No belief is neutral. Every one has the power to dictate each decision you make. For a decision is a conclusion based on everything that you believe. It is the outcome of belief, and follows it as surely as does suffering follow guilt and freedom sinlessness. There is no substitute for peace. What God creates has no alternative. The truth arises from what He knows. And your decisions come from your beliefs as certainly as all creation rose in His Mind because of what He knows. T-24.in.2.

Our emphasis has been on bringing what is undesirable to the desirable; what you do not want to what you do. You will realize that salvation must come to you this way, if you consider what dissociation is. Dissociation is a distorted process of thinking whereby two systems of belief which cannot coexist are both maintained. If they are brought together, their joint acceptance becomes impossible. But if one is kept in darkness from the other, their separation seems to keep them both alive and equal in their reality. Their joining thus becomes the source of fear, for if they meet, acceptance must be withdrawn from one of them. You cannot have them both, for each denies the other. Apart, this fact is lost from sight, for each in a separate place can be endowed with firm belief. Bring them together and the fact of their complete incompatibility is instantly apparent. One will go, because the other is seen in the same place. Light cannot enter darkness when a mind believes in darkness, and will not let it go. T-14.VII.4-5

The ego's whole continuance depends on its belief you cannot learn this course. Share this belief, and reason will be unable to see your errors and make way for their correction. For reason sees through errors, telling you what you thought was real is not. Reason can see the difference between sin and mistakes, because it wants correction. Therefore, it tells you what you thought was uncorrectable can be corrected, and thus it must have been an error. The ego's opposition to correction leads to its fixed belief in sin and disregard of errors.

It looks on nothing that can be corrected. Thus does the ego damn, and reason save. Reason is not salvation in itself, but it makes way for peace and brings you to a state of mind in which salvation can be given you. T-22.III.2-3

The Helpful Use of Belief

This course is perfectly clear. If you do not see it clearly, it is because you are interpreting against it, and therefore do not believe it. And since belief determines perception, you do not perceive what it means and therefore do not accept it. Yet different experiences lead to different beliefs, and with them different perceptions. For perceptions are learned with beliefs, and experience does teach. I am leading you to a new kind of experience that you will become less and less willing to deny. Learning of Christ is easy, for to perceive with Him involves no strain at all. His perceptions are your natural awareness, and it is only the distortions you introduce that tire you. Let the Christ in you interpret for you, and do not try to limit what you see by narrow little beliefs that are unworthy of God's Son. T-11.VI.3

Like you, my faith and my belief are centered on what I treasure. The difference is that I love *only* what God loves with me, and because of this I treasure you beyond the value that you set on yourself, even unto the worth that God has placed upon you. I love all that He created, and all my faith and my belief I offer unto it. My faith in you is as strong as all the love I give my Father. My trust in you is without limit, and without the fear that you will hear me not. T-13.X.13

Examples of Specific Beliefs

* scarcity T-1.IV.3
* deprivation T-1.IV.4
* space and time T-2.II.4
* that error can hurt you. T-2.II.2
* that miracles are frightening T-2.IV.4

- death T-3.VII.5. 11
- that darkness can hide T-1.I.22
- differences T-22.in
- superiority and inferiority T-4.I.7
- physical sight T-2.V.7
- that the body can be used as a means for attaining atonement T-2.III.1
- separation T-6.II.1.
- you are a body W-91.9
- that God rejected Adam and forced him out of the Garden of Eden T-3.I.3
- more, less and selectivity T-3.V.7.5
- attack and rejection T-6.V.B.1
- physical illness T-2.IV.2. 7

The fear of God and of your brother comes from each unrecognized belief in specialness. For you demand your brother bow to it against his will. T-24.1.8.

5) Desire

The memory of God can dawn only in a mind that chooses to remember, and that has relinquished the insane desire to control reality. T-12.VIII.5.

Your practice must therefore rest upon your willingness to let all littleness go. The instant in which magnitude dawns upon you is but as far away as your desire for it. T-15.IV.2.

The willingness to communicate attracts communication to it, and overcomes loneliness completely. There is complete forgiveness here, for there is no desire to exclude anyone from your completion, in sudden recognition of the value of his part in it. In the protection of your wholeness, all are invited and made welcome. T-15.VII.14.

Hear Him gladly, and learn of Him that you have need of no special relationships at all. You but seek in them what you have thrown away. And through them you will never learn the value of what you have cast aside, but still desire with all your heart. Let us join together in making the holy instant all that there is, by desiring that it be all that there is. T-15.VIII.2.

You have accepted God. The holiness of your relationship is established in Heaven. You do not understand what you accepted, but remember that your understanding is not necessary. All that was necessary was merely the wish to understand. That wish was the desire to be holy. The Will of God is granted you. For you desire the only thing you ever had, or ever were. Each instant that we spend together will teach you that this goal is possible, and will strengthen your desire to reach it. And in your desire lies its accomplishment. Your desire is now in complete accord with all the power of the Holy Spirit's Will. No little, faltering footsteps that you may take can separate your desire from His Will and from His strength. I hold your hand as surely as you agreed to take your brother's. You will not separate, for I stand with you and walk with you in your advance to truth. T-18.III.4-5.

We are made whole in our desire to make whole. Let not time worry you, for all the fear that you and your brother experience is really past. Time has been readjusted to help us do, together, what your separate pasts would hinder. You have gone past fear, for no two minds can join in the desire for love without love's joining them. You and your brother are coming home together, after a long and meaningless journey that you undertook apart, and that led nowhere. You have found your brother, and you will light each other's way. T-18.III.7-8

The holy instant is the result of your determination to be holy. It is the answer. The desire and the willingness to let it come precede its coming. You prepare your mind for it only to the extent of recognizing that you want it above all else. It is not necessary that you do more; indeed, it is necessary that you realize that you cannot do more. T-18.IV.1.

I desire this holy instant for myself, that I may share it with my brother, whom I love. It is not possible that I can have it without him, or he without me. T-18.V. 7

The desire to get rid of peace and drive the Holy Spirit from you fades in the presence of the quiet recognition that you love Him. T-19.IV.D.5

Seeing adapts to wish, for sight is always secondary to desire. And if you see the body, you have chosen judgment and not vision. For vision, like relationships, has no order. You either see or not. Who sees a brother's body has laid a judgment on him, and sees him not. He does not really see him as sinful; he does not see him at all. T-20.VII.5.

Truth is restored to you through your desire, as it was lost to you through your desire for something else. Open the holy place that you closed off by valuing the "something else," and what was never lost will quietly return. It has been saved for you. Vision would not be necessary had judgment not been made. Desire now its whole undoing, and it is done for you. T-20.VIII.1.

Your brother's sinlessness is given you in shining light, to look on with the Holy Spirit's vision and to rejoice in along with Him. For peace will come to all who ask for it with real desire and sincerity of purpose, shared with the Holy Spirit and at one with Him on what salvation is. Be willing, then, to see your brother sinless, that Christ may rise before your vision and give you joy. And place no value on your brother's body, which holds him to illusions of what he is. T-20.VIII.3.

You made perception that you might choose among your brothers, and seek for sin within them. The Holy Spirit sees perception as a means to teach you that the vision of a holy relationship is all you want to see. Then will you give your faith to holiness, desiring and believing in it because of your desire. Faith and belief become attached to vision, as all the means that once served sin are redirected now toward holiness... Those who would free their brothers from the body can have no fear. They have renounced the means for sin by choosing to let all limitations be removed. As they desire to look upon their brothers in holiness, the power of their belief and faith sees far beyond the body, supporting vision, not obstructing it. But first they chose to recognize how much their faith had limited their understanding of the world, desiring to place its power elsewhere should another point of view be given them. The miracles that follow this decision are also born of faith. For all who choose to look away from sin are given vision, and are led to holiness. T-21.III.6-8

The constancy of joy is a condition quite alien to your understanding. Yet if you could even imagine what it must be, you would desire it although you understand it not. The constancy of happiness has no exceptions; no change of any kind. It is unshakable as is the Love of God for His creation. Sure in its vision as its Creator is in what He knows, happiness looks on everything and sees it is the same. It sees not the ephemeral, for it desires everything be like itself, and sees it so. Nothing has power to confound its constancy, because its own desire cannot be shaken. It comes as surely unto those who see the final question is necessary to the rest, as peace must come to those who choose to heal and not to judge. T-21.VIII.2.

What is the holy instant but God's appeal to you to recognize what He has given you? Here is the great appeal to reason; the awareness of what is always there to see, the happiness that could be always yours. Here is the constant peace you could experience forever. Here is what denial has denied revealed to you. For here the final question is already answered, and what you ask for given. Here is the future, now, for time is powerless because of your desire for what will never change. For you have asked that nothing stand between the holiness of your relationship and your awareness of its holiness. T-21.VIII.5.

Beyond the body that you interposed between you and your brother, and shining in the golden light that reaches it from the bright, endless circle that extends forever, is your holy relationship, beloved of God Himself. How still it rests, in time and yet beyond, immortal yet on earth. How great the power that lies in it. Time waits upon its will, and earth will be as it would have it be. Here is no separate will, nor the desire that anything be separate. Its will has no exceptions, and what it wills is true. Every illusion brought to its forgiveness is gently overlooked and disappears. For at its center Christ has been reborn, to light His home with vision that overlooks the world. Would you not have this holy home be yours as well? No misery is here, but only joy. T-22.II.12.

How willing are you to forgive your brother? How much do you desire peace instead of endless strife and misery and pain? These questions are the same, in different form. T-29.VI.1.

There is no miracle you cannot have when you desire healing. T-30.VIII.4

What you desire you will see. Such is the real law of cause and effect as it operates in the world. W- 20.5.

You have not lost your innocence. It is for this you yearn. This is your heart's desire. W-182.12.

It is impossible that anything should come to me unbidden by myself. Even in this world, it is I who rule my destiny. What happens is what I desire. What does not occur is what I do not want to happen. This must I accept. For thus am I led past this world to my creations, children of my will, in Heaven where my holy Self abides with them and Him Who has created me. W-253.1

You are my goal, my Father. What but You could I desire to have? What way but that which leads to You could I desire to walk? And what except the memory of You could signify to me the end of dreams and futile substitutions for the truth? You are my only goal. W-287.2.

It is not easy to realize that prayers for things, for status, for human love, for external gifts of any kind, are always made to set up jailers and to hide from guilt. These things are used for goals that substitute for God, and therefore distort the purpose of prayer. The desire for them is the prayer. One need not ask explicitly. The goal of God is lost in the quest for lesser goals of any kind, and prayer becomes requests for enemies. The power of prayer can be quite clearly recognized even in this. No one who wants an enemy will fail to find one. But just as surely will he lose the only true goal that is given him. Think of the cost, and understand it well. All other goals are at the cost of God. S-1.III.6

Very simply, the resurrection is the overcoming or surmounting of death. It is a reawakening or a rebirth; a change of mind about the meaning of the world. It is the acceptance of the Holy Spirit's interpretation of the world's purpose; the acceptance of the Atonement for oneself. It is the end of dreams of misery, and the glad awareness of the Holy Spirit's final dream. It is the recognition of the gifts of God. It is the dream in which the body functions perfectly, having no function except communication. It is the lesson in which learning ends, for it is consummated and surpassed with this. It is the invitation to God to take His final step. It is the relinquishment of all other purposes, all other interests, all other wishes and all other concerns. It is the single desire of the Son for the Father. M-28.1.

Epilogue

The life of Mysticism is one of devotion and reverence to God and therefore to all. It is a discipline of mind, of training the mind to hear and follow only the Voice for God. The goal is everlasting peace of mind and the humor, gentleness, happiness, freedom, and joy that flow from such a State of Mind.

The life of Mysticism is as spontaneous and playful as it is serene and tranquil. Alive and energized by the living moment, the need for rituals and rules and structures falls away from the mind. Mysticism learns mastery through love and compassion and kindness; everyday is like a painting full of opportunities to extend the Love of God.

Mysticism is not ruled by fear of consequences. The Law of Love reigns supreme in the Divine Mind, and there is no other. Love is without opposite, and this spiritual fact is finally approached and accepted without exception or compromise. In the Awakening it becomes clear that doubt is impossible.

Willingness to humbly accept oneself as a Child of God, created perfect in the likeness of God, grows and grows with each Holy Instant. The world of idols loses all of its former attraction as the Heavenly light enfolds the heart of the mystic. When such vastness and magnitude become apparent, there is need of nothing else.

Meditation on the Divine is at first a practice, then a continuous living experience, until it finally yields to an eternally blissful and completely unalterable State of Being. Such is the State of Grace. To move in the direction of this State of Absolute Being, the desires of the world of multiplicity must fall away.

Miracles lead the way, for the way of the true mystic is approach to God through attraction, not through avoidance or opposition. As error is seen as false and without a real cause, its foundation disappears in the light of truth. Perfect love casts out fear, for belief has been withdrawn and replaced by the Knowledge of Life in God. There is no battle to be fought, only a gentle awakening to the truth of what always was and always will be so.

All things are accepted exactly as they are, for that which is eternal is unchanged, unchanging, and unchangable. It is understood that no arrangement of circumstances and no amount of gain or personal improvement is necessary to attain the peace and happiness that is available now. Only a yielding to truth, a surrender of the belief in illusions, a stepping back and putting full trust in God is required. This is no sacrifice. It is the giving up of nothing for the remembrance of Everything. Joy has no cost, for Love is without an opposite.

Mysticism is finally yielding to Absolute Happiness in God and Self. Only the Mind which knows "I and the Father are One" knows Absolute Happiness.

Thank you God, for leading us all home to You. Your way is certain, for your plan cannot fail. Hallowed be your Name O God of eternity, and hallowed be the Name of your Beloved Child.

My heart is beating in the joy of God. My mind is resting in the peace of God. My soul is invulnerable in the strength of God. Mine eye is single in the light of God.

We are One. God is One. All is One.
Amen.

Resources

Instrument for Peace
Working through upsets and healing your mind

The mind at peace is healed. The mind at peace has whole-heartedly welcomed peace. In this world, lack of peace appears in many forms. For permanent healing to occur, lack of peace must be traced back to its singular cause in the mind. Use of this instrument for that tracing back can help a willing mind let go of what it thinks it knows, see the world differently, and experience a present state of peace and joy.

A = Past or future action, situation, or event
B = Upsetting emotions
C = Name and/or future consequence
D = My belief in lack (taking the form of an image of self/other/ the world)
E = Wanted and expected action, situation, or event

1. When I think about **A**: _____
_____, I feel **B**: _____
_____ because I think that
C: _____ is to blame and/or
I'm afraid that **C**: _____
will occur in the future.

2. **A**, **B**, and **C** prove that I am right about **D**: _____
_____.
I do not like how I feel now, so I am ready to consider the possibility that the way I am perceiving this is not the way it really is. As part of the healing process, I am willing to look beyond my perception of this upset (the meaning I have given it) and look within my mind.

3. I want to learn that there is a way that I can, without guilt, see the part I play in thinking **A**: _____, in feeling **B**: _____ in blaming **C**: _____, or in fearing **C**: _____.

4. I release my wanting to be right about my perception of **A**, **B**, **C**, and **D**. I want instead to be happy. Through the ego (distorted thinking/seeing), I perceive the cause of my upset and its resolution as outside my mind. This projection seems very real; its purpose is to distract my mind from looking inward.

5. If the cause of my upset and its resolution were outside my mind, I would, in fact, be powerless to change it. My use of projection (seeing outside what I don't want to see within) is why I seem powerless, why **C**: _____ _____seem(s) to be the cause of my upset.

6. Thinking **A**: _____, feeling **B**: _____ blaming **C**: _____, or in fearing **C**: _____ result from my belief in D: _____ _____.

7. I am only upset at someone or something when they/it mirror(s) back to my mind a belief which I have denied from awareness. When I blame/fear something in the world, it is to avoid seeing the upset and resolution as they really are (a decision in my mind) and to instead maintain an image of self/other/the world as I wish. This mind trick seems to displace guilt and fear, but actually maintains feelings of upset. To blame or fear an image of self/other/the world requires that I believe I am limited to a body and world of bodies and denies the spiritual abstract reality of my being. As a first step in letting go of all upset, I want to see in my mind what I thought was outside it. Being upset about **A**: _____

is only another attempt to make **C**: _____
_____ the cause of my guilt and fear.

8. Upset seems valuable and justifiable when **A** runs counter to what I wanted. What I wanted and expected is **E**: _____
_____.

   I still believe in **D**: _____
so I think I need **E**: _____
_____ to be happy, complete, and at peace. Is this belief in lack, and the resulting expectation, more important to me than peace of mind?

9. Everything in the world works together for my good. What I think is the cause of my upset is not the cause at all. The choice to be upset is a choice not to see the cause, my belief in separation/lack, as a present decision in my mind. It's an attempt to see the cause in the past/future and the present as its effect.

10. What I want RIGHT NOW, above all else, is peace.

    I question my belief in **D**: _____ and I voluntarily let go of **E**: _____ in order to reconnect with my one goal: peace.

11. Peace of mind is a present decision which I gratefully choose RIGHT NOW! Guilt, and fear of consequences, only seemed possible because I was determined to hold on to a belief in past/future cause. I let go of the meaning I gave to the past/future and open my mind to the present. I am absolved and innocent.

12. I am grateful for the realization that the cause of my upset, which I thought was in the world, was actually only an unquestioned belief and decision in my mind. I have decided anew for my PEACE OF MIND.

Notes on the Instrument for Peace

"Lack of peace must be traced back to its singular cause in the mind." The singular cause is your mind's decision for the ego at the instant of separation, from which arises all your various "lack" beliefs. But don't get ahead of yourself and just write that in. Do your own tracing back, step by step. For it to be effective, be completely honest with yourself as you use this Instrument.

1. What is your ego's perception of this? Write down the first things that come to your mind regarding **A**, **B**, and **C**.

2. "**A**, **B**, and **C** prove *[to me]* that I am right about **D**"... look within my mind. *[at my beliefs]*

3. It is OK to adapt or refine your thoughts as you go along.

4. Read and think.

5. Read and think.

6. Think about **D**. What is the nature of your belief in lack that might be behind **A**, **B**, and **C**? Lack of control? Vulnerability? Lack of a certain quality in yourself? Body identification? Linear time?

7. Step 7 clarifies the nature of your projection.

8. In step 8, you do not need to be realistic about **E**. If you had a magic wand and could change anything, what would you ideally have wanted or expected?

9. In step 9, the Instrument addresses the higher mind, "and the present *[upset, your present state of mind]* as its effect."

10. "I voluntarily let go of **E** *[your hope to change a person or the world]* to reconnect with my one goal: peace *[of mind, joy]*"

11. All the images are false. None of it ever was. Nothing in the past is real or true.

12. I am the Son of God: free, whole and happy!

"The cause of my upset was only an unquestioned belief and decision in my mind." *[**D**, which you may reflect on and trace back even further, are you a person or spirit?]*

Projector Chart

The Mechanism of Projection
Perception is an effect of an unreal idea

"Dreamer of the Dream"

"Cause"

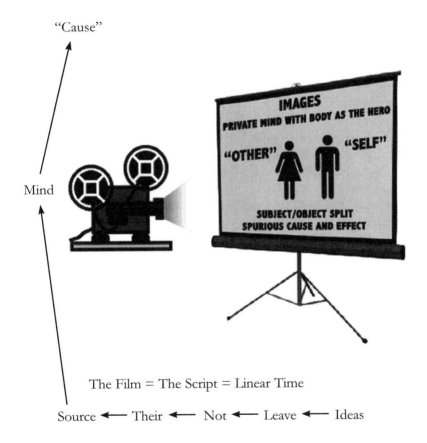

Mind

IMAGES
PRIVATE MIND WITH BODY AS THE HERO
"OTHER" "SELF"
SUBJECT/OBJECT SPLIT
SPURIOUS CAUSE AND EFFECT

The Film = The Script = Linear Time

Source ⟵ Their ⟵ Not ⟵ Leave ⟵ Ideas

Notes on the Projector Chart

Mind is the cause of everything. But in the sleeping mind only the ego thought system (projector) is active. The Holy Spirit, although always present in the mind, is unheeded and forgotten. It would be represented on this chart as the light before it goes through the film.

Seeing itself as the agent of the separation, the ego is filled with intolerable amounts of fear. In an attempt at control it projects fearful thoughts as images onto the screen of the world. Ego confuses the mind about cause (content) and effect (form) by drawing all its attention from the mind to the images on the screen (form). Ego thinking upholds belief in separation by seeing victimization, competition, bodies, and all that comprises the self-concept as real. You identify with the body self, the hero of the dream, and believe that you (subject) have a separate, private mind. You believe that each other person (object) also has a separate mind and can cause things to happen to you. This is spurious (false) since cause is only in your mind. There is no causation on the screen of the world. You are doing it to yourself. Although the film was scripted in an instant, as it runs through the projector it gives the illusion of linear time unfolding. In a state of sleep or mindlessness, your perception is unreliable and continually changing.

In a state of alertness or mindfulness you can be aware of and detached from ego thoughts and see everything and everyone differently. You look through the lens of the Holy Spirit. With this change of mind, your perception changes and the world you see is different from the way you saw before. The Holy Spirit consistently brings everything perceived on the screen back to the mind, where it can be seen as what it is: the out-picturing of the mind's false thoughts and beliefs. The Holy Spirit sees only wholeness, and two orders of thought: love or a call for love. When the Holy Spirit's thought system has the mind's allegiance, it is at peace. And peace of mind is the goal of life. You will see that all things work together for good.

Main Awakening Mind Sites
http://awakening-mind.org
http://miracleshome.org

Awakening In Christ Yahoo Group
http://groups.yahoo.com/group/awakeninginchrist

Awakening Mind ACIM Global Community link
http://acim.me

Additional Awakening Mind Resources

Online Video
www.acim-online-video.net
www.jesus-christ-videos.net
www.video.yahoo.com/search?ytag=1&p=david+hoffmeister
www.video.google.com/videosearch?q=david+hoffmeister
http://acim.mobi

Audio
www.acim-online-mp3.net

For Awakening Mind materials and Donations
www.christ-jes.us
www.course-in-miracles.com

Independent commercial website in support of the Foundation
www.davidhoffmeistermaterials.com

Contact Us
requests@awakening-mind.org
retreats@awakening-mind.org

.